PATRICK HAMILTON
A Life

PATRICK HAMILTON

A Life

SEAN FRENCH

faber and faber
LONDON · BOSTON

First published in 1993 by Faber and Faber Limited
3 Queen Square London WC1N 3AU

Photoset by Wilmaset Ltd, Wirral
Printed in England by Clays Ltd, St Ives plc

A CIP record for this book is available from the British Library

ISBN 0–571–14353–9

2 4 6 8 10 9 7 5 3 1

To Nicci

Contents

List of Illustrations

All photographs are from the author's
collection except where stated.

THE NOVELIST

Encased in talent like a uniform,
The rank of every poet is well known;
They can amaze us like a thunderstorm,
Or die so young, or live for years alone.

They can dash forward like hussars: but he
Must struggle out of his boyish gift and learn
How to be plain and awkward, how to be
One after whom none think it worth to turn.

For, to achieve its lightest wish, he must
Become the whole of boredom, subject to
Vulgar complaints like love, among the Just

Be just, among the Filthy filthy too,
And in his own weak person, if he can,
Must suffer dully all the wrongs of Man.

W. H. AUDEN (DECEMBER 1938)

I have tried to make of you good readers who read books not for the infantile purpose of identifying oneself with the characters, and not for the adolescent purpose of learning to live, and not for the academic purpose of indulging in generalizations. I have tried to teach you to read books for the sake of their form, their visions, their art. I have tried to teach you to feel a shiver of artistic satisfaction, to share not the emotions of the people in the book but the emotions of its author – the joys and difficulties of creation.

VLADIMIR NABOKOV

You can define a net in one of two ways, depending on your point of view. Normally, you would say that it is a meshed instrument designed to catch fish. But you could, with no great injury to logic, reverse the image and define a net as a jocular lexicographer once did: he called it a collection of holes tied together with string.

You can do the same with a biography.

JULIAN BARNES

The intellectual surface we offer to the dead has undergone a subtle change of texture and chemistry; a thousand particulars of delight and fellow-feeling and forbearance begin reformulating themselves the moment they cross the bar. The living are always potentially thinking about and doing just what we are doing: being pulled through a touchless car wash, watching a pony chew a carrot, noticing that orange scaffolding has gone up around some prominent church. The conclusions they draw we know to be conclusions drawn from how things are now. Indeed, for me, as a beginning novelist, all other living writers form a control group for whom the world is a placebo. The dead can be helpful, needless to say, but we can only guess sloppily about how they would react to this emergent particle of time, which is all the time we have. And when we do guess, we are unfair to them. Even when, as with Barthelme, the dead have died unexpectedly and relatively young, we give them their moment of solemnity and then quickly begin patronizing them biographically, talking about how they 'delighted in' x or 'poked fun at' y – phrases that by their very singsong cuteness betray how alien and childlike the shades now are to us. Posthumously their motives become ludicrously simple, their delights primitive and unvarying: all their emotions wear stage makeup, and we almost never flip their books across the room out of impatience with something they've said. We can't really understand them anymore.

NICHOLSON BAKER

Aided by a vigorous imagination and a subtle sensibility, he was able to distil the essence of his life into his books. Biographical details (his raffish father and pretentious mother, his sexual experiences, various social and financial insec- urities endemic to the British middle class of his time) provided the raw material from which he created a world so distinctive that the 'Patrick Hamilton atmosphere' seems as palpable to his readers as any in fiction, and as mysteriously familiar as a recurring dream. Why attempt to reduce such an elaborate, coherent and consistent construction to its dull (and often debatable) original components?

FRANCIS WYNDHAM

The problem of Patrick seems to need some exploring. I believe very strongly, and have to some extent conveyed to him my belief, that he is on a wrong track. But the feeling is so often mixed up with small personal annoyances, and is so liable to be tinged with jealousy, that I need to go very carefully, not only in speaking about it to him, but also in satisfying myself that my opinions about so very important a matter are as objective as possible.

BRUCE HAMILTON (PATRICK'S BROTHER)

Arthur C[alder]-M[arshall]'s description of me as he first knew me (at the Wells Hotel, Hampstead) makes very amusing reading. I've got a copy of his talk, which I'll show you when we meet. He talks of my 'reticence and charm' and says that I looked like an 'office-worker'! What *weird* impressions one must always be making upon different people.

LETTER FROM PATRICK HAMILTON TO BRUCE

Such were the psychological accidents, errors, and complications which governed a person's movements and destiny.

PATRICK HAMILTON, *The Slaves of Solitude*

Introduction

When W. H. Auden came to revise the version of 'The Novelist' which is reproduced as an epigraph, he drastically altered the final line. Reflecting his changed views about the role of the writer, his conviction that 'poetry makes nothing happen', the phrase, 'Must suffer dully', became the wilfully bathetic, indeed almost self-sabotaging:

> And in his own person, if he can,
> Dully put up with all the wrongs of Man.[1]

But for Patrick Hamilton it was the original version that remained true: he would not mock or condemn anything that he had not undergone himself. His great achievement was to portray, and to create, a vivid, fantastic world of comic horror, of rented accommodations and temporary refuges, lodging houses, pubs, cinemas and tea houses, where the lost, failed and forgotten meet and bore each other and seek some respite. It was also the world that, for much of his own life, he chose to inhabit.

In 1935 Cyril Connolly wrote a jocular essay, 'Defects of English Novels', in which he enumerated the attributes of native fiction that rendered it irredeemably marginal and trivial. The first he labelled 'Thinness of Material':

English life is on the whole without adventure or variety, 90 per cent of English authors come from the mandarin class, the experiences from which both sexes can draw are limited to three or four – a peaceful childhood, a public school education, a university, a few years in London or the provinces in which to get a job, a wife, a house, and some children. Material for one book, perhaps, which publishers and the need to earn one's living will drag out to three or four. A rigorous class system blankets down all attempts to enlarge these barriers. The English mandarin simply can't get at pugilists, gangsters, speakeasies, negroes, and even if he should he would find them absolutely without the force and colour of the American equivalent.[2]

Connolly's notion of what constituted authentic experience was of course a self-conscious absurdity, derived from Hollywood movies and Hemingway short stories. His derisive litany is itself an enactment of why he and his kind could not write such fiction. In fact it is a defensive denunciation of the attempt even to do so. Real life was something to be portrayed by other people, by American or French writers, whose real life was more picturesque than the dreary black-and-white English world of bypasses, Lyons corner houses and men in bowler hats.

Patrick Hamilton decided to be a writer at a very early age. Unlike Connolly, he was, and was to remain, an opponent of experimental writing of any kind. 'Filthily modern incomprehensibility' was his phrase for it.[3] His literary tastes were insistently and increasingly reactionary, but from the cradle, he was set on a course that kept him systematically clear of Connolly's diversions. If, in the end, Hamilton's literary productivity petered out, this was not a result of the traditional enemies of promise. It was not the temptation to review novels or attend literary parties that kept him from his fiction. There was to be no pram in the hall.[4]

Hamilton's unwillingness to live a traditional literary life, to inhabit any literary group or coterie, was a mark of his integrity. It also deprived him of support late in his career. John Betjeman's praise for Hamilton's shunning of the limelight[5] was never accompanied by the slightest attempt to emulate the man he described as one of his literary heroes. Indeed, Betjeman followed an entirely opposite course in his own career, becoming the first English literary figure to establish his reputation largely through television.

Hamilton is an eerie non-presence in modern British literary history. He is often thought of as a quintessential writer of the 1930s, yet in Valentine Cunningham's massively inclusive study of the decade, he does not feature among the hundred and twenty-odd novelists in the bibliography or even in the index.[6] In much the same way Hamilton is often talked of as a Fitzrovian, and he is mentioned three times in Hugh David's study of the loose-knit bohemian group that straddled Blooms-bury and Soho, but only with references to his fiction, some of which happens to portray the same sort of world.[7] Fitzrovia's best and wittiest chronicler, Julian Maclaren-Ross, was a keen admirer of Hamilton's fiction, and frequently talked about him but never met him.[8]

Partly because he published his first novels so young, Hamilton's literary acquaintances belonged to an earlier generation of writers, men like W. W. Jacobs, Compton Mackenzie, Edward Marsh, Hugh Walpole. His closest literary friend, Michael Sadleir, had started a literary magazine with John Middleton Murry in 1911.[9] Hamilton was praised by many writers of his own age or younger – Walter Allen, Graham Greene, Doris Lessing, Anthony Powell, Julian Symons – but only from a distance.

This life, devoted to work, reading, drinking, listening to conver-sations in pubs, presents certain problems to a biographer. Hamilton had no direct descendants and few of his own papers and virtually none of his possessions seem to have survived. The dozen or so people who knew him intimately are all dead. Some valuable sources remain. Most important are the hundreds of letters over almost forty years that he sent to his brother, Bruce, mainly when Bruce was living in Barbados. After Hamilton's death, Bruce wrote a memoir of his brother, originally titled, *Patrick: A Tragedy*. A version of this, *The Light Went Out*, was published in 1972 by Hamilton's old publisher, Constable. Bruce did much rewriting, sometimes for the better, but the book was also very heavily cut, from around 165,000 words to 60,000. The original version – rambling, digressive, unstructured, uneven in tone – could never have been published as it stood, but the editing was maladroit, to say the least. Tedious details of Hamilton's schooldays were left intact while whole chapters describing the life of the extraordinary Hamilton family were cut. Bruce had already published ten novels, but the biography was far and away his finest work, the only one where he broke through the layers of reserve that he felt had blighted his life, and it must have been heartbreaking to lose so much of it.

It remains a valuable source of material; often, it must be said, because it brings Bruce's judgement into question. Hamilton once observed in a letter to his brother that 'To discuss your or my personal affairs is, really, a bore – and this is because it is totally impossible for either of us to get any sort of picture of what really goes on in the other's life.'[10]

There is, I understand, a theory of scientific inquiry known as the 'Lamppost Theory'. The idea is that if you have lost your keys one dark night on the way home, your best strategy is to look for them under a lamppost. There is no greater likelihood that they are there, but it is the only place where you will be able to see them. There are a few scattered lampposts throwing light on particular aspects of Patrick Hamilton's life, tempting the biographer to assume that the illuminated areas are the ones that matter and to forget about the inaccessible darkness. Nor is everything in the light always quite as it seems. Bruce had his own life and his own priorities, and it is at least arguable that these decisively influenced his view of his brother.

There are other sources. Near the end of his life, Hamilton made two fragmentary attempts to write a memoir, largely as a way of exploring the causes of his alcoholic compulsion. Many letters to and from his close friend and publisher, Michael Sadleir, were preserved in the Constable archives. There is some interesting correspondence in the BBC archives. The correspondence with other close friends apparently does not survive. Alexander Cockburn, son of Claud, wrote to me as follows: 'Alas, my father's "papers" are mounds of the sort of junk you probably have on your desk and I certainly do on mine. There may be a letter from Patrick H in there, but I've not seen it, and the exciting bit probably would have been torn off to make a spill for lighting a cigarette or reckoning up a canasta score in the 1950s.'[11]

Then there are the books. Between them the Hamilton family published over forty books: plays, novels, a political pamphlet and a 'psychic history'. The literary success of Hamilton seems all the more remarkable set against the dogged literary failure of the rest of his family.

A particular problem in treating Patrick Hamilton's life is that of attempting to put back together what was never together in the first place. When his life functioned, it was largely because of Hamilton's temporary success in keeping its different areas precariously separate. Not only does it lack a satisfying unity but its downwardly curving trajectory makes it the reverse of the exemplary, allegorical lives that, since Keats at least, we have expected from our authors.

Yet there has been too much talk among Hamilton's critics and chroniclers of tragic failure. This is the Hamilton to be found in his brother's memoir, a work of piety that is also an act of belated revenge. Patrick might have been grimly amused to be accused of being a failure by his brother, who didn't produce a single novel of the quality even of *Craven House*, his second novel, written at the age of twenty-one. For Patrick Hamilton, always and above all it was the work that mattered. Against the odds, in the most unpromising of circumstances, his was a life of resource, resilience, fortitude and humour. He suffered terrible troubles, some of his own making; he did some inferior work. But he had a steely sense of literary integrity and he never violated it. Hamilton received no honours or awards; he sat on no committees; he was never interviewed on television or radio. When he died he left half a dozen first-rate novels and two of the most commercially successful plays of his time. That is the success that matters.

I owe many debts of gratitude. Benjamin Glazebrook, the chairman and managing director of Constable, was helpful, though sadly his company's archives had been sold. Christopher Edwards of Pickering and Chatto helped me to track them down to Temple University in Philadelphia, Pennsylvania. I am very grateful to Thomas M. Whitehead, the Head of the Special Collections and Programs Department at Temple, who went to a great deal of trouble on my behalf.

Trevor White and Joanne Cayford at the BBC Written Archives Centre in Caversham aided me beyond the call of duty.

Paul Taylor of Samuel French Ltd steered me in the right direction, most usefully towards Timothy Boulton, the executor of the will of Patrick Hamilton's first wife, Loïs, and one of the trustees of the Patrick Hamilton Estate. Boulton has been generous to all Hamilton students, with his time and with the scrapbook he inherited from Loïs. I thank him for the loan of both, as well as for his own memories of Hamilton.

The letters and papers that Bruce Hamilton saved, piled randomly in a suitcase, can scarcely be called an archive in any traditional sense of the word. But they survived, and after Bruce's death, his widow, Aileen Hamilton, kept them safe. She was slightly baffled by their attraction for me, though wistfully hopeful that they might be valuable some day. She was truculently dismissive of her late brother-in-law, but let me see whatever I wanted and was most hospitable to me while I was on her premises. She died in early 1992, after years of illness borne with stubborn courage.

Aileen Hamilton bequeathed her papers to Nigel Jones, whose own 1991 biography of Patrick Hamilton, *Through a Glass Darkly*, had already made valuable use of them. In these potentially awkward circumstances, Jones acted in the best traditions of disinterested scholarship and allowed me full access to the papers now in his charge. Other Hamilton experts were helpful in different ways. Andy Croft was encouraging early on and sent me copies of his own copies of letters from Bruce Hamilton's collection. Brian McKenna, author of the first doctoral thesis on the works of Patrick Hamilton, discussed the subject with me when I was still a novice.

Ara Calder-Marshall generously talked to me, shortly after the death of her husband, Arthur, who had also been an acquaintance of Hamilton's. Sir Kenneth Robinson spoke to me of Hamilton in the 1930s and 1940s. Rosamund John acted in a revival of *Gaslight*, though sadly, if characteristically, she made more of an impression on Hamilton than he on her. The Earl of Shrewsbury and Talbot, now owner of two-thirds of the rights to Hamilton's literary estate, wrote to me of his personal encounter with Hamilton which was brief, but more important than he knows.

At a late stage of my work, I was fortunate to discover that the distinguished biographer, Fiona MacCarthy, was able to provide me with a new vantage point from which to observe my subject. I am grateful for her help. At an even later stage, Hugh Whitemore put me in touch with a resident of Overy Staithe who knew Hamilton, and whose wish to remain anonymous I have respected. And at the eleventh hour Victoria Hill kindly gave me some valuable manuscript material in her possession.

Tim Miller kindly showed me around Albany and Elizabeth M. Oliver provided me with information about Hamilton's tenancy.

When Loïs Hamilton died, she thoughtfully left her one-third share in the Patrick Hamilton estate to the Society of Authors. In its turn, the Society of Authors generously made me an award, without knowing how appropriate it was.

Dr Patrick French supplied me with information about ECT

treatment and I discussed alcoholism and liver disease with Dr Graham Butcher. Needless to say, the responsibility for any errors in my account, or my interpretation, of Patrick Hamilton's medical history is entirely mine. I am grateful to the trustees of Patrick Hamilton's Estate and to Temple University, Philadelphia, for permission to quote copyright material, published and unpublished, by Patrick Hamilton.

The first draft of this book was read by Karl French and Nicci Gerrard, the second draft by Kersti French, Philip French and Tracey Scoffield. All made valuable, detailed suggestions. This book was Tracey Scoffield's idea in the first place and it benefited greatly from her knowledge of and enthusiasm for Patrick Hamilton, his work and his world.

To Nicci Gerrard my debt has been the greatest of all. Line ten of the Auden poem that is this book's first epigraph seems apposite. She could never *become* the whole of boredom, but at times during the elephantine gestation period of this book she has known what it is to be married to it.

I

Family

I

Patrick Hamilton's alienation began at home. Ever since Aristotle's *Politics*, it has been argued that the family is the embodiment of continuity, stability and order in a society. And since possessions are handed down through succeeding generations, a deep connection has been asserted between the relations of family affection and our entire notion of private property.

If happy families are at the heart of the conservative idea of civil society, then unhappy families are at the root of the novel. Patrick Hamilton was born into an age struggling to find its feet in awkward modernity, into a middle class whose privileges were under challenge. Far from being a support, his own family was an emblem of the discontinuity between generations, of the instability of our hold on society, of the insecurity of private property in a fluctuating economy. Family tradition was nothing more than a dream – from which he was never able fully to awake.

Hamilton never denounced his family, and he never escaped it. Instead he clung on to it, however incomplete or inadequate it was in its various forms. Nor do families appear in his fiction. His characters don't get married or have children, they are stripped by their author of parents or siblings. Hamilton's imaginative world is one from which all the ideas of refuge and security that the family represented had been removed, leaving its characters scattered and homeless.

Radical reformers from Rousseau to Engels saw the family as a source of oppression that had to be swept away. Hamilton made the same discovery. In an Edwardian England that placed an almost desperate value on ideas of respectability, decorum and class stratification, all of which were locked in place by the mechanisms of the family, Hamilton saw his own family and its traditions to be a sham.

Ernest Ralph Gorse was Hamilton's study of a psychopath and also, in a characteristically complicated way, a self-portrait. *The West Pier* (published in 1951) is the story of Gorse's painstakingly executed scheme to deprive a pretty and foolish young girl, Esther Downes, of her life savings. At the crucial moment of betrayal, Gorse obtains Esther's trust by removing a ring from his finger and giving it to her as security:

Just as Gorse had adopted an old school tie which he had no right to wear, so he had adopted, falsely, a family relationship – a relationship with the peerage.

The ring he wore was of gold, with a cornelian stone, upon which was engraved the image of a horse's head – a head like that of a chess knight. A person related to Lord Belhaven and Stenton might have worn such a ring.[1]

The ring was Hamilton's own, inherited from his father, Bernard. It has not survived but the image of the martial-looking horse's head, accompanied by the motto 'Ride Through', is still to be seen on Bernard's bookplate. He used to claim to his disbelieving sons that only the accident of being born a few days late had prevented the peerage of Belhaven and Stenton returning to him.[2] When Hamilton's brother read *The West Pier* and reproachfully pointed out the connection, Hamilton admitted that it was deliberate and also that he had been tempted to use 'Hamilton' as the family name, were it not that 'For some reason one must *never* in fiction, use one's own name – not even for the name of a grocer over the way. Why is this?'[3]

Just as myths may be considered true in a poetic sense, Hamilton was to consider even the authentic aspects of his father's life and heritage as essentially false, just further props of a life without a centre, precariously built on fantasy, impersonation, constant improvisation and re-invention. As Hamilton later wrote to his brother, 'it must be remembered that Bernard was in the habit of relating himself to almost *anybody* who took his fancy at the moment – this *including* King Bruce of Scotland!'[4].

Towards the end of his life, Bernard published a book in which he proposed to recount his 'Psychic History'.[5] It began with a worldly enough chapter about his forebears, telling tales that were familiar to his family:

On my father's side we were a Border family – Scots, of course, – for generations. But intermarried with English – 'border-rievers' also. My father, as a child, had taken four days to go from Carlisle to London in a stage-coach. He used to tell how his grandmother, Mrs Fawcett of Scaleby Castle, used to dine, with all her household at one long table in hall, feudal fashion – above and below 'the salt'.[6]

Bernard's sentimental Scottishness was never far below the surface. As Patrick Hamilton later recalled,

He had a 'Hamilton' mania, and like so many Stewarts, he was, really, when everything was worked out, the rightful heir to the throne of Scotland. As such, he once explained to me, in complete sobriety, that the Hamiltons were the peremptory foes of the Douglases, and that it was really my business, if I ever met a Douglas to 'run my sword through him'. He also once ended a dramatic disquisition to me in the 1920s with: 'And if it ever comes to war between England and Scotland – you and I go over the border!'[7]

In Bernard's view, all his ancestry – and, indeed, he himself – stood in the shadow of his maternal grandfather, Colonel Edward Wildman, a lifelong soldier, who fought in the Napoleonic Wars. He would proudly tell his sons how Colonel Wildman had been wounded at Albuera, in the Peninsular campaign. His arm was nearly severed and his head wounded by a sabre so grievously that he wore a gold plate in his head for the rest of his life. He was taken prisoner but fortunately returned at the end of hostilities so that he was able to participate in the Battle of Waterloo where 'he had three horses killed under him'.[8] Bernard recalled that:

Colonel Edward, my progenitor, took over the command of the Carabiniers (6th Dragoon Guards) of which he was Colonel for sixteen years – still with his gold plate in his head. I rather think his service comes very near being a 'record'. They were pretty tough officers in those days – the last of the gentlemen of the sword. They could use it then; for old muzzle-loading 'Brown Bess' only carried eighty yards at Waterloo.[9]

Until the end of an active and varied life, Bernard Hamilton was haunted by his military ancestor and by Colonel Edward's brother, Thomas, also at Waterloo, also a Colonel, who is now remembered only for having bought Newstead Abbey from Lord Byron. In later years Hamilton wrote to Bruce, who was then living abroad, including a series of amusing cartoons depicting the decoration of their Chiswick home. The right-hand wall of the entrance hall is decorated with a picture of Newstead Abbey, with a rifle on either side. Below is a Waterloo sword and below them two claymores and a Scottish beret. On the right is a picture of Colonel Wildman.[10]

Patrick Hamilton himself was always conscious of the family's past. In his mid-forties he remarked to Bruce, in only half humorous defence of the family honour: 'By the way *I* (and I *think* you as well) did a grave injustice to Colonel W. in blaming him for all those horrid renovations at Newstead. On that trip I discovered that it was all done by the rich Webbs, who bought the place from Col. W.'[11]

By contrast with his martial forebear, Bernard's actual father was a disappointment. When Walter Bernard Hamilton was born, on 26 March 1863, his father was the Rector of Waldershare in Kent. The Revd Walter Hamilton had been married before and, after Bernard's mother died, when Bernard was seven, he married again. In Bruce's words, 'his father never supplied the need for affection of a boy who felt almost suffocated by the strictly religious atmosphere of a mid-Victorian parsonage.'[12] Recalling a childhood dominated by a love of nature and a hunger for books, Bernard saw himself as a rebel against the 'stilted mid-Victorian period', especially against its religious orthodoxies. In particular, the rituals of Sunday made that a day of suffering for him.[13]

He was educated at Repton, 'a hard-bitten, manly school' and then matriculated at Trinity College, Cambridge, his father's old college, where he studied history. There, for the only time in his life, he was happy and fulfilled. At university he was free to assume as many selves as he wanted: 'There were boats, bump-suppers, stupendous Cambridge breakfasts, topped up with audit ale, balls, tennis, football, Freemasonry. There was too the cult of the *vendeuses*, fox terriers.'[14] He also acted. He and his friends felt that 'the old A.D.C. [Amateur Dramatic Company] was too slow' and so they founded the Footlights, where they could perform revues. In November 1883 W. B. Hamilton featured in the cast list of the society's production of *Aladdin*.[15]

On leaving Cambridge, he found it impossible to settle down to any one career. For a time he worked at Toynbee Hall, 'ostensibly founded to bring university influence to bear upon the East End of London, for the East End's good. But I soon discovered that it was an endeavour only to bring "cultchair" there.'[16]

Bernard was bitterly critical of any attempt to improve the condition of the poor. He argued both that the poor needed no help – 'I found that the life of the People was perfectly happy, if they could be allowed to live their own lives – without being "improved" '[17] – and that they were beyond help: 'We must accept facts as they are. The "submerged tenth" will always remain submerged.'[18]

In his spiritual memoir Bernard omitted to reveal two pertinent facts which might have coloured these observations. The first was that on his twenty-first birthday he inherited £100,000, a substantial fortune in Britain in the early 1880s. The second is that, on that same birthday, he met a prostitute at the Empire Theatre in London. His own most direct attempt at helping the submerged tenth involved marrying her and hoping to reclaim her. In Bruce's words, 'This quixotic idiocy, so fully creditable to him as a human being, was only terminated years later [after the couple had separated], when the unfortunate woman threw herself in front of a train at Wimbledon Station, leaving behind a letter exculpating her husband as the only good thing in her life.'[19] Bruce's and Hamilton's novels teem with gibes at their father, but one of the sourer examples was when Bruce began his 1936 novel, *Middle Class Murder*, with a man composing a fake, exculpatory suicide note by his wife as a prelude to killing her.[20]

'Unstable as water, thou shalt not excel,' a prophetic teacher had quoted at the young Bernard,[21] and even to his own family he was to seem an amorphous figure. What exactly was he? He was called to the Bar at the Middle Temple, and was photographed in his barrister's robes, sporting a monocle, but he never practised. He 'dabbled in journalism', writing for the *Daily Telegraph*. He considered, then rejected, the idea of teaching. 'I think I can fairly claim to know more about the theory and practice of teaching than most Ministers of Education,' he observed.[22] He was briefly seduced by the modish mystical attractions of Theosophy, until, by his own account, he spotted its founder, Madame Blavatsky, removing a spiritual message not from the ether but from a chandelier in Ostende. He became a religious controversialist, constantly protesting against religious authority: 'The belief in a so-called Book is surely inferior, intellectually, to a system.'[23]

Mostly he spent his money on his recreations: climbing in Switzerland, sculling, squash, tennis, golf, fishing, shooting, hunting, rose-growing, 'above all, travel in old Europe. All *châteaux* and cathedrals have a perennial interest.' Inasmuch as he was doing anything, he was preparing himself for the novels to which he would devote his middle age. He began to grow fat, a man with the eccentricities of genius but no genius, nor even talent. He was more fitted, as the future would show, to be a character in a novel than an author of one. Then, in the mid-1890s he met and married Ellen Adèle Day, also known as Nellie, the first of those female 'L' names that would be so prominent in Hamilton's life.[24]

She had been born, in 1861, Ellen Hockley, daughter of 'a fashionable London dentist',[25] and, like Bernard, had been married before. All that her children knew of this first husband was that he was called Day, was charming and, 'after an uneasy year or two of married life, spent . . . largely in a house on the Upper Thames', unfaithfulness had been proved against him. Divorce followed axiomatically.[26] In appearance, Ellen was somewhat like her husband, with soft, rounded features (on the evidence of surviving photographs, the Hamiltons and their children seem not to have had a facial bone between them). She was also talented, in a fairly traditional way. She played the piano competently, sang music-hall songs, copied old-master paintings and wrote fiction.

The first years of their marriage were auspicious. At their first marital home in Hindhead, in the very south of Surrey by the Sussex border, the two ageing novice writers were on the fringe of an artistic community. Bernard became friendly with Arthur Conan Doyle, who had only recently – and, as it was to prove, temporarily – rid himself of his lucrative creation, Sherlock Holmes, and was endeavouring to establish himself as a serious author. George Bernard Shaw married in 1898 and settled nearby. Both Hamiltons embarked on literary careers and by 1904 Bernard and Ellen had produced not just three children, but five novels and a political pamphlet.

Bernard's first book, *The Light?*, was a vast baroque religio-historical

novel, beginning in Ancient Egypt and ending with a call for the reform
of the Anglican church, the abolition of the thirty-nine Articles and the
'direct representation of the Laity in Convocation'. As Patrick Hamilton
later commented, 'The leading character, after several incarnations,
turns up towards the end at the Battle of Waterloo. Here he does
amazing things, but this is the best: – *Then, with an amazing piece of
audacity, (what an American would call "bluff") he* . . . etc, etc.'[27]

Bernard begins by assuring the reader that, 'To insure accuracy, I
have, where possible, personally inspected the sites of the principal
scenes described.' In a further, ominous prefatory note he announces
that he has marked sections of the narrative that can be omitted by
readers. The story itself, 'of the eternal struggle between the Ideal and
the Carnal in man', is a barely readable version of the religiose exoticism,
occasionally becoming eroticism, that was such a feature of late-
Victorianism. The recognition by the priest Rahmer of his love for the
priestess Zillah gives a fair example of Bernard's use of archaic
language: 'The love of God yielded to the love of woman [. . .] "I am
aweary of all this strife," he said. "Do thou thy will with me." '[28]

In future years, the book was to be the subject of derision among the
younger generations of the Hamilton family. When, as cited above,
Patrick attempted to sketch the decoration of the Hamilton household,
he included witty versions of his father's pictures, military, religious,
semi-erotic, Biblical and, best of all, a sketch of two ancient pagan
worshippers praying to the dawn. One is saying to the other: 'I wish we
could preserve the words to this hymn.' And the other pagan replies:
'Don't worry. I expect Bernard Hamilton will in a few hundred years
time.'[29]

Bernard's second novel, *A Kiss for a Kingdom, Or a Venture in Vanity*
(1899), is more readable. It is an adventure story about a handsome
young captain, late of the Dragoon Guards, who is enlisted by an
American to invade San Marino. He becomes a ruler himself when the
American – King Jones the First – is killed, and then gives up his
kingdom for love of the beautiful Viola. It must have been immediately
obvious to the book's few readers that it was nothing more than a dull
reworking of two of the popular successes of the decade, Rudyard
Kipling's *The Man Who Would Be King* (first published in book form in
1890) and Anthony Hope's *The Prisoner of Zenda* (1894).

The novel also reveals the first glimmer of Bernard Hamilton's homespun political programme. 'One man *does* things, sir,' says the American, Julius C. Jones. 'Governments *talk* about 'em.'[30] This *aperçu* is the germ of Bernard's exhortatory political pamphlet of the following year, *Wanted – A Man! Apply John Bull & Co: (Late of Dame Europa's School). A War Story for Big Boys told by Bernard Hamilton*. This laborious allegory of Europe as a boys' school was a swift response to the Boer War, which had begun on 11 October 1899. Bernard's subject was not the conduct of the war but rather the flabbiness of Britain which had made the war possible ('William' is Germany):

When William went out into life he was quick to see that he had not had enough education at Dame Europa's, so he has gone on steadily fitting himself for future work by a great deal of private study; in fact by reason of this rigid self-discipline, he is now a good deal better educated than John although John does not like to hear this fact when told of it.[31]

Bernard's awakened John Bull protests against the constraints of money, law, democratic accountability,[32] or the British cabinet and Parliamentary system. He attacks the influence of the Press ('suppose the complete Liberty of the Press is contrary to Public Policy, what then?'), the 'permanent officials',[33] and the trade unionists.

Bernard's solution was an early form of what would later be codified by Mussolini as fascism, of which Bernard was to be a fervent admirer. 'It is a man we want, in these matters,' John Bull cries, 'not a committee.' The solution is an Imperial Council free of Parliament or Cabinet control which will produce a country fit for the greater Darwinian fight: 'Life is strife, whether we like it or no. And soon there is coming – sure as tomorrow's sun – a Greater Fight – a fight nearer home.'[34]

In 1902, Bernard's friend, Arthur Conan Doyle, would publish a pamphlet of his own, *The Cause and Conduct of the War in South Africa*, so patriotic that it became a bestseller and resulted in a knighthood for its author shortly afterwards. There is no evidence that Bernard's pamphlet had any impact whatever, but the author himself must have been satisfied with it, because his four remaining published novels would have just one subject, the power of a great man to embody a nation's destiny and seize control of history.

In *Coronation* (1902) the thesis was applied to Merrie England

(Bernard uses the very phrase)[35] in the patriotic story of Henry V. Bernard assured his readers that 'there is certainly no king, nay, nor man, more worthy than English Harry to rank as our national hero of romance.'[36] In other hands the story of Hal and Falstaff has met with some success, and Sir Arthur Conan Doyle, among many others, had shown there was an eager market for historical adventure stories in a Britain passing the zenith of its imperial power. There was no market, however, for historical novels consisting of over three hundred pages written in the style of the following. The scene is early fifteenth-century Oxford. Clynton is a student:

At length, impatient of his companion's book-poring, he touched him on the shoulder.

'Worthy John Dodde,' said he, 'Set thee up! Enow of clerk-work; let us out – to friends who lack us.'

The other sighed and looked up wearily. 'Nay, nay, Clynton,' he said in a sort of sing-song, ' 'tis well enow for thee, who are a knight's son, to prate of roaming streets; but for me, who came to Oxford chanting "Salve Regina" at rich men's doors that I might crave a crust; ay, and who, e'en now, have the half of my goods in pledge to our Academie, this the logic-book of the learned Shyreswood is my best friend. And with him I bide indoors.'

'Tush thou chamberdekyn!' cried Clynton.[37]

The language may be mock-medieval but it is spoken by Victorian gentlemen. In one scene a Lollard is burned at the stake: 'But he kept a determined front – the front of the typical Englishman, who will not allow his spirit to be beaten, whatever may happen to his flesh.'[38]

The novel ends at Agincourt as Clynton rescues the national Banner, 'the emblem of his country', and is knighted by King Henry on the battlefield,[39] winning a recognition that would be denied to his creator. Bernard's literary career now came to a standstill.

II

Ellen Hamilton, who wrote two novels under the pseudonym of Olivia Roy, was, in her way, a far better novelist than her husband. Bernard's fiction is irredeemable literary sludge. Its traces are to be found in

17

Patrick Hamilton's work only in the form of the jocose archaicisms for which the more grotesque characters are sometimes mocked. Olivia Roy's novels make no pretence of being anything but popular fiction for an undemanding female audience, but they display a technical skill and an acute ear for dialogue beyond anything that Bernard would ever manage.

Her first novel, *The Awakening of Mrs Carstairs*, begins on the wedding night of its heroine, Alys. She does not love her husband and the expression of her repulsion clearly anticipates all those female Patrick Hamilton characters who view sex with distaste, from Diane de Mesrigny in his first novel to Ivy Barton in his last:

I don't fancy it can be in my nature to love a man seriously. I can flirt and encourage men; I like them to admire me and make a fuss of me; but there it must end. I cannot endure to be kissed, or to have my hand pressed, or any of those uncomfortable little overtures a certain set of men make use of to show their feelings towards you – or, perhaps, to see what your feelings are towards them.

All this is not affectation on my part; to me it almost amounts to physical repulsion.[40]

The attempts of her husband Bob to arouse her are counter-productive: 'Bob thinks I do not mind him kissing me. An icicle – a refrigerator – he calls me; but, uncannily enough, all this seems to stimulate him to extra devotion; and that was not needed.'[41]

Alys begins a flirtation with handsome Major Rowan, which soon turns into love and the beginnings of an affair. When she is on the point of eloping with him at the climax of the novel, she becomes pregnant. Her confidante, Aunt Blount, greets the news with joy: 'It's exactly what was wanted, Alys – to put everything straight. Exactly! I told you something must be done and you've done it.'[42] The imminent arrival of the baby, 'An angel from God, "with healing in his wings" ', is presented with sugary sentimentality, even by the standards of the genre in which Ellen is writing, but the view of the possibilities of marriage is as stoically sombre at the end of the novel as it was at the beginning: 'Who has perfect happiness? There is no such thing. Passion is fleeting; friendship only endures.'[43]

By the time the novel was written, these were Ellen's own feelings about a marriage which had been entered into with low enough expectations in the first place. Bruce recalled a story she had told her children from the early years of their marriage which, she said, caused her for the first time to turn against her husband:

They were staying in the country with some titled people, whose daughter made friends with our mother and told her, in the deadliest secrecy, of vows of love exchanged with some quite ineligible young man. With perfect trust in his discretion, and after exacting a solemn promise, Nellie passed on the bit of gossip to Bernard – who promptly informed the parents. There was a terrible row, and the poor girl, after one look of burning reproach, never spoke again to her false friend.[44]

Olivia Roy's second novel, *The Husband Hunter*, is a much more light-hearted romance, utterly absurd but with some charm. Joanna March is a spinster, her best friend, Lady Lalage (those 'L's again), has lost her husband, apparently killed in the Libyan Desert. 'Each still admired in the other that which she did not herself possess. Lalage loved Joanna for her sterling sincerity, and Joanna loved Lalage for her lithesome beauty.'[45] Lalage aims to help her friend find a husband. Meanwhile she takes on a new butler, to whom she becomes shockingly attracted.

After an expedition to the Libyan desert, it emerges, needless to say, that Sir George Chester not only survived but is none other than her butler. For a year the 'vile Arabs [. . .] kept him with chains on his feet as a servant, or attendant slave to one of the head men. That, poor dear, is where he learned all his nice docile manners, which have held him in such good stead when he took to butlering.'[46] Meanwhile, her friend has found a Lord of her own.

An advertising brochure issued by the publishers did not concern itself with matters of literary merit: 'The devices by which the heroine and her friend work their wiles might well be an object lesson for many a modern woman who is "husband hunting".'[47] In fact, the moral of the book, such as it is, is the opposite: that it is no good hunting for a husband; all a woman can do is wait for a man to find her.

Ellen gave little serious thought to writing for publication again. Instead she chose to repose such hopes of romance and happiness as she retained in her children. In 1898 she gave birth to a daughter, christened Helen Dorothea Elisa, but always known in the family as Lalla. In 1900 a son was born and christened Arthur (after his godfather, Arthur Conan Doyle) Douglas Bruce (after Robert Bruce). When Bernard wrote the preface to his novel, *Coronation*, he signed it from Hindhead, 1901. Soon afterwards, the family moved to Dale House in the village of Hassocks, just seven miles from Brighton and the English Channel. There on 17 March 1904, when Bernard was forty and Ellen was forty-three, they had a son, and named him Anthony Walter and, after the day on which he was born, Patrick.

On the birth certificate, under 'Occupation of Father', Bernard wrote 'Author'. When he next published a book, he would be in competition with his youngest son.

2

Childhood

I

In the first decade of the twentieth century, Hassocks was a village of considerable attractions. Though just a couple of stops from Brighton on the railway line to London, it was in the middle of beautiful countryside, shielded from the sea by the high northern flank of the South Downs. It would be remembered with affection by both Hamilton brothers. The false alibi of the murderer in Bruce's first novel, *To Be Hanged*, depends on his appearing to have boarded the Brighton train at Victoria when, in fact, he has motored from London and met it at the 'cheerful little township of Hassocks'.[1] At the climax of Hamilton's bleakest book, *Hangover Square*, the doomed hero, George Harvey Bone, walks from Brighton to Hassocks on his way to London and experiences a rare, and brief, moment of exaltation: 'he knew this part of the country, and he had a fancy to see Apple Lodge, a little farmhouse, with cows and a donkey and ducks, where he had stayed as a child and been happy, before they sent him to school and made him miserable.'[2]

Dale House was a substantial dwelling with a beautiful garden, demanding a staff of maids, governesses and gardeners. Though they were not to live there for long, Bernard had time to order the installation of a stained-glass window containing the heraldic devices of the Hamilton and Wildman dynasties. For Bruce, Lalla and Patrick, in their later childhood it was to be a summer escape from urban life, an idyllic, privileged rural world of walks and horse rides.

When Hamilton wrote of his childhood experiences, he was concerned with those which dated from after his fourth birthday. Dale House had been let and the Hamilton family had moved to number 12, First Avenue in Hove. The distinction between Brighton and Hove is far from obvious, the one indistinguishably becoming the other. But the Hamilton brothers repeatedly insisted on the difference between the two districts. Writing much later (at the height of his Marxist commitment, in 1938), Bruce was contemptuous of his boyhood home: 'As was to be expected in an area where a great part of the population lived by ministering to the luxuries of well-to-do rentiers and holiday-makers with money to burn, the ground was ripe for Fascism of the purest and most uncompromising type.'[3] Writing a few years later, he showed himself also alive to its attractions. The hero of his novel *Pro* arrives at the front and finds 'the scene enormously stimulating. There was something exciting, boldly erotic about it.'[4] Yet a few minutes walk takes him to 'a very different town surrounding the County Ground at Hove – quiet, dignified, spacious.'

Already at the age of four, Hamilton found the conflict that was to stimulate and torment him for the whole of his life, almost literally on his doorstep. Barely a minute's walk to the left out of the front door of his house would have brought the young Hamilton to the seafront, and there, along to the left again, the view was dominated by the now ruined West Pier. Behind him in First Avenue, a constrained, unhappy, respectable household; before him, 'this sex-battleship',[5] tawdry, glittering, lower class, forbidden and fun.

In 1958, Hamilton was being treated in a nursing home after an 'extended period of almost unintermittent drinking' when two medical students entered his private room and took a casual interest in his case, assuming 'justifiably but inaccurately' (Hamilton's words) that he was an alcoholic. They questioned him about his drinking:

Was it hereditary? Did I think it was something caused automatically by the constitution of the body, or was it the result of nervous strain – of some underlying frustration – or major disaster in my life? Could it be traced to unhappiness in childhood or boyhood? And many other rather naïve and delightful questions of the same sort – all equally impossible for a conscientious witness to answer with a straight yes or no.[6]

Hamilton's drinking – which was to prove physically, psychologically and financially ruinous to him – is one of the enigmas of his life. There is no single answer to this and it may be that he was more revealing asking the questions than when he set about answering them. His immediate response to the questions of the two students was blandly discouraging, 'that I had been offered, on the whole, about as happy a childhood as one could reasonably hope for, and I think that this was true.' However, he at once began to write, for his own purposes, an account of that childhood, as if to search for what had brought him to the hospital bed:

At the age of four I was the youngest member of a well-to-do middle-class household of about nine people (mother, father, sister, brother, three or four servants and myself) established at First Avenue, Hove.

I have often thought that First Avenue, Hove, could be adequately described by only one living writer – Osbert Sitwell – and I can, actually, remember this writer's eye lighting up, with a sort of novelist's relish, when I told him that this had been my early background.

I myself can only say that it is quite unlike anything else I have ever seen on earth. The grey, drab, tall, treeless houses leading down to the King's Gardens and the sea convey absolutely no social or historical message to me. They are not even funny, or ostentatious, or bizarre, or characteristic, so far as I know, of any recognised form of taste or type of dweller.

There are good reasons for believing, though, that in 1908 the residents, so far from showing any sort of amazement or bewilderment at what they saw from their front windows, were complacent and even vain about their houses – regarding the Adelaide Crescent and Brunswick Square areas which lay eastwards as being inferior not only from the point of view of convenience and beauty, but also socially.

Certainly the houses had all modern conveniences – these including house-telephones and genuine sea-water obtainable from one of the bath taps. You could telephone almost any room from almost any other room, and you could have, in the bath, the crude equivalent of a delightful splash in the sea. There was, however, no domestic sea-bathing or telephoning that I can call to mind.

There was, too, an enormous amount of space – enough to contain four or five capacious flats. And nowadays, of course, the flats are there, with curiously dreary little announcements of their occupants' names stuck into equally dreary little frames above or below electric bell-pushes. The gardens at the back were disproportionately small. But the houses and the gardens taken together gave an enterprising child ample room in which to entertain himself – in which easily to invent territories of adventure and fright.

Here I was well fed, well cared for, and well clothed: and I suffered no physical violence of any sort. But this does not mean that there was any absence of anxieties and neuroses of all sorts, which were made more oppressive rather than disentangled, by various nurses with whom I spent most of my time – at that period and in that class called Nurses (not 'Nannies').[7]

The young Hamilton's capacity for deriving anxiety from the most seemingly harmless of nursery experiences was, by his own account, almost limitless. He was particularly distressed by the 'ponderous drolleries of these humourless women' into whose charge he was placed. He was told, as all children are told, that if the wind changed while he was pulling a face, the expression would be frozen for ever: 'To believe was to accept the existence of a constant personal danger: to disbelieve was to realise that one's powerful, bonnetted informant was a liar, and therefore hateful, or idiotic, or both.'[8]

He was told, as all children are told, that, for the sake of the rhyme, his toes were pigs: 'But what was "market"? Why did one pig have roast beef, and the other none? Where did justice lie? Which pig gained? Could toes, in fact, be pigs?' He was to decide from a very early age that his destiny was to be a writer, and the nascent poet was particularly offended by the nursery rhyme's failure of rhyme and scansion: 'I was disturbed by the complete and ugly abandonment of scansion in the last line, by the knowledge that "home" did not rhyme with the word "none", and that the final use of the word "home" was a repetition and not a rhyme.'[9]

His nurses told him that he was composed of slugs and snails and puppy dogs' tails, that eating mustard with mutton was the sign of a glutton, that if he ate too many potatoes, eggs or peas he would turn into a potato, an egg or a pea. When the nurses were asked for a story, they were 'hatefully disobliging', and instead of cordially declining resorted to their usual unpleasant mental trickery:

I can remember two particularly below-the-belt ruses they used when I asked to be told a story. In one case, pretending to consent, they would say 'Very well . . .', and I was waiting eagerly for what was to follow. Then, slowly and pointedly recited, came the following rhyme: –

'I'll tell you a story of Jack O'My-Nory,
    And now my story's *begun*.
I'll tell you another of Jack and his *brother*,
    And now my story's *done*.'

In the other case they would again feign consent and begin, with a heavily dramatic air which filled me with pleasure and hope: –

'It was a cold and frosty night! . . . And the King of the Castle said to his Servant "Tell me a Story! . . ." And this is how he began: – 'It was a cold and frosty night! . . . And the King of the Castle said to his Servant "Tell me a Story!" And this is how be began: – "It was a cold and frosty night! . . . And the King of the Castle said to his Servant "Tell me a Story!" And this is how he began: – "It was a cold – " ' and so on until my patience tired. And no amount of entreaties brought forth anything but the same cruel, deliberate formula.

All this sort of thing, almost certainly, helps to nourish in a child's mind those plants of doubt, distrust and anxiety which are ultimately the main causes of heavy or excessive drinking – as will be shown later.[10]

The disproportion between the normality of the events described and the Dickensian horror of the effects they produced is exteme. And there were other 'neuroses' (Hamilton's term) for which the nurses could not be held responsible. He had, and retained all his life, the inability to engage himself 'in any task or pleasure' without the door being shut, a common enough compulsion:

But in my case it was carried to extremes. Not only did the door have to have the appearance of being shut: it was necessary to ascertain that the knob had been properly turned. And even when this had been ascertained it had to be ascertained over and over again: I would go to the door to do this as often as half a dozen times in half an hour. Here, without any encouragement from nurses or anything external, were the beginnings of the malady of doubt – the desire for the insurance of insurance of insurance indefinitely.[11]

When Hamilton told the medical students of his happy childhood, what he seems to have meant is that he had all the furnishings, the props and the backdrop that is generally supposed to accompany that state. But the actual activities, the essence of being a child, he looked back on with loathing:

Young people when together often make a lot of noise and clamour, and unthinking people assume that this signifies happiness. Nothing could be further from the case: there is a lot of hysteria, distress, insincerity and devilishness in the noise, and it is more often than not all part of the miserable muddle in which the children are trapped. The noise, indeed, is as ugly and unhappy as that made by adults at a cocktail party.[12]

Hamilton never wrote about early, pre-school childhood in his fiction, a strange omission for a writer so steeped in Dickens. To read his first memories is to recognize that what he did instead was to preserve them and then dramatize them, refracted through adult experience. There is something child-like about Hamilton's innocent heroes and heroines with their compulsions and observances, their dismay in the face of the big world's deafening noise and baffling rituals. The germ of those vividly realized anxieties can be seen in the following passage:

This way of thinking and behaving was very much more painful and harmful when it was combined with a fear of the dark, of isolation in the dark. Thus, when I was put to bed by my nurse with the assurance that if I needed anything I had only to summon her from the kitchen far below, I was soon, strenuously as I tried not to be so, agitated and really afraid. Was she really in the kitchen? Would she reply to a call? It was necessary to assure myself of the truth of her assurance, and soon I would be out on the half-lit landing, which frightened me more than ever, and listening for any sounds of human activity which might come up from the kitchen. Hearing nothing satisfactory, I would shout – and before long she would come upstairs, put me to bed again, and leave me with fresh reassurances. But they were valueless, hardly worth a thing, an empty formality. In ten minutes' time I was out on the landing and again shouting – yelling, indeed, if there was too long a delay before her next journey upstairs. I do not know how many times each night this nurse (Nurse Swain, I remember – an exceptionally good nurse, who, like my mother, never told me fraudulent stories or harmful lies) had to climb, at the end of her day, from the basement and up through the equivalent of two capacious flats, to soothe me. I should say half a dozen at least. But she knew as well as I did that this was not caprice, self-indulgence, imperiousness or foolishness on my part: it was panic.

A night-light was given me, but this made matters worse. For the night-light in its saucer on the mantelpiece – dim, wavering, and sinking – was even more suggestive and anticipative of evil than darkness itself.

Finally it was arranged that another bed should be set up in my room, and that Nurse Swain should sleep in it at the end of her day, which was, I think, at about ten o'clock.

It is difficult to believe that even this was useless: nevertheless it was: for Nurse Swain was a quiet sleeper, so quiet that as soon as she was in the first stillness of sleep she gave me a vivid impression that she was dead. Had she snored no doubt I should have thought she was choking. 'Nurse – are you all right?' and 'Nurse – are you dead?' were my sincere, serious and incessant enquiries in the darkness. Once, I remember, she lost, or pretended to lose, her temper with me. 'Don't be so *stupid*, Master Pat!' she said, almost angrily. She pronounced the word 'stupid' in an odd way. She said 'styöopid' – the 'oo' sound being uttered as in 'book' or 'cook'. And I was aware of this, just as I had been earlier aware that the last line of 'This little piggy went to market' did not scan.[13]

Hamilton himself wondered whether this 'ultra-anxiety' might be evidence of 'some constitutional defect which might lead finally to excessive drinking'. Or could it have been inherited from Bernard, 'who at certain periods of his life, was often remarkably drunk'. Hamilton dismisses both possibilities, but it seems at lest plausible that Bernard was, in one way or another, the principal source of his anxiety. As Hamilton grew older and was able to supplant his father in his own profession, he also began to forgive him, partly by attempting to understand him, but also by diminishing him into a comic figure. 'On the other hand,' he was able to say when he was in his mid-forties, 'as I grow older I see, of course, more and more his pitiable side. And I, at any rate, must at times have been *infuriating*, even to a normal father.

'Furthermore, the amount of *laughs* I have had subsequently out of this man makes me feel that I have been compensated, almost fully, for what I suffered.'[14]

But what was this 'on the other hand' *from*? Bernard was a snob, as he demonstrated by telling his wife's secret to a titled acquaintance, humiliating her and losing her a friend. Yes, 'Social snobbery was, I fear, one amongst the least of the faults of the author of "The Light?" He made us all suffer intensely – Mummie, Lalla, you, and myself.'[15]

Bernard was obsessed with the idea of the great man of destiny, and the tragedy and comedy of his life was that he could never, as his fantasy demanded, take this role on the stage of letters or public affairs. But for a few years, to an audience of his three young children, he could be God, and the two figures became confused in the mind of the young Hamilton. During thunderstorms, Bernard would flamboyantly conduct while counting after each lightning flash in order – though the children did not then understand this – to calculate the storm's distance. Such was Bernard's incantatory vigour that his son derived the impression that he was actually creating the storm, and calling forth the thunder and lightning.

Even as an adult looking back on a father long dead and forgotten by everyone except his children, Hamilton's problem was that, though he was able to see through the charades of his father's life, he could not shake him off because he was so profoundly a part of the experiences that had made him a writer. Throughout Hamilton's life, Shakespeare is a curious presence, disparaged, patronized, resented, grudgingly praised, finally yielded to. The root of this was in his introduction to the writer by his father, one Sunday evening. After mentioning the name, Bernard suddenly embarked on the 'Friends, Romans, countrymen' speech that was a traditional recitation piece in Edwardian England:

Underneath the dazzling white table-cloth used for meals, there was a permanent cloth of dull green. This he snatched from the table, and briskly threw round himself – thus representing himself as one wearing a Roman toga. Then he took a dining-chair, stood upon it, and, with the aid of a volume of Shakespeare's works, delivered the famous speech.

On the reiteration of the words 'Brutus is an honourable man', he put on a leer more a slow, horrible, and sardonic than I have ever seen on any man's face in my life – even on his own. This, I know now, was to convey the bitter ambiguity of the words, but at the time it seemed that the impersonator in the green table-cloth had gone mad.[16]

Appalled and captivated by his demonic theatricality, all three of Bernard's children were to write plays, all three of them would act on stage. The audience of Hamilton's first novels was composed of Ellen, Lalla and Bruce, as their author performed them aloud. As an adult, Hamilton would view his father with more sympathy:

When he was not making a fool of himself, he was reasonable, kind-hearted, generous and even wise in the ways of the world. And although, when making a fool of himself, he caused a great deal of distress and pain to his family, it would be impossible for any of them to feel any resentment.

Moreover, his constant condition of absurd inflation and the abandonment of reality naturally brought with them their opposites – periods of fearful deflation in the presence or the suspicion of reality. And at such times he had as he sat thinking, a staring look – almost unbearably childish, simple and unhappy.[17]

This magnanimity was easier to summon up in later years, when Bernard had lost his capacity to do harm. As children, they felt not so much resentment, which would suggest they could imagine life being otherwise, as 'complete dread and consequent absolute hatred'. In her secret teenage memoir, written when she was fifteen years old, Lalla recalled, 'I have always been told and I'm afraid I know that I am fearfully old for my years – but then there has been something to make me so, but I shall never write about that as it is not my secret.' This presumably refers to her childhood perception of Bernard's other life when he was away, out of the country with his mistress, Marthe, in Paris, or taking a cure at the waters in Karlsbad. Even when he was in England he would spend the weekdays in London where he had chambers.[18] His arrival on Fridays was awaited with apprehension, 'indeed it seemed as if the whole house shuddered feebly'. Hamilton's innovation as a play-wright would be to strip melodrama of its reliance on gimmicks and crude effects. Instead he found horror in a drinks party or an apparently normal marriage, produced by the simplest effects, such as the footsteps from above heard by a disbelieving Mrs Massingham in *Gaslight*.[19] It was the apparent security, the lack of overt conflict, that was so disturbing to Lalla, Bruce and Hamilton. Confined to their 'schoolroom', at the back of the ground floor, the children listened, terrified, to the arrival of Bernard, drunk and resentful, from London:

What happened then, as overheard with dreadful intentness from the school-room, varied considerably. Sometimes there would be a long and inexplicable silence: the sound of his footsteps giving no clue to his actual movements or intentions. Sometimes he went to the top of the basement and shouted for a servant, who would quickly appear and at whom he would shout. But all the curious variations were certain to end with his slamming open the dining-room (he had the gift of slamming doors open) and greeting my mother.

What then happened in the dining-room, over his dinner with my mother, could not be ascertained from the schoolroom. Only an incessant mumbling sound could be heard from the other side of the thick wall – mumbling, mumbling, mumbling, mumbling, going on and on and on – and on and on.

To listen to this was somehow even more terrifying than the earlier anticipation of the entrance, and the eavesdropping and its variations.[20]

As it became clear that the marriage was a sham, the children were forced to take sides. The contrast was striking. Their father was generally in a 'bad temper', the family euphemism for his drunkenness, and picked quarrels with both friends and strangers. When he paid attention to his children it was to subject them to a lawyer's inquisition or a parade-ground inspection. Their mother was 'attractive in her plump piquant way, and chock full of volubility, vehemence, and emphasis, with her sensibilities lying close to the surface.'[21] And she was at home.

The children naturally took her side, though Bruce suspected, with no evidence, that she might be sexually frigid and therefore that the 'bubbling energy of plump, pretty little dark-fringed, snub-nosed Nellie', as he put it, was channelled into motherhood.[22] As might be expected from the author of *The Awakening of Mrs Carstairs*, Ellen was both a solicitous and a passionate mother, finding solace for the failings of a second marriage in her three children. Like many women of her age and class, she could be over-solicitous, plying her children with medicines and tonics.[23] Patrick was fifty when he recalled her having plied him with laxatives as a boy, thus, in his view, almost making him constipated for the rest of his days.

Ellen was, as Bruce later recalled, 'neither more nor less than most of her kind, highly class-conscious.'[24] She treated servants and trades-people with uneasy thoughtlessness, or even brutality. The children recalled nurses being dismissed for trivial offences. Yet her snobbery was of the most superficial variety and if her children gradually came to recognize and criticize, then so did she and in later years 'finally came to deplore and even ridicule her former pretensions.'[25] The children saw no comparison between the affectations of their mother and those of their father and all three remained devoted to her. Hamilton affectionately used her expression, 'd.v.' (God willing), in his letters until the end of his life.

From an early age, when Hamilton was approaching the age of seven and the prospect of preparatory school, the relationship between the two brothers was complicated. Bruce had been dominant. He taught Hamilton to read and to ride a bicycle. But quickly they became more equal. They shared a bedroom and each night would talk after the light had been switched out, inventing stories for each other. Soon Bruce became jealous of Hamilton: 'He had an engaging quality that I lacked; people were more attracted to him than to me.'[26] Sixty years later, with his brother dead, Bruce recalled seemingly trivial events – a dentist citing Patrick's fortitude in comparison to his own cowardice, a childhood friend spurning Bruce for Patrick – that still tormented him. The latter failure was commemorated by Patrick and his new friend going through a playful marriage ceremony before Bruce and some amused adults: 'There was a great deal of laughter from our grown-up fellow-guests, but I didn't join in it, not even on the wrong side of my face.'[27]

II

In 1912, when Hamilton was eight, he began school for the first time, at Holland House, a mere five minutes' walk away, in the opposite direction from the seafront. The best description of this institution is his own, when he portrayed it with a change of name in *The West Pier*:

Rodney House was a preparatory school for about forty boys, accepting pupils from many different classes of parents in the town. What may be roughly called an aristocracy of five or six boys came from the squares and avenues – Brunswick Square, Grand Avenue, First Avenue, and the like: what may be roughly called a *bourgeoisie* (the sons of merchants, dentists, estate agents, doctors, clergymen, retired officers, and well-to-do local tradesmen) came from the roads – Wilbury Road, Holland Road, Tisbury Road, Norton Road: while the rest came from the villas – Hova Villas, Ventnor Villas, Denmark Villas – or from obscure crescents and streets at the back of Hove or of Brighton, or from humble western regions verging upon Portslade. A few of this third class approximated to the *sansculottes*: at any rate, their clothes were laughed at, and they were known to be 'common'.[28]

Hamilton's educational career was to be superficially successful and happy. In middle age he was to insist to his brother in nervous double negatives that 'I was not unhappy there (as *you* were not)'[29] and the school itself, though far from the first rank, socially or intellectually, had its own enticing privilege for a young boy, which is recalled with pleasure in the novels of both brothers: pupils were entitled to free admission to the nearby ground of Sussex County Cricket Club. Ernest Ralph Gorse takes advantage of this privilege to commit his first assault on a young girl. In Bruce's words the two brothers came to look back on this venue as 'as a lost Elysium where, in the summers immediately before the first war, so many golden days had been spent.'[30]

Hamilton was less nostalgic than Bruce, and it is significant that he accorded his scholastic experiences to a man destined to be hanged for murder. Some years after he had abandoned the Gorse tales, when he was recovering from a psychological crisis, Hamilton found himself, in a letter to Bruce, reconsidering some of his prep-school experiences. The earlier must have occurred in his first summer term at Holland House:

I shall never forget a particular moment of misery, which I didn't tell you about, when (I *think* on our first day of watching cricket at the County Ground) you and I stopped at the nets and saw, among others, Longridge bowling at somebody, and me realising how utterly, *utterly* uninterested I was in Longridge, and in the game we were going to watch.[31]

The second episode presumably occurred towards the end of his school career, when he was twelve or thirteen:

Again I shall never forget a moment after tea at the C.G., when I had left you (I left you as much as possible, you will remember, for to inflict my own misery and restlessness on you considerably *added* to my agony of my mind) and sat on the south side of the ground (near the 'pennyworth of squashed flies' place, and tried, tried, *tried* to interest myself in a chess-problem, but at last gave in and walked round and round the ground with my mind set on my first whiskey at that pub (whose name I've forgotten). Drinks, at this time, used to give me a faint, *faint* relief, you may remember.[32]

Hamilton was never to lose his pained perception of the meaninglessness of the structures and customs of school society. That he, on occasion, achieved success in them made no difference. Even when he had adopted a passionate Marxism, he, in his English way, would always be indulgent, even affectionate, towards what Marx called the idiocy of rural life. But he was repelled by the idiocy of school life, which he exposed both in *The West Pier* and the earlier *Craven House*. In the latter novel the young hero, Master Wildman, arrives at his new school, Lyndon House (also based on Holland House), where in his first few days he is mercilessly bullied, accused of being a sneak, of cheating and cribbing, of stealing, put on trial, reduced to tears, tormented.[33] By the following week, however, he is perfectly happy:

Master Wildman was not sorry to get back to school at the end of it. He was by now well trained in the usages and idiom that had so distressed him on his first day, and was, in the habits of barging, punching, slandering or pure reviling, together with the easy interchange of such epithets as Sow, Pig, Swine, Hog, Cad, Cheat, Sneak, Cur, Fool, Liar, Ass, Cow, Beast, Insect, Worm, practically the equal of his companions.[34]

Master Wildman has not conquered the bullies, but become one of them. Hamilton himself presided over a strictly hierarchical secret school society called the Sporting Club, which made mischief in the environs of the school after hours. Bruce praised Holland House because it gave Hamilton the chance to exercise power, but for Hamilton, as he was to show in book after book, when one person exercises power over another, it is to do harm. Bruce was well aware of this. The earliest surviving letter by Hamilton, on the evidence of the wavery writing which it would take him another fifty years to re-acquire, must have been written even before he began school: 'I promise on my honour that I will not quarrel with Bruce if we go into rooms, while I'm in the bedroom, at meals, or any other time. I've fixed it up with him, and I really don't think we will if we try.' And Bruce testifies that Hamilton early became an expert in quietly teasing him, and then calmly observing the effect he produced. As he grew older, he became more skilfully manipulative still. In a late letter, Hamilton recalled: 'We must not forget what a blackmailing little shit [I] at one time was – particularly to [my] brother! [. . .]

'I have a feeling that my horribleness at that time was mostly due to *illness*. From 10, or 12, to 20 is a very sick time for most of us.'[35]

3

Leaving School

One sunny evening in August 1914, Hamilton and Bruce were watching the cricket at the county ground, when they heard the sound of a brass band. According to Hamilton's recollection, it simply marched noisily around the 'outer path encircling the seats and the stands'.[1] He had a further memory which haunted him because he didn't know whether it had really happened or whether it was a dream. He and Bruce were seated on the front steps of their house 'and the two umpires, *dressed in their white coats* (this certainly sounds dream-like and impossible) passed us on their way to the sea, presumably for a stroll. And either you or I asked them what had happened about the match. And they replied, in a kindly and rather shame-faced way, that it had been thought better to drop it.'[2] Britain was at war with Germany.

Bernard had not made good use of the pre-war years. His literary career had become dormant, except for one absurd and brief incarnation as a playwright. He wrote a one-act play called *The Combat*, concerning the gladiatorial form of combat in Ancient Rome involving a net. The play was produced for an inconsequential week at a music-hall in Bournemouth while Ellen was away in Lausanne supervising Lalla's education. Bernard appeared at the family home with a potential young actress for the play, chaperoned by her mother. However the suspicious housekeeper, a Mrs Hancock, discovered what Bruce termed 'conclusive evidence of adultery'.[3] Ellen was informed and immediately returned to confront her husband. A second divorce would have seemed an unpalatable option and instead she shrewdly used the shaming discovery to secure a more generous settlement on her and the children.

The war must have come as a relief to Bernard, who had been waiting for this epoch-making military conflict since the turn of the century. He first found humble enough employment as a special constable but soon, though he was now in his early fifties, obtained a commission in the Territorial Division of the Royal Warwickshire Horse Artillery in 1915. He played the military role with theatrical gusto. Hamilton wrote of one afternoon, in 1916, 'he was having tea and taking it fairly easy while on duty at his office in Leamington, when his orderly brought in an evening newspaper which announced the death of Lord Kitchener. On seeing this he at once rose to his feet, stood at attention, saluted and said, 'Carry on".'[4]

Men of Bernard's age were used to release younger officers for the front line, but as casualties mounted, their duties brought them closer to the action. In 1917 he and other 'Senior Officers' were ordered to France to take administrative positions in towns to the rear of the fighting. Bernard recalled his experiences with the laconic modesty of an old military man: 'After becoming a casualty, when in command in Peronne in 1917, I took over, in January 1918, sixty camps in the Favreuil and Bekugnâtre area, in front of Bapaume (Fourth Corps: Third Army).'[5]

Bapaume figures in Siegfried Sassoon's 1917 poem, ' "Blighters" ', in which he rages at a patriotic music-hall show:

> I'd like to see a Tank come down the stalls
> Lurching to ragtime tunes, or 'Home, sweet Home',
> And there'd be no more jokes in Music-halls
> To mock the riddled corpses round Bapaume.[6]

Bernard felt no such qualms. By his own account, he was living in poor conditions. In March 1918 his command came under attack. Yet he seems to have enjoyed his part in the action as he had enjoyed nothing since he left Cambridge. It might be thought that the war would furnish Bernard the writer with some much needed authentic experience, and while he was stationed in England he began to write a book about the war. In March 1917, Hamilton wrote home from school asking if it was finished. After his service nothing more is heard of it and the account of his military experience in *One World* is perversely lacking in vividness. As a creative writer, Bernard was hampered by a total lack of interest in the surfaces of life, its sights, sounds and smells.

Nevertheless, he had had a good war. But, like many soldiers, he returned in 1919 finding children very different from those he had left.

Shortly after the war began, the Hamiltons had given up the First Avenue house and rented a house of a similar size in Chiswick in West London. (Ellen bought a sixty-year lease on the house in 1919.) Bruce, now fourteen years old, had begun to attend Westminster public school and Hamilton moved to Colet Court preparatory school in Hammersmith as a day boy, starting in the summer term of 1915. The move to London proved to be only temporary. Bruce became ill with 'congestion of the lungs'[7] and it was decided he needed to return to the healthier sea air of Brighton. The Chiswick house was sub-let and the family returned to lodgings in Hove, but at the end of the summer Hamilton chose to return to Colet Court as a boarder. One product of this arrangement was his first work of literature to survive. At Colet Court he wrote a poem about August of which he was so proud that he copied it out for his mother. He was about ten years old:

> Then August comes, clothed in her golden robe,
> When one remembers nothing but clear skies,
> Green fields, and the sweetly perfumed flowers.
> And thought of cold has faded from our minds
> Complete as 'tis departed from the earth.
> The corn in graceful stacks is piled up.
> Or waving in the breeze as if it wooes
> The sickle. And the trees do bend beneath
> Thick clusters of rich fruit, which almost bow
> Their branches to the ground. The wagon, thus,
> As moving slowly o'er the well reaped field,
> Before so harsh, adds beauty to the scene.
> A Mellow softness covers all the earth.
> 'Tis now that Nature show[s] her beauty best.[8]

This routine anthology of images and words from the ode 'To Autumn' demonstrates nothing except the extent of Hamilton's juvenile preoccupation with Keats.

At the end of his second term, Hamilton spent the Easter holidays with Bruce, who had not returned to Westminster and was making futile attempts at a correspondence course which would qualify him for a lowly

Second Division clerkship in the Civil Service. Hamilton confessed to Bruce that he had been made very unhappy by the fetid sexuality of dormitory life at Colet Court. He had been disturbed by an account of how babies were born: 'It appeared that a man and woman got married, and when they decided to have a child they came genitally together (under medical supervision) and "drew spunk", out of which fluid the doctor in some uncertain way fashioned a baby.'[9] Hamilton was more disturbed still by the sexual activities of the dormitory:

Mass masturbation, individual or reciprocal, was practised by the older boys, sometimes under cover of sheets rigged up as tents, and any children unwilling to join in this, or backward in using the painfully crude vocabulary of incipient sexuality, were held in contempt and even bullied. Hamilton was as yet quite undeveloped sexually. His attitude was one of fascination, tempered by some disgust and strong moral reprobation.[10]

Hamilton was asking for help that his older brother was not able to give. Though Bruce was now fifteen years old, this account of the mingling of genital fluids was the first he had heard of the details of human reproduction and he was as amazed as his younger brother. More urgently, Hamilton wanted Bruce to tell his mother what he had been suffering. But Bruce admitted to Hamilton that he was so guilty about his own compulsive masturbation that he felt unable to intervene on Hamilton's behalf. The disastrous interview ended with Hamilton counselling Bruce against self-abuse. It was then left to Hamilton himself to communicate the truth to his mother and Ellen immediately removed him from the school.

Hamilton left no record of this time and he never refers to it in any of his surviving letters, but it is noteworthy that Hamilton's two most evil characters are people who have never adequately grown out of childhood. Of Mr Thwaites in *The Slaves of Solitude*: 'The trouble with that man was that he had never stepped beyond the mental age of eleven or twelve, nature having arrested him, and preserved him, at a certain ugly phase – the phase of the loquacious little braggart at school so often met with at that age.'[11] And in *Hangover Square*, the protagonist's tormentor, Netta, 'had never got out of being the bad-tempered, haughty, tyrannical child she was at the beginning. She lacked the imagination and generosity to do so.'[12]

Hamilton and Bruce spent an aimless few months in Hove, much of it with their easy-going cousin, Frank Bridger, only son of Ellen's sister, Elizabeth, visiting cinemas and music-halls. Then in the autumn, Bruce enrolled at Brighton Technical College, Ellen having resisted Bernard's urgings that his eldest, who suffered seriously from respiratory disease, go down the mines as an engineer. This also failed and Bruce left for an army crammer with the idea of taking the Army Entrance Examination in 1918. Hamilton returned to Holland House, where he continued to board, surprisingly enough, and the rest of his preparatory school career passed with no apparent trouble. One surviving report, on the autumn term of 1916, is favourable in an unremarkable way. A. W. P. Hamilton is described as 'a good N. C. O. and he should make a good Prefect when his time comes.'[13] In 1918 he began at Westminster school, which Bruce had just left for the army.

In one of the few press interviews of his career, Hamilton gave a brief account of his formative years to an American journalist:

'I was born in Hassocks, Sussex, and externally grew up much as all boys do, taking my surroundings for granted, but I always had a more or less vague notion that I wanted something that my surroundings did not quite supply.' So he began his story. 'While I lived the life of an ordinary boy, a poetic yearning developed by degrees until, all unconsciously as to how I reached that state of mind, I was sure that some day I was going to be a great poet. There was not the slightest doubt of it in my mind,' and he laughed as he said it.[14]

Hamilton's brief time at Westminster – under two years – left far less of a mark on him than his experiences at Holland House. His fictional portrayal of school life was to be restricted to the pre-pubescent, pre-sexual world of prep schools. But his literary ambitions were not discouraged as they might have been at other English public schools. He won an essay prize. He wrote poems, and when he was still at school, one was published in a supplement of new verse accompanying the journal of the Poetry Society. It was titled 'Heaven', and was no worse than its dismal fellows:

> They say, my dear, that far from here,
> And we shall meet again.
> There is no death, it's a loss of breath,
> And an end to the bitter pain.

And there shall be (wise men agree)
    A better land than this.
Oh! Far above, and only love
    Shall enter to our bliss.

But shall we meet what we used to greet:
    The slumbering English hills,
The open seas: the willow trees,
    And the laughing daffodils?

And shall we find the autumn wind,
    The talk of men who are witty,
The splashing rain, won't these remain?
    And will you be as pretty?[15]

Looking back, Hamilton would recall that he had been ill for much of his school life, though this seems to have amounted to little more than an adolescent disgust with his surroundings. He was certainly not afflicted as Bruce had been. But in March 1919 he became ill with the influenza that was then a world-wide epidemic and he left Westminster for the last time at around the time of his fifteenth birthday. His school days were over.

4

Adolescence

I

The fifteen-year-old Patrick Hamilton, an aspiring poet, physically and mentally unstable, with no qualifications and no job, now cut a disturbingly eccentric figure. His brother later recalled his curious garb: 'A bright green sports coat would, for example, surmount well-worn grey flannel trousers; additional colour might be supplied by a scarlet knitted tie, and a further touch of oddity by his poking three dents in a greasy old felt hat, giving him the look of a rather skinny cowboy.'[1] His social circle consisted of two people: his sister, Lalla, and his brother, Bruce. His friendship with Bruce, who had just been demobilized from millitary service that had never taken him out of London, was based on their shared passion for literature. Their taste was doggedly conventional, and would not have been out of place in a middle-class household of fifty years earlier: Palgrave's *Golden Treasury*, and in that spirit the lyrics of Wordsworth, Shelley, Tennyson, Milton, Spenser, with just cursory nods elsewhere, to Pope and Browning. Hamilton wrote the first two chapters of a novel, called *Disillusionment*, and a long 'essay in verse' called *Modernism*, which was an assault on that movement, such as he understood it, 'an indictment of all those trends, chiefly in poetry but also in the whole field of contemporary creation, that seemed to him to be leading away from simplicity and sincerity.'[2] He worked on it for several years, and made a serious effort to have it published, offering it to Jonathan Cape, who turned it down, though with words of encouragement appropriate to such a young aspirant author.

If Hamilton's relationship with Bruce was based on adolescent ideals about art, his relationship with Lalla, six years older than himself, was very different. She was far less emotionally constrained than her bookish, self-conscious younger brothers, as well as better looking, and had a succession of boyfriends from the age of thirteen onwards. Writing in her 1914 memoir, she observed of herself:

So far through my life I have never been without one girl friend, two or three girl enemies and two or three men or boys fond of me. I am a tiny flirt I know – but can I help it? The majority of men are devils or rotters and I think the male sex deserves to be teased.

When she was sixteen, she became temporarily engaged to a young businessman, and this was succeeded by two more engagements over the next couple of years. As she began to have more serious affairs, she chose to confide not in her mother, nor in Bruce, but – to Bruce's considerable chagrin – her youngest brother. Hamilton was to have few close women friends in his life, and this relationship, in his insecure, formative years, was a crucial influence both on his life and his work. Hamilton's early novels prominently feature attractive young girls alone, planning the strategy of their love lives, and his experience of this consisted solely in his mother's first novel and his discussions with Lalla about how to deal with her importunate suitors.

Lalla also provided glimpses of another, less ethereal, form of artistic endeavour. She had had hopes of a singing career and, at the end of 1916, narrowly failed to win a scholarship to the Royal College of Music. Instead she went to London in January 1917 to study with Miss Nellie Rowe, an expensive singing teacher who lived in the Cromwell Road in Kensington. Though a captivating performer, Lalla did not have the technical gifts to make a career in music, but in the following year she obtained, through an actor friend of Bernard's, a bit part in a touring play. She got regular work in the theatre, where she acted under the name of Diana Hamilton. Early in 1920, while appearing in a small role in a play called *Mumsie*, she met and fell in love with Vane Sutton Vane, thirty years old and unsuccessful both as an actor and playwright. He had been a distant family friend in Hove. In Bruce's view he was, though striking in appearance, decidedly not handsome: 'Although his prominent eyes were appealing, his small beaky nose and close-lipped downward curving mouth were not specially attractive; his light brown curling hair had receded far from his forehead, and an almost comic plumpness of face and figure led Lalla to address him affectionately as "Fatty".[3] He became a close associate of the two brothers. He shared their attraction to popular culture, music-hall rather than opera, and a taste for drink. Yet, though he remained something of an enigma to them, his commitment to their sister and the couple's mutual love was not in doubt.

Vane was already married and it would take two and a half years and considerable expense for a divorce to be obtained. In the meantime, to Ellen's great alarm, the couple lived together in rooms on the Edgware Road, then in Maida Vale. Both Vane and Lalla attempted to write plays, Vane with moderate success. In mid-1922 they were finally married.

Looking back at this period from the vantage point of success, ten years later, Hamilton spoke lightly of this period to his American interviewer:

I did all sorts of things, anything I could get hold of; worked for the army and at law. Had a sister who was on the stage, and that led me into that sort of life. Took perfectly rotten jobs in the theatre, nothing that amounted to anything more than giving me barely enough money to live, and not a good living at that, but it did give me a pretty clear knowledge of the life of that class of people. Finally I decided there wasn't anything in it for me. I must have more money, so I learned stenography and typewriting by correspondence and got a job in the city. This would keep me from starving while I was getting to be that great poet.[4]

This has the detached and slightly mocking self-deprecation that he was to deploy to endearing effect in his first novel, *Monday Morning*, and disguised what he was really feeling. The year after the interview in which he spoke with such insouciance, Hamilton would write to Bruce of their 'nerve-wracking, ill-adjusted, wretched early youth', in which they had 'battled with and been tortured by the monsters'.[5] For both brothers, amid their traditional anxieties, there was the practical question of what they would now do. They had the artistic temperament, but were they artists?

Meanwhile, the primary source of their anxieties returned into their lives. Bernard had survived the war physically almost unscathed, but he suffered from what was considered to be, in Bruce's phrase, a 'shattered nervous system"[6] in reparation for which he constantly appealed to the Ministry of Pensions. He was a diminished figure, his military demeanour comical, his violent temper no longer a threat, his habitual drunkenness now recognized for what it was. For the first time the brothers found themselves on equal terms with their father, and able to view him with affection, or contempt. Behind his back the family began to refer to him as the Old Devil, then just the O. D. Hamilton recalled a typical occasion, one afternoon when he returned from the Savage Club

as he so often did, 'on' (as my mother called it) and quarrelsome. What his quarrel was I cannot remember but I know that he ended it by skidding his tea-cup and saucer along the table in the direction of my mother with the words 'And you can *take* your tea!' At this my mother said – without anger: 'All right – there's no need to throw the tea in my face': and he spotted her inaccuracy without difficulty: 'I did *not* throw the tea in your face,' he said, and added, with obvious pride, 'I am an Artilleryman – and I took a low trajectory.'[7]

Hamilton was now more aware of, and amused by, his father's compulsively protean nature:

He took, then, keen pleasure in being a soldier, which he was: but he took even keener pleasure in being a Frenchman, which he certainly was not.

His performances as a Frenchman took place mostly when he was 'on' but they were not at all uncommon in everyday life – particularly when he desired in speech to be either sardonic, sentimental or pithy. He resembled, then, when being a Frenchman, (1) the popular idea of Voltaire, (2) Victor Hugo in his unhappy passages of voluptuousness in *Les Misérables* and (3) Miss Agatha Christie's Hercule Poirot in his moments of triumph. Properly to impersonate either of these characters it was absolutely essential to leer, either horribly and slowly, or faintly and brusquely.

There was one fatal flaw in these impersonations: for my father (who actually could speak French quite adequately) constantly had the impression that he was speaking French when in fact he was speaking broken English – that is to say, in the accent of a Frenchman attempting to speak English. 'And after ze soup,' he would say to baffled French waiters, 'I haf ze omelette.' And zen he would have something else, expressing his delicate understanding of, and anticipation of the perfection of French cooking by raising his hand in the air, and joining his second finger and thumb with infinite suggestiveness.[8]

Bernard seemed to have lost the core of his identity, and could only compile an ersatz personality from his surroundings: 'On returning from a trip to Canada, for instance, he became Canadian, smoked small cigars, said "Yep", and without actually sending forth saliva, spat cleverly in the direction of an imaginary spittoon.' And in Bruce's words, 'he returned from the Scillies practically a deep-sea fisherman or a smuggler. From France he brought an ineffable Gallic strain, talk of elegant little eighteenth-century *dames galantes* whose heels he could almost hear tap-tapping on the *parterres* of Versailles, and a stage French accent. Italy turned him into a Roman patrician with a dash of Mussolini, whom he almost worshipped. Spain gave him grave courtesy and a grandee's dignity; from Scotland he came canny, pawky, "metapheesical", and practically a Presbyterian.'[9] He joined the Fabian Society and attended one meeting. He read to his family passages from unpublished novels. He unavailingly urged his wife to collaborate with him on a putative bestseller, titled *Daphne Dale, Typist*, under the joint pseudonym of A. Myrtle Brown. A film scenario called *The Devil on Two Sticks* came to nothing. It is no wonder that in moments when he found himself without a role, or without drink, he was reduced to despairing emptiness and inaction. At home his appearance was 'slovenly in an old dressing-gown stained by food and tobacco'[10] but for his appearance at the Savage Club, or later – after being asked to resign from the Savage after breaking a glass over the head of a fellow member – at the Reform, he would assume a costume of military correctness.

By 1920, a good deal of Bernard's substantial fortune was gone, spent on his regular foreign excursions and diminished by the effects of the war. Hamilton was working hard, reading and writing, to prepare himself for his artistic vocation, and Bruce had similar, even less plausible, ambitions. Bernard Hamilton MA, as he signed himself even on his bookplate, was dismayed by the academic failures of his two children and understandably unwilling to subsidize their nebulous ambitions. He argued, not implausibly, that commerce or engineering offered opportunities for intelligent young men. His sons never accepted this argument; their lives – especially Bruce's – might have been happier if they had. A reluctant Bruce was forced into the City, which he swiftly left for that traditional intermediary job in the twenties and thirties for aspiring young writers, a job at a prep school.

Hamilton wished to devote himself to his writing, but in the end Bernard insisted that his younger son should educate himself, repeatedly stating that 'literature could be a walking-stick but not a crutch.'[11] Aged sixteen, Hamilton agreed to enrol at a commercial college near Holborn, though on the condition that he be allowed to leave the family home at Chiswick and move into lodgings. Bernard had cracked the whip, as can be judged from the letter he sent to Hamilton at the start of his new academic career:

On Sabbath mornings you will sit, regularly, under the minister of the Scots Presbyterian Kirk near St Pancras. This is a *parade*. You will then proceed to Chiswick, reporting here for Dinner at one-thirty, military time – i.e. five minutes early. Your costume will be such as befits a gentleman, not a neophyte of Mr Vincent Crummles, a socialist agitator, or a denizen of the Wild West. You will bring with you a weekly report on conduct and progress from your tutors, endorsed by the Principal. If any difficulty should arise you are to say that, I, your father, [the author and barrister,] require this.

You will make enquiries as to membership of the City Volunteer and Cadet Companies; I believe such bodies still exist. Understand this is an *order*; excuses will have no more avail with me than the preachments of Mormon missionaries.

For exercise I recommend rowing. Ascertain the conditions of membership of the London or Thames Boat Clubs; you cannot hope for Leander.[12]

The latter phrase became a joke between the two brothers. A few years later, when Bruce was working in Barbados, he sent Hamilton his diary to read and Hamilton wrote back enthusiastically praising it: 'You may not be able to hope for Leander, but you'll make a *writer*, my boy.'[13]

II

Despite these injunctions, the commercial college was an immediate failure. Hamilton left and went instead to Bruce's old army crammer, in the hope that he might eventually be able to enter the University of London. At the same time he moved into a residential hotel, the White House, in Earl's Court Square. The educational benefits of the crammer were nugatory, though its eccentricities would furnish Hamilton with valuable material for his first novel. The White House

Hotel would do the same, but it also provided him with two friends whose importance to him would be very different, the one symbolic, the other practical. They were brother and sister in a prominent Peruvian family, Charles and Maruja Mackehenie.

Hamilton fell in love with Maruja, or, to be more precise, he used her as a pretext for falling in love with the idea of being in love, an experience for which his sentimental poetry reading, and writing, had prepared him. She was, in Bruce's words, 'exquisitely pretty', but Hamilton never permitted Bruce to meet her, as if his brother's experience of her would violate the idea of her he had created in his mind. Bruce saw her once from a distance 'and I could see that her mere appearance made him almost faint with longing',[14] but it was not a longing for anything that could be gratified.

Yet if this was a first adolescent crush, it was a crush on a spectacular scale. Nearly forty years later, Hamilton was writing about Shelley in a letter on literature to his brother when his boyhood passion came into his mind: 'I have an idea that he was rather oddly sexed – in rather the way that I am. Although, clearly, he slept with girls, I don't think this was what he was *really* after. I think he liked *yearning* for them – *spooning*. What he *really* enjoyed was the emotion I had for Maruja.'[15] The conventional taste in poetry that Hamilton displayed was to stay with him for his entire life – in his bulky writing to Bruce on the subject, he never even mentions the name of any twentieth-century poet except Rupert Brooke. Similarly, passion was something that, at its best, was distant, ethereal, and utterly hopeless. The year before his death he admitted to Bruce that, 'I'm afraid to say that I still like looking at little girls from the window of the room I'm writing from.'[16]

He tried to explain to the baffled Peruvian teenager the subtle distinction between his loving her and being *in love* with her. Later she would remember Hamilton as 'extremely shy, unsure of himself, and unhappy'.[17] He was intoxicated, bewitched, but it doesn't seem that he ever had much contact with her as a person. She was a boarder at a Catholic school and only lived at the White House during the holidays, where Hamilton achieved his only physical contact at the weekly dances held in the hotel's ballroom. She soon married someone else, which caused no pain at all to Hamilton, who had encouraged the match. He also stayed in touch with her for some years, because of his more durable friendship with Charles, and in 1933 he reported to Bruce, almost in an aside (calling her by her pet name): 'Oh! – I saw *Marya*! Not changed a bit, looking very attractive. It is *I* who have changed. Was bored to extinction.'[18] The following year he was even more severe, dismissing his former idol as 'extremely *stupid* and *immature* – in fact I should say *backward* – a veneer of Paris-London sophistication not having really affected the good old imprisoned Shavian type one hears about.'[19] This is not so much the bitterness of a spurned lover, as a romantic for whom the world can never match the emotion he expends on it. Maruja herself was undamaged by these extreme emotions, indeed she was largely unconscious of them.

To Hamilton, Charles Mackehenie represented everything that he was not. He was handsome, urbane, cheerfully cynical, confident, an uncomplicated and untormented womanizer. He was free of troublesome idealism, and punctured Hamilton's with affectionate scorn. He was to lead a successful public life that would culminate in his being appointed Peru's ambassador to the United Nations. Much later, in a letter to Hamilton, he amiably observed: 'I am fortified in my belief that you should have been the diplomat and I the writer. My violence might have served me better as a writer and your exquisite sense of good-mannerliness would have made you an ambassador long ago.'[20] This was playful nonsense. It was Hamilton's incapacities, with women, drink, life in general, that made him fascinated by their intricate workings. For the rakish Mackehenie, life was not enough of a problem for him to peel back its surface. He was content, as the elegant English of his letters shows, to skate across it.

The influence of Charles on Hamilton was more tangible than that of Maruja. He was a friend, of a sort Hamilton had never had; he introduced him to social drinking, and a taste for the seamier side of life in general. And the friendship was fully reciprocated. 'No one has ever been so close to me as Patrick,' Mackehenie would later recall. 'He was my confidant and my support and I believe there was little about each other that we did not know.'[21] Meanwhile the crammer was proving little more enticing than the commercial school, but he was now to be provided with an opportunity to fail at something else. In the autumn of 1921 Lalla's husband, Sutton Vane, gave him a job in the theatre.

5

Apprenticeship

I

Vane immediately concealed the sole qualification Hamilton had for his job in the theatre by changing his name from Hamilton to Henderson. He was seventeen years old, and he worked immediately not just as an assistant stage manager but also in small stage roles. In the autumn of 1921, Vane had raised the money for a tour of the provinces with his play, *A Case of Diamonds*, in which he also starred, with Lalla, and Hamilton, in a silent role as 'a negro of gigantic proportions, wearing a cummerbund'.[1] In a second tour, he had two lines as a comic clergyman in a saloon bar scene in *The Squaw Man*, a melodrama set in the American West.

After this unpromising start, Hamilton was hired as the lowest member of a company presided over by the notoriously parsimonious Andrew Melville, one of the last great barnstorming, melodramatic actors in England. He worked on tour, and in repertory, with unpretentious vehicles like *The Count of Monte Cristo*, *The White Man*, *Her Marriage Bells*, *The Great World of London*, *The Monster*, and *On His Majesty's Service*. He would rehearse plays for the next week in the mornings, then play several parts (he had three in *On His Majesty's Service*)[2] and work as ASM in three performances on the same day – matinée and twice nightly.

It was hard work, badly paid, but it provided practical lessons in the business of making art: 'While prompting and ringing the curtain up and down, I watched the technique of melodrama closely, and realized how successful such plays might be if written and presented in a sophisticated way.'[3] This was the lesson he drew from his experiences, and whatever else might be thought of Hamilton's first play, it was obvious that the young author of *Rope* had a professional's grasp both of his material and the business of what would work in front of an audience. And he learned more than that. Hamilton tended to be dismissive of the stage. Even when recalling his first job with some pride, he anxiously insisted that, 'First and foremost, though, I always wanted to succeed as a novelist.'[4] But it wasn't the poetastic experience of writing 'Heaven' that was to make Hamilton a novelist. His finest fiction, his stories of fallen women, of murder and deceit, are rooted in the popular forms he first witnessed from the wings of provincial theatres.

The raffish life of train journeys, shared boarding houses, one-week engagements was a new world for a boy not long out of public school, but there was one form of experience which Hamilton did not gain from this bohemian life. A female member of the cast once attempted to seduce him but he was not interested and rebuffed her. On this non-occurrence, Bruce later made the curious observation that this 'difficult process of avoiding commitment to an undesired affair taught him a great deal',[5] though Hamilton never needed much instruction in the art of avoiding sex with women. Bruce reports that Hamilton was once assaulted by a fellow actor who suspected him – wrongly, says Bruce – of being a homosexual.[6]

There was never the remotest possibility that Hamilton would make a career for himself as an actor, and the money he was earning was barely enough to support him. Formal education had failed him but he was always to be a tireless, if erratic, autodidact. Making use of the breaks between his three shows a day, he took a correspondence course in typing and shorthand and in late 1922 he took a job in the City as a shorthand typist. Bruce was now in his first year studying for an arts degree at London University and the two of them shared a squalid room together in Delancey Street in Camden Town.

Hamilton's first day at work was, with a measure of Dickensian hyperbole, inserted into his second novel, *Craven House*, in which Master Wildman takes up his employment as a shorthand typist at the Xotopol Rum Company:

Mr Creevy then began to 'show' Mr Wildman a few things. He was shown the filing cabinet, and the Books, and where the stamps were kept, and where the ready cash was kept, and where the stationery was kept, and where (incidentally) the Tea, and the Sugar, and the Biscuits were kept; and he was shown the press-copying apparatus, and told how to use it, and how not to get the rags too wet, for 'Our Worthy Boss,' said Mr Creevy, 'is very particular about his copying.' Lastly he was shown the typewriter and given a shorthand notebook. He sat down looking and feeling uncommonly like the little boy who was fixed up by Mr Staines of Lyndon House School, some fourteen years ago . . .

And the glorious spring sun shone through the window, just as it did on that entrapped little figure long ago, and as there were no letters to do at present, he sat checking some neat figures in Mr Creevy's hand, for about an hour, until Mr Shillitoe arrived . . .

Master Wildman's shorthand was well able to keep up with Mr Shillitoe's dictation; and with a few odd letters for Mr Casing, and a few odd jobs for Mr Creevy, the morning dragged on – the clock standing at the wrong side of twelve, when at Craven House it would have been well the right side of one, but at last reaching a quarter past one, when Master Wildman went out to lunch. This he took in the atmosphere of a Wilkinson's round the corner, and returned sharp at a quarter past two, having drearily inspected the Tower of London in the interim.

In the afternoon there was an amount of routine letters, memoranda, and minutes of the last board meeting awaiting Master Wildman's typewriter, which lasted him over the digestive and office-deadly hour of three. And outside the glorious day declined to a mellow, full gold on the jolt and roar of the City traffic; and inside the typewriter hammered away, or abruptly ceased hammering (when Mr Creevy, out of Master Wildman's view, fluttered a paper against the charge of sleep), and then started again with redoubled ferocity . . .

And such was every one of Master Wildman's days at the office of the Xotopol Rum Company, Ltd., from half-past nine in the morning to seven in the evening – the after-tea period being spent in a thick, wakeful, and electric-lit bustle over the post. Then Master Wildman would find his way down the blackened stone landings, come out into the flow of a burrowing humanity, throw his letters upon other and less fortunate shoulders, buy his evening paper, and burrow himself, for Southam Green.[7]

At this transitional period in his life, Hamilton was working at a job that was itself archaic. Office life had been permanently changed by the First World War, and the irreversible entry into the labour market of women. The old male clerk and copyist were being replaced by a new cohort of female shorthand-typists who earned less money and had virtually no prospects of promotion.[8]

Hamilton had found himself in another dead end, but it enabled him finally to decide what he must do. In August 1923 he wrote to his father telling him that 'I must follow my own career in my own way, without hindrance or help, standing or falling by myself.'[9] His fate was not entirely in his own hands. On 17 September 1923, Sutton Vane's play, *Outward Bound*, opened at the Everyman Theatre in Hampstead. This skilful piece of commercial drama begins like an orthodox shipboard tale, but it soon emerges that the passengers have all died and they are being transported to the other side. The necessary element of pathos is generated by two lovers who have attempted suicide, and who face the option of returning to life to carry on. One of the lovers was played by Lalla, under her stage name of Diana Hamilton. The play was an instant success. It transferred to the Garrick Theatre in the West End and, though it ran for only six months, it established itself as a popular classic, being performed all over the world by professional companies, and later by amateurs. (It was to be filmed in 1930, starring Leslie Howard.)

This had profound and various effects on Lalla's youngest brother. Up to now, the Hamiltons had seemed like a family of cranky failures, nurturing unattainable fantasies. Now, finally, the Hamilton name was visibly connected to a prominent success, and the two brothers had a tantalizing taste of its fruits. Several times a week they would visit the Garrick to call on Lalla in her dressing room and inspect the length of the queue, a science they christened 'Comparative Queueology'.[10] Neither Hamilton nor Bruce had any respect for the sentimental message of the play, but both were impressed by its theatrical effectiveness. Hamilton had learned about stagecraft on the road, but the plays themselves had been nothing but crude vehicles for melodramatic or comic turns. In *Outward Bound* he saw how effective a strong, simple central idea could be with a single set and a small cast. There were one or two ominous events. Lalla discovered empty brandy flasks secreted in their elegant new South Kensington flat. Bruce also observed that Lalla herself was starting to drink more heavily.[11]

Hamilton was now subsidized by the Vanes, which allowed him to leave his job in the City and concentrate on his writing once more. He moved into some austere lodgings in Comeragh Road, West Kensington, and embarked on a programme of dedicated work that was to dominate his life for the rest of the decade. This monastic activity was at the centre of all that would be most important to him. Hamilton was, in his way, a sociable man, yet he would always resist the attractions of collaborative, public work in favour of the exigencies of his craft. Some years later he wrote on the subject, its paradoxes and logistics, to Bruce:

You know, I have an idea that it's this *writing* business that is so tough. I suspect that it's something requiring infinitely more labour and pain than what the average person thinks of as 'work'. 'Work' to so many people is a question of sitting in an office, phoning, making contacts, getting ideas, chatting, overcoming difficulties, meeting new people, above all *being stimulated by the presence and activities of others*. There is no reason why 'work' of this kind should not be pleasurable to any one with a reasonably active mind (which you and I have). But working at writing it seems to me, in comparison, is like hard labour in 'solitary' – something to which even illness is preferable. Perhaps this is at the root of one's trouble.

Of one thing I am certain, and that is that one cannot run away. If one tried *complete* escapism – gave up everything save golf, reading, and sleep, one would still be in an awful fix. For one has to make contacts in order to live comfortably, and contacts involve letters etc. and the small amount one had to write would give one all the same acute torture – more, in fact.

No – one has got to have a *daily machine* capable of digesting easily the particles of soul-discomfort alighting on one all the time in the natural order of things in this terrestrial sphere! If you let that machine stop they collect and irritate *unbearably*.[12]

In August 1924 Bernard made a final attempt to order his son to get a job, but the spell was broken. Hamilton wrote a chillingly firm response:

My dear Father,

Many thanks for your letter which I have read carefully over many times. I very much appreciate your kindness and care for me, but I must ask you *on no account to attempt to get a job for me, as I would not take it, however good it might prove.*[. . .]

You can know at least that I am a very, very hard worker now, and that in itself is a justification to me for my present course, even if I had any doubts of the ultimate wisdom of it, which I have not.[13]

Bernard now accepted the inevitable, and when he acknowledged it to Hamilton, he happened to be employing his French persona:

On finally realising that I had, in spite of his discouragement, an unquenchable ambition to be a writer, he one day invited me, in complete sobriety, into his room to talk about writing and to give me advice about its technique. 'Very well,' he said, 'You have the music. But now it is necessary to learn to play the piano.' I do not think that he said ze music or ze piano but his whole accent and manner were those of Hercule Poirot.[14]

Bernard had been in France, researching an historical novel about Danton. He had left with the name Captain Bernard Hamilton painted on his trunk but he later wrote from Grenoble asking that letters be addressed to Colonel Hamilton, since this was the rank by which he was known by fellow guests at the *pension*.[15] In the same year, Bernard was to suffer a terrible humiliation, at least in the eyes of his family. His old friend, Sir Arthur Conan Doyle, still one of the most famous writers in the world, published his autobiography and it contained a single, cruel reference to Bernard. He appeared as a minor character in an anecdote about Sir Henry Irving, the great late-Victorian romantic actor:

Irving had a curious dry wit which was occasionally sardonic and ill-natured. I can well believe that his rehearsals were often the occasion for heart-burnings among the men and tears among the ladies. The unexpectedness of his remarks took one aback. I remember when my friend Hamilton sat up with me into the 'wee sma' hours' with the famous man, he became rather didactic on the subject of the Deity or the Universe or some other tremendous topic, which he treated very solemnly, and at great length. Irving sat with his intense eyes riveted upon the speaker's face, which encouraged Hamilton to go on and on. When at last he had finished, Irving remarked: '*What* a low comedian you would have made!'[16]

A devastating dismissal, and yet one of the most perceptive comments ever made about this music-hall clown condemned for ever to mistake himself for a sage, an artist or a man of action. It humiliated Bernard at a time when he was planning a revival of his literary career. Irving's phrase was to haunt Hamilton, and years later he was to use it of two of the great men of his time, as if, in a final, touching act of filial piety, he could transform the insult into an oblique tribute. In the 1950s, Hamilton found himself living opposite the Hyde Park Gate house of the aged Winston Churchill, and he wrote about him to Bruce:

Talking of this man, have you ever realised how splendidly *he* (like B*.H.) resembles a low comedian? I can see him coming on at the Chiswick Empire and bringing the house down. I have a feeling that it is this quality which made him such a success in the war. At that time what was *wanted* was a low comedian. Things were so grim that nothing else would *do*. Now, of course, he has degenerated into an inferior clown. (* 'ernard – not 'ruce! [Patrick's note])[17]

And four years later he found himself making the same comparison about the man he admired more than any other, the leader of the Soviet Union:

I find myself liking and admiring [Nikita Khruschev] more and more. It seems to me that Russia, at the moment, has got something very much like what England got in the war – i.e. a *superb* low comedian – like *Churchill*.

I particularly like the way in which he is incessantly rebuking those who go too far in their denigration of Stalin.[18]

If his father was absurd, Hamilton may have thought, he at least had the absurdities that in other men accompanied greatness.

While Bernard was writing in Paris, Hamilton was making good use of his time steadily completing *Ferment*, his first novel. When it was finished, he retitled it *Adolescence* and, with the help of Vane and Lalla, it was sent to the literary agent, A. M. Heath & Co., and then on to various publishers under the name *Prelude to Misadventure*. In turn major publishers such as Jonathan Cape and Heinemann rejected it.

In late 1924, Hamilton suffered an attack of dysentery – judged by Bruce to be the result of an inadequate diet. The Chiswick house was being sub-let, and Hamilton moved with his mother as a paying guest to a guest house in Kew Gardens Road, Richmond, where they were soon joined by Bruce. Hamilton's relations with his fellow guests, a tyrannical old man and two American women from Wilkes Barre, Pennsylvania, were not good, though he would recall them as a source of material twenty years later.[19]

Early in 1925 a telegram arrived informing Ellen that Bernard had suffered a stroke in Paris, brought on, it was thought, by his heavy drinking. His children took it in turns to visit him there and Bruce found him 'being treated with some noisome looking black leeches clamped to his neck and shoulders'.[20] As soon as he was better, he was escorted back to London where he took up residence in a hotel in Bayswater. Both in Paris and back in Richmond, Hamilton, who was barely out of his teens, was also having regular drinking sprees with Bruce and friends like Charles Mackehenie. Bruce and Hamilton began to feel that they could not face either lunch or dinner in the staid guest house without two or three large glasses of port in a local saloon bar. Hamilton's lighthearted irresponsibility was much like that of the undergraduate life that he was missing out on.

After some disheartening rejections Hamilton's novel was accepted by Constable. On 20 March 1925, three days after his twenty-first birthday, he agreed to a contract entitling him to £50 on the day of publication. Perhaps nervous, he signed himself A. W. Patrick Hamilton (the only time he seems ever to have used that particular form of his name). Just before the contract was completed, *Prelude to Misadventure* was crossed out and a final title, *Monday Morning*, written in by hand.

II

Hamilton never made great claims for his first novel: 'It was never meant to be a great book, but it is honest and honestly written,' he said later.[21] It is unquestionably honest in its fidelity to the details of Hamilton's own life.

The hero, Anthony Forster, aged eighteen, leaves a hotel overlooking King's Gardens, Hove, and arrives at an Earls Court boarding house. He has just left Westminster School and is to study at an army crammer in Kensington. The title derives from his constant resolve that on Monday morning he will truly start his life and become a major novelist. He falls in love with Diane de Mesgrigny, a young French girl who also lives at the boarding house.

Anthony's employment prospects look bleak until the actor, Sydney Brane, comes to stay at the boarding house and one day, suddenly, he offers to make Anthony an actor. He becomes an assistant stage manager and has a small part in a trial run of a new play in the provinces. The novel consists principally of skilfully written set-pieces, a twenty-page account of a train journey with the theatrical company up to Sheffield, a drunken attempt to return to his digs, a trip to Paris with Brane/Vane. Then at the end of the novel, Hamilton ties up the loose ends in his own life and provides himself with a happy ending. Diane has told Forster that she is engaged to somebody else, but this turns out to be untrue and they end up together. The one substantial difference between Anthony Forster and Anthony Walter Patrick Hamilton is that Forster's parents are both dead.

Monday Morning is a deft first novel, remarkable for a twenty year old, produced in blissful ignorance of what we now, with retrospective partiality, consider to be the *zeitgeist* in the mid-twenties. *The Waste Land* and *Ulysses* had been published three years earlier, *Mrs Dalloway* and Ernest Hemingway's revolutionary collection of stories *In Our Time* would appear in the same year. But when Anthony wants to be a great writer he is thinking of Compton Mackenzie and Alec Waugh. The poets he reads are Swinburne and Rupert Brooke.

Hamilton displayed a professional shrewdness in writing a novel about callow adolescent ambitions, taking his own serious preoccupations about his failure to begin life and rendering them with a comic detachment. Looking back, Bruce – the novel's dedicatee – was scathing about the book's limitations, but what was more significant, in such a young author, was its technical strengths: the delineation of character, the ear for dialogue, the skill of transition between scenes, the sense of pace. In a book that is reminiscent of P. G. Wodehouse, it is remarkable how much of the Hamilton world is already there in embryonic form. There are the settings, Hove and Kensington, the lodging house, theatres, trains and pubs. When Anthony fails to get a job he seeks refuge in a pub and we see Hamilton learning what he can do best:

'I'll go and have a drink,' he said. He went into the saloon of the nearest public-house. It was ill-lit by daylight. There was the soft murmur of men's voices, and the noise of levers jerking, the ring and clatter of the till. He ordered a double whisky, and took it without the offered water. The first sip was very bitter – then fine warmth inside him. The rest of the sips were bitter and nasty.[22]

There are anticipatory details. Anthony's preoccupation with spelling words backwards ('Doctor Collis Browne was good – Enworb Silloc Rotcod') was close to an obsession of Hamilton's. His letters addressed to 'Dear Ecurb', are a harmless private joke, but in 1939 he also based almost an entire novel on the idea, *Impromptu in Moribundia*.

Most striking of all, in such a lighthearted novel as *Monday Morning*, is the bleakness of its portrayal of the relationship between the sexes. Anthony is at first attracted to Cynthia, the sister of a college friend. They both want to kiss each other but the first attempt is an embarrassing disaster. The chapter ends with Anthony leaving the house: 'Anthony stood quite still, at the bottom of the steps, for a quarter of a minute, and looked at the pavement.'[23] And the next chapter begins: 'Anthony never saw Cynthia again.'

The object of Anthony's adoration is not a portrait of Maruja. Of Diane, Hamilton writes, 'Sweet was the word for her face. Neither pretty nor beautiful . . .',[24] but he, like Bruce, considered Maruja to be very beautiful. It is his side of the relationship that the book dramatizes. When parted from her, 'Anthony wanted to cry. That is to say, he wanted to have the desire to cry. He had no desire to cry.'[25] In a muddled way, and this is one of the few areas where the book's design is disfigured by Hamilton's private concerns, the narrator wants to despise Diane: 'She had a quick, bright mind making as fast as it could for shallowness.'[26] 'Then she reached for her writing-pad and scribbled a letter to Anthony, and put some of the most trying characteristics of Diane into it – all the uppish conceits, the half-formed, unrealised ideas, self-glorifying.'[27] But he also wants the reader to forget about these criticisms and consider her an ideal heroine as the book reaches its climax.

Monday Morning received warm, indulgent reviews. *The Sunday Times* acclaimed it as 'A wholly delightful and charmingly impudent piece of work. Its first chapter puts the reader into the best of good tempers and its last finds him in the same agreeable mood.' The *Saturday Review* considered it 'a piece of cheek, if you like. But it made me laugh aloud, and I am accordingly grateful.'[28]

The cheek was this ambitious young author mocking the ambitions of a young author. In retrospect, there is something more than cheek in the life plan that the hero constructs for himself:

Anthony had it all lucidly ordered in his mind. He imagined Life, more or less consciously, as a sort of play in three logical Acts and a Prologue. He had just done with the Prologue. The three Acts were (1) fiery youth leaping splendidly to the zenith, (2) replete, mellow middle age, and (3) sedate decay. With a wonderful curtain in Death, bang in the centre of the stage.[29]

Patrick Hamilton's first three novels have an almost incantatory power, humorously willing a success that he then immediately achieved. The first act, the zenith, would be achieved with spectacular swiftness.

6

Craven House

I

Hamilton was to remain with Constable for his entire career, and Michael Sadleir, the man who accepted *Monday Morning*, became one of his closest friends. Hamilton chose his few close friends – there were to be scarcely more than half a dozen throughout his life – for possessing qualities he himself lacked. Born in 1888, Sadleir was sixteen years older than Hamilton and socially and intellectually confident in a way Hamilton would never be. He had been educated at Rugby and Balliol College, Oxford, and when he first met Hamilton, in early 1925, he had been employed by Constable for thirteen years and had been a director for five. He shared Hamilton's predilection for literature of the nineteenth century, and did so with the reassuring weight of a major bibliographer and book collector (his classic work of scholarship, *Excursions in Victorian Bibliography* had only just been published).

Michael Sadleir was a man Hamilton could look up to and be boyishly friendly with at the same time. He put Hamilton up for membership of a famous dining society, the Omar Khayyám, at which the young author was able to meet some very old authors, and the extremely limited part that Hamilton was to play in literary circles was largely through his association with Sadleir. On Sadleir's part, it seems that Hamilton was attractive, initially at least, because of his boyish charm, with an undisturbing hint of raffishness. He appealed to Sadleir's side that displayed – in the words of Derek Hudson, author of the entry on Sadleir in the *Dictionary of National Biography* – a 'weakness for melodrama and [an] absorption in the seamy side of nineteenth-century life.' Within a year of their first meeting they were writing elaborately jokey letters to each other, frequently incomprehensible to any outsider. Hamilton loved nicknames and Michael soon became Quarles, while Hamilton was generally Hen, or Henderson, recalling his shortlived stage alias. Michael's jovial, forthright assistant, Martha Smith (nine years Hamilton's senior), who seems to have been the only close female friend Hamilton ever had, was addressed in letters as Beryl. Hamilton and Sadleir were longtime drinking companions, frequently joined by Martha.

After the acceptance of *Monday Morning*, Hamilton immediately began to work on another novel with a confidence that was for the first time justified by experience. Having fictionalized one aspect of his life, he now turned his attention to the boarding house in which he and his family had lived, and he was so pleased with his progress that he regularly read chapters of it aloud to his mother (to whom the book would be dedicated), his sister and brother, back once more in the Burlington Gardens house in Chiswick. They were delighted by his declamatory performances, and Bruce, who successfully passed his final examinations at London University in the summer of 1925, recalled these months as among the happiest the family ever spent. Yet at the same time, Hamilton and Bruce developed together – though largely prompted by Hamilton – an austere philosophy to lift themselves out of despair, a 'life-of-labour-from-day-to-day gospel, the utter safety and haven of expecting nothing from life but using oneself unremittingly and fighting with endless courage a winning or losing battle.'[1] Bruce may well have lacked the will necessary for such a gamble of everything against the prospect of literary success. In any case, such a commitment was now easier for Hamilton to make. When he submitted the new book to Constable they were so pleased that they signed a five-novel contract. If Hamilton delivered one novel a year, he would be guaranteed an annual payment of £100. The outlay was not huge but it was a solid assertion of confidence by the publishers in the future of their twenty-two-year-old author.

This is scarcely surprising, because *Craven House* was patently an impressive advance on what had been a promising enough début. The hero is Master Wildman, an ironic acknowledgement of his author's military ancestor, whom we see growing up as one of the paying guests in

Miss Hatt's Chiswick boarding house, Craven House, in the fictional Keymer Gardens (the Hamiltons' Hassocks house had been on Keymer Road). During the course of the book he gradually realizes that the girl he is really in love with is not the more obviously alluring Miss Cotterell, but his nice fellow lodger, Elsie. It is a story of a whole household, and Hamilton created and manipulated a large cast with a skill that no longer needs to be judged as the precocity of a young man. Reading it years later, Michael Sadleir praised it in a way that shows the book's limitations as well as its considerable virtues: 'I have now read *Craven House* really carefully. It pleases me better than ever, as a delightful story with a charming love-interest and as something laugh-aloud funny.'[2] This slightly understates the book's virtues. It is also a domestic horror story. In the book's early pages Mr and Mrs Spicer are living together with Miss Hatt and this had produced the Long Evening Problem:

For it had taken only three months' residence at Craven House to exhaust the little fund of external entertainment remaining in each other's personality. And though there was the Piano, upon which Mrs Spicer could deliver an unimpeachable performance to her placid and respectfully alert man; and though there was the Southam Green Empire, to which they paid a weekly visit; and though they sometimes turned the lights down in the drawing-room, and sat about the glowing fire wilfully to exude middle-aged comfort and romance (with an occasional rather ghastly and aghast interlocking of hands from the mated pair), the evenings on the whole were reaching a pitch of *ennui* and amiability almost intolerable – if not positively approaching the danger mark. For one evening the Spicers took their courage into both hands and read a newspaper and a novel for an hour and a half by the clock, like perfect limpets against the bright conversational wrenches of a knitting Miss Hatt; until at last that lady, after poking the fire with an efficiency and rapidity that carried an unquestionable Hint, was driven to say, 'Well, then, I'd better be going up to bed, then,' to which Mrs Spicer replied, 'Very well, my dear,' without raising her eyes. The first cross word between them.[3]

Hamilton was now writing with authority. The prose is brilliant, but sometimes it is the brilliance of pastiche. The history of Dickens's influence is a subject in itself. In the 1920s there is a modernist Dickens, author of the hallucinatory *Our Mutual Friend*, which T. S. Eliot drew on for *The Waste Land* (whose original title, *He Do the Police in Different*

Voices, was drawn from that novel). And there is a traditionalist, retrograde, no-nonsense J. B. Priestley Dickens, good ale and good humour, used as a bluff, comic antidote to any notions of modern art, and it is this latter figure which haunts the pages of *Craven House*. Elsie, for example, is,

this little victim of Bringing Up. For Elsie is being Brought Up – exactly wherefrom or whereunto neither of them could tell you, but they are both quite complacent in an apparently self-contained process.[4]

Or, even more unignorably Dickensian:

With respect to Mr Spicer's Business we may say at once that Mr Spicer was widely (if rather ungracefully) known to be In Tea. How far Mr Spicer was involved in this comforting commodity, how far Mr Spicer had committed himself to Tea, how far Mr Spicer was compromised by Tea, whether Tea was Mr Spicer's master, or whether Mr Spicer was the master of Tea, were problems alike in the shadow. Mr Spicer was in Tea.[5]

It is well done, but the question is whether Hamilton ought to have been doing it at all. The answer of the press was generally in the affirmative. The *Times Literary Supplement* asserted that 'In English fiction there will always be room for the novel of which *Craven House* is the type. It is the garrulous, communicative, knowingly-facetious, all-comes-right-in-the-end type in which Dickens sometimes indulged and in which William de Morgan scored his chief successes.' The *Christian World* observed that 'Mr Hamilton is in the line of descent from Dickens,' the *Manchester Guardian* that the characters 'all are drawn in that vein of heightened risibility beloved of Dickens.'[6]

Hamilton retained a great affection for *Craven House* and a high opinion of it. It was the only one of his first books that he later chose to revise and have re-issued. Yet within a short time he also developed a sense of the book's limitations: 'The truth is that *Craven House* was not, never pretended to be, a magnum opus.' He needed 'a corrective to that tendency to virtuosity which had always been with me. I think that this has been a weak point with me hitherto – that I have dwelt too strongly upon and become too masterly at the handling of pure *scene* and as long as that has been going all right felt myself justified in letting the rest go hang.'[7] *Craven House* is crammed with these set-pieces. Some of them –

a pub crawl by Mr Spicer, a disastrous dinner which finally breaks up the entire household – are comic masterpieces; others, including the climax in which Master Wildman and Elsie finally acknowledge their love for each other, are wildly miscalculated. Hamilton decided that both were wrong. He felt intuitively that he had to strip himself of what he was being most praised for and attempt something rougher, more amorphous.

A final detail: Hamilton faced the problem of establishing Master Wildman as a success. With what seems like the height of implausibility, Wildman writes a play and sends it off to Mr Eugene Layburn, of the Express Theatre, Charing Cross. A few days later he is summoned there: 'When Master Wildman at last emerges from the Express Theatre, he carries all the natural stupefaction of a young man hearing on a Friday that his play is to be produced, by one of the best-known (if most critic-scoffed) actor managers in London, on a Monday.'[8]

In *Monday Morning* Hamilton had playfully anticipated success as a novelist. Now he was anticipating instant West End success as a playwright.

II

The publication of *Craven House* coincided with the reappearance of another novelist from the Hamilton family. In a letter to Michael Sadleir, Hamilton included a leaflet announcing the imminent appearance of Bernard's *The Giant*. The italicized words represent Hamilton's handwritten addition: 'Bernard Hamilton (Major R.H.A., Rtd.; Trin. Coll., Camb.; Barrister, &c), who has now returned to writing (after a *somewhat remarkable* silence of twenty-five years)'.[9]

This was not entirely true – Bernard had been reading the books to his family for many years. But he approached this new opportunity with a due sense of occasion. *The Giant* is dedicated 'To the great people of France', and accompanied by a grandiloquent epigraph from Victor Hugo, whose influence, Hamilton would later feel, 'led our poor father astray in literary matters'.[10] In a letter he helpfully provided the publishers with advice about publicity: 'As a puff preliminary you may say that this is the greatest novel ever published – which indeed it is.'[11]

According to his own preface the book 'may be described as the romantic biography of the inner life of this prodigious Danton – whose fiery eloquence, ardent passion, sincere patriotism, and magnanimous courage have never been surpassed by any man – at any time.'[12] Apart from being 'the backbone of the new State' and a 'capable giant [who] contrived order out of chaos',[13] Danton is a mouthpiece for Bernard's already well-rehearsed views: 'A nation in this plight needs one man to rule it – absolutely – instead of a multitude of weaklings. *One* man!'[14]

Bernard's was a politics of gesture, and after Danton has died because of his chivalrous efforts to save Marie Antoinette, his lover meets, in the very shadow of the guillotine, a young Corsican who proclaims that he will fulfil his, Danton's and Bernard's idea of destiny: 'It is Danton who really has created this new epoch. In it I shall rise. I am a man destiny drives forward.'[15]

This diffuse sense of destiny reduced Bernard to numbed passivity or pointless activity. In different ways this was always to afflict his sons as well. Bruce was never to lose the anxiety about what he was actually going to do with his life. Unlike his brother, he had mustered some academic qualifications and he now began to receive the first of their benefits, a three-year attachment as a teacher of history and general subjects at Harrison College in Barbados. On the day before his departure, shortly after the publication of *Craven House*, Bruce and Hamilton met in a Lyons Corner House, followed by a pub in the Strand, to talk about their future. They decided, or Hamilton decided on his older brother's behalf, that they were now in their prime, and they were already a year late in starting life. The two of them possessed a 'brilliant *intelligence*' and to make full use of it they must both 'work unremittingly and live abundantly'. When they met again, they must have something to show for the time they had spent apart.[16] They made a pledge that the two of them, at whatever sacrifice, would achieve literary success. Bruce's failure to keep his side of the bargain can be seen as the great unspoken theme of his memoir of his brother.

After making this weighty commitment, Bruce left, and took the first steps on a path which would keep him out of England for much of the rest of Hamilton's life.

7

The Young Novelist

The Hamilton household was a strange organism, constantly shifting, dispersing and reconstituting itself. Bruce was gone, but Lalla was often back, retreating from her own unstable marriage. The domestic environment enabled Hamilton to lead the life of a professional novelist. Each day he got up at half past six in the morning and went to bed at half past nine in the evening. While writing he didn't smoke, and in the evening, even if he went out with Charles Mackehenie or Michael Sadleir, he tried to limit himself to three drinks, though here his self-discipline was less secure, and with Charles he developed extravagantly complicated strategies to limit their consumption. Bruce described one of them:

The two bases of this plan were christened 'the Hamilton Drop' and 'Charles's Principle'. The first, a physiological experience that I shared, was a sharp fall in our spirits if, having taken one drink, we did not have further ones at intervals of not more than half an hour until a meal was taken or a point of surfeit reached. 'Charles's Principle' was devised to combat this inducement to excess. They would start off with, say, a double Scotch apiece; when about a third of the drink had been absorbed they would top up glasses with further soda or water, and repeat this process perhaps twice more. The theory was that while the illusion of drinking was preserved the consumption was greatly diminished; one double might last over an hour, and a long evening got through on not more than five or six. The trouble, as I found the only time I was with them when the Principle was in operation, was that though it was honoured in the letter, in practice the dilutions followed one another so swiftly that almost as much Scotch was drunk as in the unregenerate days. No food was eaten except the odd sandwich or scrap of provender of the kind found under glass on bars; anything like a real supper or dinner would have put a complete end to the serious business of drinking.[1]

With more success Hamilton forbade himself any reading, though he did admit to 'a little gazing at gas fire'.[2]

He was painfully conscious of the struggle needed to turn a couple of minor successes into a substantial writing career, as if he was still wary of his father's self-delusion masking a capacity for failure. As he concluded a letter to Bruce, 'In fact I'm getting down to it, because I know that the difference between the failures or half-failures and the successes in this life is *the difference between mild self-control and something partially fanatical*.'[3] He and – in Hamilton's view – Bruce were different from others. Though talented, they also lacked the security of less gifted insiders: 'Some are born with a strain of energy and healthy resistance which makes it easy. Vide Michael [Sadleir]. But then will he be one of the big successes?'[4] Hamilton was an adherent to the romantic notion of art as a calling to which you sacrificed yourself. His admiration and friendship for Sadleir was based precisely on Sadleir's stolid refusal to sacrifice himself to anything, perhaps out of the conviction that in the end art wasn't worth the ruin of one's life.

Hamilton compiled a chart to mark his progress, but despite his punishing schedule, his creative energy was uncontainable. For the only time of his life, his letters were self-consciously literary, as if he was gradually fashioning his imaginative world and couldn't prevent himself from describing it: 'As I passed Turnham Green the grass was glistening wet, and the drops were like diamonds – but rather shoddy yellow diamonds against a sickly green – depressing.'[5] Even in an evocation of life for the benefit of the absent Bruce, there is a sense of Hamilton flexing his developing literary muscles:

Life is going on just as usual here. We come down every morning to the usual breakfast, and meet again at every lunch, and make jokes and slyly look up to see how Annie's taking them – that pastily spectacled and non-committal creature in brown giving nothing away as usual. And Mummie's listening in the dark when you come back from your movie, and Lalla looks as bleared as ever in her old silk kimono, and irons unceasingly. There's not much hope in life.'[6]

Above all, the Hamilton world, that nightmarish yet palpable vision, eerily composed from the most mundane and trivial incidents and objects was taking shape:

I'm sure your scenery is much finer than the Chiswick High Road, and the noises beating on your ears much pleasanter than the everlasting rumble therefrom. And Mrs Buck is no pleasanter to see coming down Sutton Court Road towards you than she ever was, and the pasty pudding girl at the library and Mr Black or rather Grey Beard have all their old sinister Chiswick flavour. And the dark young man at Percivals, and the funny looking women at Needhams, and the criminal news-vendor, and the jolly Pub manager, and Mr Shattock, and Mrs Stanham (whose son, I understand, has 'his own views on Religion' whatever that may mean) and the sporting little barber, and the 27 buses, and the Trams, and the cars taking revolting females to Twickenham – all, all go on with their dreadful immutability, like obsessions in a sick madman's brain. And if you came back, in a week's time you would be crawling out to movies and abhorring them all in just the same old way.[7]

He began to form ideas, about art and life. Some of this was merely a restatement of his adolescent views on aesthetics. He found time to compose a skilful verse for Bruce on how to write that could have appeared in a mid-Victorian issue of *Punch*:

> In our fair craft three rules there be –
> The first of these Lucidity,
> The next of these Economy,
> The third of these Propriety,
> Three in one and one in three,
> The author's holy trinity!
> Be *clear* – without prolixity.
> Be *spare* – without obscurity.
> And *choose* discriminatingly.
> The sole Parnassian Mystery!
> Of Prose's doors the Master-keys,
> Thou hast, in taking these with these.[8]

He read *Also Sprach Zarathustra* (the name of whose author he was never able to spell) and for a time the book became an obsession. Hamilton decided he was no longer a mere writer, but a philosopher destined to write nothing less than an Apology for Art, one of a number of non-fictional works he was to embark on during his life, not a single one of which was ever completed. Whole letters to Bruce became extended pastiches of the aphoristic Nietzschean style. With the impetuosity of an auto-didact, the megalomania of his father and a reading of Nietzsche and Samuel Butler, he concocted a version of the previous fifty years in which Darwin and Huxley had destroyed religion, Neitsche [*sic*] had destroyed morals, Bernard Shaw had destroyed science and now it only remained for Schleswig (one of the nicknames with which Hamilton signed his letters to Bruce) to destroy art.[9]

Much of this was just the thinking aloud of a boy intoxicated with early success and a consciousness of his growing powers. But *Zarathustra* was also a help to the young author in reinforcing the intuitive decision to change the course of his writing. In his early novels Hamilton felt a conflict between the way he saw the world, the infernal vision that confronted him even on a walk down Chiswick High Road, and what he felt was called for in fiction, a world with its own rules, where nice men fell in love with and ended up with nice women, and where, in general, the world was a benign, ordered place. Nietzsche freed Hamilton's imagination, and he quoted with delight the assertion: 'I love the great despisers, for they are the great adorers: they are arrows of longing for the other shore.'[10] Here was a philosophy that justified the expression of the dark side of ordinary life that had preoccupied Hamilton since he was four years old.

Nietzsche permitted Hamilton to redeem his experience by rendering it honestly, rather than transforming it into glib comedy. At the same time, the message of assertiveness allowed Hamilton to free himself from his past, and in particular from his father; he articulated this in one of his more lighthearted parodies of a Nietzschean aphorism, labelled TODAY'S THOUGHT: 'Any nation in which the sons do not, on reaching a given age of discretion, kick their fathers with the utmost ceremony downstairs, is a nation without a destiny.'[11] More materially, Hamilton's interest in Nietzsche would, within two years, lead to a financial prosperity that would secure his future for a decade.

In his enthusiasm, Hamilton was also urging on Bruce's dormant literary career. Hamilton's tone, as if Bruce were a recalcitrant younger brother instead of four years older, and his perverse assertion that all the things that were preventing Bruce from finishing his novel were actually a help rather than a hindrance, must sometimes have been difficult for Bruce to bear, far away in Barbados, struggling with a new teaching job. In the following letter Hamilton refers to a novel about teaching, based on Bruce's first prep-school experiences, that would occupy him for many years:

My boy, for heaven's sake take notes (it's so easy to forget things) from the journey over to the last moment. Note every piquant scene – human or natural. It's a chance in a lifetime. It would sell, too. Now *do* take notes. Don't *think* of doing it. I notice that your style is as limpid and exquisite as ever – even in your letter. You're a natural born writer – even more than I am. And that you can tackle a Novel, the first section of The Term has proved. Though I still think you'll have a lot of struggles – more than I have to put up with now.

God! What an Epic of schoolmastering you'll turn out one day! And what a valuable subject to handle too. You've been through the mill from beginning to end.[12]

When Bruce wrote a minor newspaper article, Hamilton overwhelmed this tiny flame of literary endeavour with his extravagant claims of what it promised for the future:

Oh, Bruce, make use of your *Natural Gift* for writing. It is a thing which a man either possesses or doesn't, and *you* do, and *I* don't. And to one who possesses it, and is yet aware of the pitfall of glibness, it is inestimably valuable. I may have other gifts (the comic gift, for instance) but I envy you this.

But apart from the article itself, the mere fact of your having started to do something out there, is so wonderful.[13]

Yet there was always something ambiguous about the enthusiasm with which Hamilton would hail Bruce's writing throughout his life. It was partly encouragement but there is sometimes a sense that Bruce is being taunted. As far as it can be established, it seems that Hamilton did not take Bruce's work seriously. Much later, Bruce would hear from their cousin, Frank, of how he had mentioned Lalla's writing to which Hamilton had brusquely replied: '*I'm* the only writer in this family.'[14] Bruce was to become uneasily aware that he was a victim of Hamilton's increasing tendency to divide his life into compartments, whose several inhabitants were virtually unaware of each other's existence. It was to

Bruce that Hamilton liked to talk about ideas, literature, sport. For other aspects of his life he turned to other people. He was now seeing Michael Sadleir more frequently. He attended lectures, a Trollope dinner, the Omar club. He was also invited by Sadleir to a significant PEN dinner. This international association of poets, playwrights, editors, essayists and novelists had been founded just six years earlier, in 1921, and its president was John Galsworthy, author of the then recently published *Forsyte Saga*. The dinner provided for Hamilton a rare encounter with the avant-garde: 'James Joyce was the guest of honour, and he gave a little speech. Quite unlike what you'd expect. Red longish face, moustache, quite clean, tortoiseshell spectacles. And a good speech too, terse, and with obvious loathing of the whole affair, even if civil. For these affairs *are* loathsome. To a philosopher anyway.'[15] Despite the half-humorous tone of his disapproval, there is no evidence that Hamilton ever attended another such dinner, and he resolutely remained free from any literary scene, cliques, groups, dinner parties of any kind. Far more visible writers, Arthur Calder-Marshall is an example, have praised Hamilton for this.[16] Some might accuse Hamilton of selfishly refusing to identify his interests with those of writers as a group, though even if this were true, the PEN was an inadequate vehicle for solidarity of that kind. In the following year, the association would disgrace itself by its refusal to support Radclyffe Hall, one of its members, when her novel, *The Well of Loneliness*, was prosecuted and convicted for obscenity.[17]

In any case, it seems that Hamilton's motives were more personal. He was genuinely ill at ease on public occasions and he admitted to Bruce that he was in a 'great state of doubt as to whether (now that I seem to have made my debut in the literary world) I ought to try and put my own excited as-to-you-and-Carlitos personality across, or shut up altogether and keep close. Advise me . . .'[18] As if, still under the influence of his father, personalities were to be assumed and discarded for different occasions. Bruce wrote back insisting that Hamilton should not '[put] a personality across in public' but Hamilton was unconvinced:

I'm not sure that this is right, because when I start being a propagandist in real earnest, and am speaking as well as writing, I shall have to develop something to put across. But whether I should try to put the thing with which you are familiar across, is certainly doubtful. I think I could read, in between the lines of your advice, the heartfelt thought, 'For God's sake let the arrogant little bastard keep his excitements to himself and his family.'[19]

Brigid Brophy has plausibly suggested that Hamilton was addicted to family even more than to drink.[20] It may have been that it was only among his close family circle that he felt no need to construct masks for himself. But addiction is the right word, because it was in the family that the need had been created in the first place.

One significant, and pleasurable, mask which was acquired for the first time in May 1927 was a made-to-measure suit obtained at Charles Mackehenie's West End tailors for ten guineas, more than a tenth of his yearly stipend from his Constable contract. Hamilton made a slightly nervous defence of this extravagance to Bruce, stressing the economy from the added wear you get from such high quality and the 'enormous confidence anywhere' that derives from 'perfect cut and irreproachable-ness'.[21] His views on the subject were expressed much more cogently in the following year when his alter ego, Bob, the hero of *The Midnight Bell*, makes the mistake of purchasing an off-the-peg suit. The difference between the argument above and the argument below shows Hamilton's accelerating skill at inserting his experience into his books while decisively altering and enriching it. His life is still being turned into comedy, but of a darker, more disturbing kind:

Now the tragedy and evil of buying a ready-made suit is this – that it ends, just like that, in 'Yes . . .' You think it would be a good idea if you bought a suit; you delightedly resolve to buy a suit; you work yourself up into a heavenly climax about a suit – and then suddenly it is all over and you are merely saying 'Yes . . .' You stare at it. You pat the pockets; you turn round and look at yourself sideways; you see what it would look like if it wasn't buttoned. But whatever you do, there is nothing else to be said. 'Yes . . .' You look at the cuffs – but they are no help to you – they're excellent. You examine the lining – it couldn't be better. Perhaps it is too tight under the arms. But it is not. It is no good. You are faced by the depressing fact that you are going to buy it.

'Yes,' said Bob.[22]

8

Twopence Coloured

I

Hamilton's third novel, a theatrical story provisionally titled *The Player's Scourge* had a far wider scope than *Craven House*. By May 1927 the first book of three was finished: 'Unspeakable labour is ahead, but I feel sure of bringing it off.'[1] He was writing an impressive 1,500 words daily and occasionally wondered if he had taken on too much, but Michael Sadleir soothed his doubts and encouraged him to 'go all out epically and make a big book of it.'[2]

By the summer he was more aware of the book as something different from what he had previously written: 'It is a much grimmer book, and not nearly so specialised. And it's much longer, and more amorphous, and interesting in itself. You could rob it of its humour, style, and piquancy (let us hope they exist) and it might still remain interesting as a document.'[3] In September he went with his sister, Lalla, whose experiences had provided the core of the book, to stay in Cardiff. He tried to cut down on his smoking while alternately rewriting the book and reading it aloud, receiving a 'quite satisfactory reception'.[4] By the end of the month he was able to report that the book was finished and that he was spending eleven hours a day copying it out.

He assured Bruce that he was working so hard that he wouldn't even go to the lavatory until he had a word he wanted to look up, and he would then retire to the closet with the dictionary. Hamilton included with one letter eleven abandoned sheets of typescript, teasing fragments which must have baffled their recipient, to which he added jocular titles like captions for illustrations in a Victorian novel: Learning Chorus Work, The Importunate Drunkard, A Flighty Actress, A Landlady's Daughter and one page which contains only the typewritten words 'she would pick it up again and handle it slowly and luxuriously' accompanied by PH's handwritten addition, 'Don't Ask Me!'[5]

The novel was delivered to Constable under the title *The Aspirant* and within a few days Hamilton was nervously soliciting Michael Sadleir's opinion: 'There is a very particular reason for my wanting you to like this book, which I'll tell you, if all is well, when I see you next.'[6] After an initial murmur of uncertainty, the response was enthusiastic enough for Hamilton to dedicate the book to Sadleir, 'to make known my enormous debt of gratitude to you – a debt which you hideously underrate . . . and which I can only hope to repay by humbly acknowledging it, and endeavouring to justify it by my work.'[7]

By early the following year, Hamilton was able to report to Bruce:

It looks as though I have written a book called TWOPENCE COLOURED [*The Aspirant* became the title of Book One], which is to be published in March. What's your opinion of this title? I think it's damnably good from a selling point of view, but what it means, or to what it refers, God in Heaven knows. There is, apparently, a phrase 'penny plain, twopence coloured', but no two persons agree as to its origin and precise meaning. They are fairly unanimous, however, in thinking the effect of the title is one of tawdriness and cheapness and possibly pathos, and that's as it should be. To me the value of it lies in its absolute (and filthily modern) incomprehensibility.[8]

Twopence Coloured begins with nineteen-year-old Jackie Mortimer leaving Hove for London in the hope of going on the stage. In a feeble coincidence unusual in Hamilton's work, she meets Richard Gissing, a successful leading actor, on the London train. He is discouraging about her ambition but secures her an interview with Carson Lee, an agent. Against Gissing's advice, Jackie becomes a chorus-girl in a touring review, *Little Girl*. The narrative principally traces Jackie's slow progress through the provincial theatre and her relationship with Richard. He is married, though estranged from his wife who is not only living in dissipation in Paris (abroad is always a bad thing in Hamilton's work), but a Catholic and unwilling to grant him a divorce. While working in Brighton, Jackie meets Richard's brother, the dashing Charles, who secretly falls in love with her. Jackie and Richard start to live together as man and wife and she attains a certain success, including one starring role in the West End. Then, during an engagement in Sheffield, Richard suddenly dies of influenza. Her career fades then undergoes the beginnings of a revival. But Jackie has become profoundly disenchanted with the theatre and Charles has asked her to marry him. She ends triumphantly by abandoning the theatre and accepting Charles.

This cumbersome plot shows the book at its weakest and most retrograde. Ominously, for Hamilton's future, it also seems that Michael Sadleir liked the book for what was meretricious about it. As his own most successful novel, *Fanny By Gaslight* (published in 1940), was to demonstrate, Sadleir had a taste for a sort of melodramatic Victorian pastiche, and this was what he responded to in Hamilton's novel. Years later he wrote of it warmly, but perversely: 'It must be as true a picture of the stage as ever was made and Jackie holds together all through. But I can't help feeling the final chapters are an anti-climax, after the lover's death. It's odd how different is its appeal from *Craven House* – a much more specialized one – although its manner is as individual.'[9] W. W. Jacobs, in his mid-sixties and an acquaintance of Hamilton's, responded to the book in similar terms on its first publication, describing it as one of the best novels he had read for a long time: 'Patrick Hamilton's observation, irony, humour and toleration are admirable. To the "penny plain" of ordinary life he has added the pennyworth of romance which makes all the difference between a dull book and a good one.'[10]

Modern readers are more likely to respond to this novel despite the predictable love interest, to be struck by the resemblances it bears to books in the future rather than those of the previous century. There are some disastrously bad passages in the novel, far worse than the most misguidedly sentimental scenes in *Craven House* – Hamilton himself was to describe the style as 'a base, indeed at moments slightly obscene, imitation of A. A. Milnish, de Morganish sentimentality at its worst', adding reasonably enough that 'Of course one is not entirely to blame for this – the mere passage of years turns what once seemed to be light humour into "whimsy-whimsy", and unobjectionable sentiment into objectionable sentimentality.'[11]

The novel begins creakily, almost as if Hamilton were guiltily conscious that this was his third novel in a row in which a young person with no previous acting experience enters the theatrical profession. But as soon as Jackie reaches the 'vast, thronged, unknown, hooting, electric-lit, dark-rumbling metropolis',[12] we are in the urban landscape Hamilton would make his own. His panoramic vision of the sordid West Kensington, where he himself had taken lodgings, is part Dickens (the right part this time) and part cinematic montage:

West Kensington – grey area of rot, and caretaking, and cat-slinking basements. West Kensington – drab asylum for the driven and cast-off genteel! Penitentiary for misused existences; distressed haven for the house-agent-ridden, the servant-harassed! Land of geysers; rusty baths; gramophones; landladies; breakfasts in bed; meals in kitchens; dark hall-ways; dank, seeded gardens; buses; Belgian refugees; coal carts; Chinese nurse-maids; barbers' shops; West End prostitutes; cripples in Bath chairs; modish youths; chorus girls; barrel-organs, street singers, flautists, harpists (ineffectual and conflicting assuagers of the public grief) . . .[13]

Only in the final clause is the wrong note struck, with the author stepping unnecessarily from behind the curtain to provide a sentimental gloss.

Too much of the affair between Richard and Jackie is a faded melodrama, unmediated by the savagery and wit Hamilton would later bring to similar material. Even here, though, there are many fine touches. The first night they spend together as husband and wife is conveyed with wonderful grimness, particularly Richard's pathetic attempt to celebrate the occasion with fine food and champagne. The use of the word 'perky' in the following passage is wonderfully scornful: 'It was the champagne which hurt her the most. The banality of that champagne! The banality and inadequacy of those two bottles, standing with a perky air of celebration, upon the table!'[14]

What is most startling in the novel is the savagery of its attack on its main subject matter. The story has its lapses into sentimentality, but none of these occur in its treatment of the theatrical life. Even Dr Johnson was excited by the idea of meeting actresses backstage,[15] but Hamilton's description of the women's dressing room is astringently Swiftian: 'For from here the breath of languor is expelled, and all feminine blandishment replaced by a vitality and overbearing practicality that does not challenge, but implicitly refutes illusion. This is a place of flesh, and blood, and sinew, and human need. This is not Revelation; it

75

is letting the cat out of the bag.'[16] This is so excessively resistant to any illusion as to take on a psychological interest. What cat is being let out of what bag? What did the young Hamilton expect a women's dressing room to be like? Yet while writing this, he was preparing to enter the profession in triumph. A couple of years later, Brian Aherne, who was starring in a Hamilton play in the West End, was deeply shocked when he read the theatrical novel by England's most successful young playwright:

I have read your *Tuppence Coloured* [*sic*] and, still quivering with distress, I am moved to ask you – is that really what we're like?

I know – I know only too well that every slash and jab of your pen is deserved by some portion of this dilapidated profession. Mr Shaw before you tells us that it was even worse in his day.

But please, please believe that there is some corner of it where dignity and honest endeavour still maintain their being, where catchwords and empty vanity are recognised for what they are.[17]

In the final chapters of *Twopence Coloured*, those considered an anti-climax by Michael Sadleir, Hamilton circles the theatrical genre like a general ruthlessly surveying every weak point of a fortress he intends to storm and capture. Yet the energy of his scorn denotes an intense engagement with the subject, certainly far beyond his meagre published writing about the theatre. There is the audience, the 'Disinterested Theatre Lovers':

In fact, from the long queues of pasty-faced and overworked typists, dowdy and genteel young women from obscure Universities, genteel and toothless ancients from Bayswater boarding-houses, suburban harridans with canvas stools, spotty-faced young men peering at bent-back books, out-of-work actors and medical students – all lined up stodgily between the wall and the gesticulating histrionic parasitism of the down-at-heel but impudent queue performer – Jackie derived the most depressing sensations. It was not that she reacted so much against the almost plodding beautilessness of these patrons themselves (though she did do this): it was that the whole scene was antipathetic to her own concept of art.[18]

But Jackie, who is contemplating an acting career, or Hamilton, who was contemplating a playwriting career (there is no distinction in these

particular passages, since they precisely match his later statements on
the form), has further, more profound reservations:

Concerning that medium itself she had her doubts. Her medium would be a
slightly uncanny, elongated, three-walled, glue-smelling, bright lemon-col-
oured interior world (a form of symbolism, to begin with, from which the
imaginative mind recoiled), and in this world she would walk about with a
feeling of peculiar mental undress, knowing that every one of her movements
and utterances was espied, embarrassed, and generally eaten up by the spiritual
magnetism of a fourth and non-existent wall – to which wall all the settees were
obviously sprawled (like sun-rays), all the silent and dreadful speeches were
made, and all existence was subtly but inescapably referred. (Those sinister
glassy eyes of actors and actresses on a first night!)

But although this wall played so large a part, it did not really exist. You could
not even look at a picture on this wall (and Jackie had tried this) without getting a
laugh . . .

And when there were a lot of people present at the same time in this world, the
person speaking spoke three times louder than he would have ordinarily, and all
the other people either remained queerly silent and attentive, or spoke among
themselves three times more quietly than they would have spoken ordinarily,
and stood extraordinarily close to each other, like conspirators . . . With
discrepancies and eccentricities of this nature this world was filled, and it was,
on the whole, a grouped and arranged world as little resembling actual life as
Frith's selected picture resembles Derby Day.[19]

The plays themselves are no good either. As an actress Jackie is
frustrated by the inane material she is imprisoned by. She found that:

so far from being permitted to express her own self in this vehicle she had
chosen, she was to be called upon to interpret the mostly obscure and always
half-heartedly conveyed ideas of another. And more than that, these ideas,
before coming under her control, had not only to pass filtrated through the
whims and urgencies of the mime-master himself, but to be embarrassed and
effected by the exigencies of her fellow-performers. . . . It was a world in which
Comedy was either the pat utterance of humorous quips, or a series of creaking
Situations in which somebody discovered somebody else doing something he
shouldn't, and watched him toying ineffectually to hide it up.[20]

The acting profession which Jackie had hoped to join is equally at fault: 'The obvious stumbling-blocks and difficulties of this art (if it was to be an art) being so much greater than those of any other, a supremer effort (she felt) was called for. She was therefore disturbed to observe that in this, of all arts, the least effort was being made.'[21] Jackie's triumph, in what is a thoroughly happy ending, is her knowledge that 'the whole West End acting world, with its social intrigue and garrulity, remained a closed door to her – a thing beyond her.'[22] The door, that is, that would soon be swinging open for Hamilton.

II

Bernard's mild stroke had done little to stem the output of books which had anyway been in manuscript, largely completed, for many years. In 1927 *His Queen* was published, a historical novel about Columbus, another of Bernard's stories about a great individual's ability to change history. Columbus shares his creator's political optimism: 'We new men of science are all brothers. We are seekers together for truth.'[23] And, just as Bernard's Danton had been guillotined for his devotion to Marie Antoinette, so Bernard's Columbus discovers America because of his love for Queen Ysabel:

He was her Champion – her own knight, having done his devoir.
And she the Lady, to whom he had given up his life.
Is there, in song or story, a nobler example of true chivalry?[24]

This was swiftly followed in the next year by two final books from the increasingly feeble Bernard, who was in no condition to write any further, even if the publishers had wished to encourage him, which they didn't.

His last novel, an historical novel about Rabelais, *The Master of Mirth*, is arguably – though it is not clear whom one could find to argue with on the subject of Bernard Hamilton's fiction – the most ludicrous of his entire oeuvre. Early in the book, Leonardo da Vinci unveils a well-known painting to an impressed King Francis: ' "She hath the wisdom of ages in her smile," said he. "Name, Master, thy guerdon." '[25] Among the book's set pieces is an attack by a force of bandits on a convent, in response to which the author metaphorically throws up his hands in horror: 'Can there be anything more hideous than the sack of a helpless convent?'[26] Fortunately help arrives before too much harm is done: 'As yet, there had been no organised assault upon the nuns; only stray ravishes.'[27]

Bernard's own guerdon from his fiction was insignificant and his wife noted, 'There has been no success with Rabelais. It has scarcely been noticed *at all* in the papers. It is really rather sad for him.'[28] His final book was his 'Psychic History', *One World – at a Time*, dedicated 'To My Children, Diana, Bruce, and Patrick Hamilton', and published in 1928. Its purpose was to feed the 'growing spiritual hunger of the public'. Apart from the accounts of his youth cited above, and some swipes back at Sir Arthur Conan Doyle, the book is most notable for its recapitulation of his philosophy first expressed twenty-eight years earlier in his political pamphlet. The ideas were the same: 'The firm Will is essential; and an organized Leadership. We get too often instead the self-interested vote of the major portion of the ignorant mass. Men welcome a real Leader as they would a Saviour, a *man* who knows only his duty, not his personal feelings.'[29] The difference was that Bernard had now found his saviour:

Nothing short of marvellous is the career of Benito Mussolini.

I have myself stood in the Palazza Colonna and heard his modest but stern eloquence. His career is unsurpassed in world history.

But his conduct is a moral example for all the world.[30]

Bernard would not live to see the further progress of his hero's career, nor the appearance of the German leader he might have seen as an even greater man of destiny.

Hamilton and Bruce would soon be moving to the other end of the political spectrum from the theory expressed by their dying, failed father. Yet for Hamilton, at least, the idea of a strong leader would always be as potent as it had been for his father. More elusive perhaps, less openly acknowledged, but it would never leave him.

9

Courtesans and
The Midnight Bell

I

Hamilton was now living a fragmented life. The fiction that he was producing was intensely, if problematically, autobiographical. While writing *Twopence Coloured*, he was experiencing what he would adapt for his next novel, *The Midnight Bell*. His life was becoming more deliberately compartmentalized, with several relationships being conducted simultaneously and separately. He was in his final days of living at home, where he spent the bulk of his time writing frenetically. He had occasional, clubbish meetings with Michael Sadleir and Martha Smith. One letter describing an evening with the two of them deserves to be quoted in full, because here, more than in any other of his letters, the reader is at Hamilton's shoulder, travelling through London in the late summer of 1927.

Darling Bruce,

I am writing this on Chiswick Park station.

A train has come in and I am in it. I am on my way to dinner with Michael and Martha. He goes off to Scotland to-night. We are meeting at *Henckey's* in the Strand at 7.30.

It is now 10 to 7. I'll make it all right, won't I?

I shall tell you my adventures on the way, and whether by the end of the evening, I am drunk or not. I should think I would be, as Michael

RAVENSCOURT PARK

wants to get rather sodden, I think, for his long night journey.

If I *do* get Drunk

80

HAMMERSMITH

and if I get them both off in time, I shall pay a visit to *The Admiral Duncan*, and write you something from there.

BARON'S COURT

Anyway, you will be with me all the evening. I have no news. I am working *terribly hard*, and am *very very* depressed

passing WEST KEN

(I hadn't known this

was a non-stop)

by your loneliness on your holiday. I do hope, dearest, dearest Bruce, that you're

EARL'S COURT

feeling better by the time you get this. Oh, dear, I'm working so hard this end. If only I can make a lot of money, I could come out to you. I think I must try and do this in any case. Anyway I'll really write you properly when I've finished this book

GLOUCESTER ROAD

and send you books and things. Cheer up. Can't you be writing a novel or something? At black moments why don't you regard these years as *penal years*, and, since you're suffering a bit

S. KENSINGTON

suffer thoroughly, and bring back a Book. You *must must* write, dearest Ecurb.

Opposite me is a not altogether filthily ugly girl, of about 29, reading a book and further along to my left is another girl to whom the same description

SLOANE SQUARE

applies. But the latter has now put her book on her lap, along with her bag, and is looking boredly in front of her. Also thousands of other people have entered whom I cannot begin to describe.

VICTORIA

I can't think of anything to *say*. Is the next station mine? Do you know, I *really* can't remember.

NO!!

ST JAMES PARK

And the next will be Westminster and the next Charing Cross. You, with your topographical mind, knew that already.

WESTMINSTER

Well Bruce, I'll be saying good-bye for the present in a moment. I'm waiting to write the name as it goes into station. Here we are . . . Here we are . . . Here

81

CHARING CROSS

Am in the middle of the Strand, outside a pub, looking a Fool.

In Taxi

in dark,

drunk

[The above three lines are a virtually unintelligible scrawl]

Dearest Ecurb,

The last remark was

'In Taxi, in dark, drunk'

I am now at Piccadilly Station, going home.

I stood in the middle of the Strand to write that bit, then I met M & M. We had wine at Henckey's and proceeded to the Renommé, where we had wine.

Train COME IN

We got wildly drunk. We saw M. off at Kings Cross, and then I saw Martha home. Then I went to the Admiral Duncan. I was just in time to get a drink. I should have written from there but it was very crowded and I couldn't get the opportunity.

I am now at

Hyde Park Corner.

Well, dearest Ecurb, I shall go on writing this till I reach Hammersmith and then I shall read Poe's Tales of M[ystery], and I[magination], on which I have been scribbling this piffle.

When you read this, remember that *this* is the *identical* bit of paper which I have carried about with me on

An Evening in London

I hope it may have some sentimental value for you.[1]

With Charles Mackehenie, Hamilton ventured more deeply into the capital's low life. Much of this consisted of little more than visiting a series of pubs in Earl's Court, Chelsea, Soho or around Euston Road and getting drunk, rather in the manner of two schoolboys out on a spree. Though he made constant resolves against it, Hamilton was now drinking heavily and regularly for the first time in his life. In the same month as the above underground journey, Hamilton gleefully reported that he had spent the night in a 'genuine low-down slum DOSS HOUSE in Drury Lane'. In his newly favourite pub, the Admiral Duncan, Hamilton had encountered what he might now think of as a Hamiltonian character, a one time artist who now makes a pretty rotten living, at the age of sixty two, by drawing smutty, or pseudo-funny-smutty postcards and selling them in bars (I don't know whether he's got any other means of living). He's quite a well read and educated lad – but I can't go into him. Anyway he, having no means, goes to dosshouses of a night, and I asked him to take me with him. He was delighted. Charles said he would come too. I was a bit drunk, and so was Charles. 'Look here, you are really coming to this place to-night, aren't you, Charles?' I was saying all the evening. 'Axiomatic,' he replied each time. I wonder if this amuses you. It did me at the time. Anyway, when the pub closed, we walked along there, but when we got there Charles wouldn't come in, so I went alone with the man. And I paid my money, and went in.[2]

Hamilton concluded by saying that he might describe what happened in another letter, but it would have to wait until the end of *The Midnight Bell*, when Hamilton's triumphantly squalid night would be transformed into Bob's climactic disaster, losing his girl, and the remnants of his money. Bob wakes up at half past five facing 'possibly one of the most peculiarly depressing situations in the world'.[3] Hamilton woke at the same time because he had to get home before his mother missed him: 'And I had Oh such a lovely walk along the river by Westminster Bridge at six o'clock. It was divine, and I'm sure that Wordsworth's Sonnet is the best in the language.'[4]

Hamilton now began regularly to arrive back late at the family house and he stopped concealing the fact from his mother. Ellen was now moving into her late sixties, and her health had become poor. She suffered from rheumatism and increasingly from insomnia, exacerbated by her puritanical refusal to take sleeping pills. All this had to be borne in reduced circumstances. A household of servants had been affordable in the days of prosperity, but Bernard's inherited fortune was gravely diminished and like many women of her class she was forced to undertake new domestic tasks, from cooking to shopping, with nothing but a single hired help. These changes must have been difficult to tolerate but she 'remained as she always had been, at the heart of her sons' lives, always to be relied on for sympathy and practical help.'[5] Hamilton confided in his mother and she was tolerant of his nocturnal absences. On his return from the West End, with dawn approaching, he would scrawl notes for her on scraps of paper, written in the affectionate, playful language he reserved for his mother, brother and sister, and leave them for her to find in the morning:

A quarter to eight, my exquisite?
>   Your infatuated,
>   *Patrick*

My own darling,
>   Will you call me with the *gong* to-morrow and I'll have a cup of *tea*. I'm feeling ever so fit,

>   Good night my angel,
>   Patrick

And, after a specially heavy night:

My more than darling Mother,
>   I hope (even more than you do) that by the time you receive this you will have had a glorious night's sleep.
>   Don't call me *at all*, darling, to-morrow. Not even for breakfast. Let me sleep on, and I'll have a cup of tea and a digestive when I wake. But make as much noise as you like, because when I'm sleeping I hear nothing.

>   Your doting,
>   *Patrick*[6]

To friends – to Bruce, to Michael Sadleir – Hamilton admitted, with varying degrees of ambiguity, that the attractions of his nocturnal expeditions with Charles Mackehenie were not just alcoholic and seamily social, but sexual. Michael Sadleir and Hamilton used to exchange verse letters so elaborate that at certain times of their friendship they must have occupied much of their time in composing them. In 1930, Sadleir wrote a letter to Hamilton about an impending visit to Sadleir's family:

> Pee Ess: one word of caution DON'T
> shock my mamma with gross impurities
> unlock Miss Russell for securities
> or croon to plaintive melodies
> those horrid symptoms of disease
> which – nature having made you so –
> take you twice weekly to Soho.[7]

Hamilton compartmentalized his relationships with women to an even more extreme extent than he did those with his men friends. There were women he idealized, like Maruja. There were women he was friendly with, sometimes with a childish, entirely unsexual flirtatiousness, such as his sister, Lalla, and Martha Smith, who were respectively six and nine years older than he was. He seems not to have contemplated physical sex with either of these categories of women. It is notable, even by comparison with the female characters in Bruce's novels, that Hamilton's women are strikingly lacking in a female physical presence. He is haunted by clothes. Master Wildman in *Craven House* is preoccupied by Miss Cotterell's 'slim boy's shape and the Florentine bobbed hair, and the lissom dresses', but like other Hamilton heroines she appears to be without breasts or hips.[8]

For sex, even for the idea of sex, Hamilton turned to women for whom it was a straightforward monetary transaction. This was a family tradition. Bernard had married a prostitute. In an unpublished, highly autobiographical novel, Bruce describes himself having sex for the first time with a Hyde Park prostitute in 1919. In the last months of 1926 or in January 1927, they had both had some sexual experience, and by February Hamilton was feeling guilty about it: 'Isn't it awful how one blames other people in this world for doing shoddy things, or saying or thinking them, and yet imagines there is some natural explanation and excuse for all the things which one does oneself and knows would look shoddy enough in *their* eyes.'[9] Hamilton was now fascinated by prostitutes, though for most of the time he was talking, listening and looking. The following month he sent to Bruce a copy of a letter he had written to Charles Mackehenie, which shows that, for the moment, 'touching courtesans' was a merely metaphorical phrase:

Touching courtesans, it has just occurred to me that they themselves would be the last to subscribe to our theory of abstinence. 'That is all very well,' I imagine they would say. 'But what about us? Just because you get squeamish about our eyes, we've got to lose decent custom.' Directly you de-sentimentalise the position, and allow they are amply justified in pursuing that course, there is no earthly difference between a courtesan and her less adventurous and courageous sisters. From which it follows that if you reject a courtesan's commodity, you might just as well reject a poached egg from a waitress in a sweat restaurant.

They are both equally victims, and you are assisting in their victimisation. The waitress deserves rather more consideration, though, for she's having a much worse time. But she would soon lose her job if her patrons were unable to face her eyes. Now as you and I are obviously unable to exist without the waitress, if follows that, as men of honour, we cannot continue to live. But this we will succeed in doing, as will be demonstrated by the fact that when I phone you on Saturday morning you will be at the other end of the line.[10]

What had begun as sexual enticement soon became a tantalizing source of material. One side of Hamilton at least was more intrigued by the atmosphere of their world, by the idea of them, than by the erotic possibilities they offered. His assertions to Bruce that he was carrying out research may not have been the whole story, but he *was* carrying out research. In May he reports:

Lately I've been making the most extraordinary expeditions (with Charles) into Soho – mixing a great deal with the courtesans therein, and also the low life. I think I've got an idea for an extraordinary and really valuable novel. I daresay you know it's always been one of my leading ambitions to write about the life of *servants* – particularly female ones – and their oppressed hideous condition. And it's also been my ambition to write about harlots. I have two first rate novels with either of these subjects. Now my latest adventures have led me into remarkable sociological observations and enlightenments, and it's suddenly occurred to me that to write a novel which is about both servants *and* harlots (possibly the slow transformation of the one into the other) would not only be ferociously good as a novel, but really sound work. A kind of Mrs Warren's profession brought up to date.[11]

This was to be the seed of *The Siege of Pleasure*, the second volume of Hamilton's impending trilogy, *Twenty Thousand Streets Under the Sky*, whose sole subject is Jenny's transformation from domestic servant to prostitute. In the same letter, Hamilton went on to argue that prostitution was forced on working-class women by economic necessity:

The cardinal fact is that women *cannot earn a decent living* (as people vaguely think they may). Their position, in fact, if one takes the trouble to examine it, and think hard about it, is HIDEOUS. I'm going into wages and facts. They are utterly dependent on their sexual attractions for their salvation. There was never such a need for a huge feminist movement as there is now.[12]

The story survived intact but the didactic feminist purpose was entirely dropped. Twenty-five years later, though, Hamilton took up the argument in *Mr Stimpson and Mr Gorse*, and gave it a more political twist, in an account of Soho prostitution in – and the year is emphasized – 1928:

Prostitution, in fact, was just then approaching its heyday – the collapse of the 1926 strike having put the working class into a mood of dejection, apathy and submissiveness, which, taken in conjunction with increasing national unemployment, had thrown more dejected, apathetic and submissive women upon the West End streets than, perhaps, ever before.[13]

The villain of the novel, Ernest Ralph Gorse, is fascinated by Soho's prostitutes, just as Hamilton was at the same time, though it is made clear that he has no sexual interest in them:

His assured sense of social superiority made him very much at ease with such women, who, because of their low educational level and somewhat debased sense of humour, were pleased, or even delighted, by his dashing air, his monocle, and the 'Silly Ass' act in which, with them, he was able to indulge to the full. . . . A 'public-school' voice and a monocle are regarded as symbols of a 'gentleman' in such credulous circles. But he was also thought of as a 'real gentleman'. For he was generous with his money, made no amorous advances, and frequently went out of his way to do one of these girls or women a 'good turn' – such as lending her money (usually repaid), or giving her a lift in his car.[14]

By July 1927 Hamilton was insisting that sex is 'great and holy' and Bruce may have been dismayed to be told that it was 'not for you and I (our lust is the lust for thought and power) and if we can't get it we will not steal furtive little bits of it, and so torment ourselves. And it can be put aside, if it is put aside, with one noble gesture, completely.'[15] Hamilton proclaimed that he had 'committed no malpractices for months'. Though he was still visiting Soho, he had 'created the habit of celibacy, as Samuel Butler, and G. B. S. and any amount of priests and people have also succeeded in doing.'[16]

The three great crises of Hamilton's life occurred when the carefully constructed compartments of his life broke down, and his emotions spilled into each other. Celibate he may have been, but the first of his crises had already begun. Like his father before him, he had fallen in love with a prostitute.

II

Hamilton met Mrs Lily Connolly in the first week of July, 1927. In letters to Bruce he first referred to her as Esther Ralston – the name of a current Hollywood film star that they both adored – and proclaimed within a week that he was 'hopelessly and madly in love, much more so than ever with Marya'. But this was love of a truly Platonic kind. Hamilton experienced not lust but 'the vast and terrific and transcendent emotions . . . at the *pure physical beauty and the aura shining therefrom*'. He felt ennobled and awed, though more, it seems, by the force of his own love than by any particular quality of Lily, who remains undescribed.[17]

However ethereal Hamilton's original impulses, the affair, if such a one-sided, non-sexual relationship can be called that, got out of hand. In October he told Bruce that he had 'cut her out long ago'. This was either a deliberate falsehood or else, which may be more likely, he met Lily once more at the beginning of 1928 with far more devastating results. What is certain is that the relationship was at its most extreme between about March and May 1928.

Lily could scarcely have been expected to respond to the fantastic, exalted romanticism of Hamilton's emotion. She must have seen that there were no long-term prospects for the relationship and hence, understandably, she made use of his infatuation to extract money from him while she could. She also perceived, quite correctly, that the only way of continuing to extract money was to keep her infatuated suitor at a distance, while constantly offering encouragement. In February 1928, Hamilton – made ill by his work and his feelings for Lily – retreated to Brighton for recuperation. A letter Lily wrote to him there, and which he kept, examplifies the problems of interpreting Hamilton's life, even when fragmentary evidence survives. Is this a moderately affectionate letter? Or is it, on the other hand, an example of tormenting flirtatiousness, the endearments overdone (with what Hamilton was later to call 'the spontaneous and characteristic "dear" of the courtesan'[18]), the spurious note of jealousy about the 'nice *girls* in Brighton', the mention of a new coat in order to solicit money? It is impossible to say, since she survives only in Hamilton's rendering and in just three letters (I have preserved her spelling and punctuation, which Hamilton would soon mimic with cruel accuracy):

Dearest Patrick

Well dear I received your letter this morning and of course I was very pleased. The weather here is awful the wind is howling and it is raining so you can quite understand I am as fed up as you dearest but never mind we shall soon see each other again shant we honey. You write in your letter you will be back on Wedensday well dear as soon as you arrive will you Phone me as I shall not leave this address by then Well Patrick it must be awful at Brighton and I think it would be far better for your health if you returned home dont you. Well you write to ask me if I go into the Queens well I am the first one in and the last one out but I expect you are having a few drinks where you are as I know you are awful fond of it aint you.

and dear someone told me there were some nice *girls* at Brighton. I am trying to buy a new coat so I shall look quite smart when you come home but I know that dosent interest you does it. It is two o clock and I am still in bed aint I lazy but you already know that dont you Well I think

this is all
until I see you
so Bye Bye
yours with lots
of love
Lily

ps Look after yourself
darling[19]

As Bruce recalled, Hamilton's friends tried to make him see reason: 'The sensible thing, so our cousin Frank, Charles, Michael and other experienced advisors told him, would have been to possess her on her own terms, and give himself a chance of getting her off his mind. But he could not bring himself to do this.'[20]

There is an abundance of possible explanations for Hamilton's pursuit of Lily. She was genuinely beautiful, as even Bruce admitted when he later met her. Her Christian name had two 'l's in it, always a significant attraction for Hamilton. He was re-enacting his own father's doomed attempt to reclaim a prostitute. As a chronicler of the lower depths, he was also imitating the predilection for proletarian women of his predecessor, George Gissing. The very futility was as much of an incitement here as it had been with Maruja; Hamilton could play at giving himself utterly without the fear of any ultimate commitment.

There may also have been a colder, more detachedly literary motivation. Hamilton had systematically mined his own experiences for his previous three novels. He was piercingly conscious that he now had to write a major book and he knew that his subject was to be a prostitute. He wrote of this sense early in 1928, expressing dissatisfaction to Bruce with *Twopence Coloured* even before it had been published. The two novels referred to are by Sinclair Lewis (published respectively in 1927 and 1925) and were famous, or notorious, for the research they had required:

My present object is to harness my old enormous gusto to my new vehicle. This I think I shall do next time. And that brings us to the next book – which is rather ticklish. The only book of importance on my horizon is my prostitute one – but I don't think I can undertake this at once. For one thing it requires as much study as an Elmer Gantry or M. Arrowsmith, and for another I've just finished a 130,000 word novel, and I want a rest. I'm therefore going to do two books this year. I'm going to be slowly constructing the prostitute one, and writing another *short* one for publication.

The short one, I think, shall be about a pub. What a miraculous opportunity for reaping my wild oats! If ever a man knew the atmosphere and life and ethics of these places it's me. And what an opportunity for my own particular brand of fun! Drunkenness. I should be able to write a rollicking little masterpiece.[21]

In the event, the new novel he was about to begin would combine both those ideas, and it was with great self-consciousness that he abandoned himself to Lily Connolly. His first full confession of the affair is a curious mixture of agony and bathos. He begins by saying that he has had terrible problems with smoking, drinking and depression. The following quotation is accompanied by Hamilton's handwritten addition, 'Not a word to Mummie': 'In which phase I entered in upon the most DEVASTATING love affair that a man could be called upon to suffer. I can't begin to tell you about this. It's all too involved, and incomprehensible and scandalous. I can only say that I have been truly obsessed and have suffered agonies.'[22] Hamilton then claims that it is his smoking that is really at the root of his troubles, agitating him and making it impossible to conduct a love affair peaceably. His descriptions of the affair constantly undermine its reality. Attempting to describe his idealized passion, he drew on his common movie-going experiences with Bruce, contrasting the famous beauty Esther Ralston with the then fifty-two-year-old actress, Mary Carr (described by Leslie Halliwell as 'the archetypal white-haired old mother'[23]):

Now in so far as all love is, and must be, to the philosopher, of secondary importance, if I cannot have a love affair peaceably and without agony, *I cannot have one at all.* In other words, if my sentiments are for one moment going to interfere with my efficiency as a writer, then I must evade my sentiments by flight from the one who inspires them. And that is pure tragedy – the tragedy of the man whose true mistress is not Romance, but Thought. For Romance is as beautiful as Esther Ralston and Thought is as beautiful as Mary Carr. And it is my doom to be the slave of the latter. If I was only a bank-manager or a novelist or anything but what I am I would follow Romance to the death.[24]

Hamilton saw his literary calling as a form of priesthood, which may well have suited what were anyway his own inclinations. In early June 1928, in the middle of this final flurry of pain, Hamilton was able to organize a move out of the family home in Chiswick into rooms of his own in New Cavendish Street, W1, right in the heart of the West End, and he wrote eagerly to Bruce saying that they must live together there. He added, as an inducement to his brother, that he was now just a short walk and a bus ride from Lord's Cricket Ground. He omitted to mention that ten minutes' walk to the north would bring him to Lily's squalid new flat in Bolsover Street and ten minutes' walk to the south would bring him to Wardour Street, the main street of Soho's prostitution industry. It scarcely mattered now anyway. At about the same time he was able to report, without noticeable pain, that his love affair was over.[25] Hamilton was either being disingenuous, or only gradually recognizing his true gifts. His life seemed to be founded on contradictions. At this time he had the conception of himself as a man who would transcend mere art and become an artistic philosopher, like Nietzsche or, which is more likely, Shaw's domesticated version of him, John Tanner in *Man and*

Superman. The leap forward Hamilton made was to bring the two sides together, to abandon pretentious ideas either of philosophy or even of exploring prostitution as a social force, but instead to make use of his own experience.

The end of the affair was resolutely undramatic. He bounced straight from Lily Connolly to a brief infatuation with another prostitute but, while lamenting the time it took, he was grateful for the 'barrier, not of sentiment, but of mental occupation, between me and the other affair.'[26]

The other affair was now clearly revealing itself to Hamilton as potent in its literary possibilities. He wrote a letter to Bruce which is the decisive document in his literary development. Everything seems to be happening at once. His slumming is portrayed with brutal honesty and then immediately connected to his novel in hand. He reveals that he has abandoned his jejune philosophical ideas in favour of a pessimistic – and thoroughly atheistic – theology, which doesn't require to be argued but instead can hang over the story like fog. And finally, this shift has demanded a stylistic change, away from the baroque Dickensian comic style to something simpler, more classic and pared down. His own non-literary experiences had brought him to a discovery that Hemingway had made several years earlier:

That, indeed, was terrible, though I am as free as air now. I am so free that I can talk about it without a tremor. I am dying to tell you the story, and *what* a story it makes! I shall tell you all one day – of Lily Connolly (but *she* thought it was spelt Conerlly), the mad harlot from Ipswich – of Priscilla, the wearied courtesan who had seen the Isles of Greece – and of Joan, the red-haired whore of Soho. And how I had tea with them all on a foggy day in a filthy little room at the top of a house in Bolsover Street – just opposite Great Portland Street Station and not more than three hundred yards away (as I remember comprehending at the time) from your old room at Osnaburgh. They all three slept in the same bed, and syphilis was in the air. Not that there was any air, or anything but the heavy odour of carbolic soap, gone bad. By the way I have since discovered that that filthy smell we experienced at 14 Comeragh Road, and suspected of arising from urine, is nothing more than carbolic soap used wrongly.

And yet I couldn't run away. I got into brawls at restaurants, and fights in the street, and fell amongst thieves in Soho dens. You will never believe it. And yet, when you hear my story, you will not be able to detect one psychological flaw in my behaviour. You would have done exactly the same yourself, and so would anyone of lively temperament. But I've lost my taste for low life permanently, and thank God I'm out of it all.

My present book is, I think, streets ahead of what I've done before. By that I only mean as a novel. But I thought I might as well write a purely objective novel for once. I shall make a success soon, believe me, and then I shall do what I want.

But this book is fine. Its background is taken from what I have sketched, perhaps rather exaggeratedly, above, and it has gathered to itself, quite unconsciously, the theme of which all really great novels are composed. There is only one theme of the HardycumConrad great novel – that is, that this is a bloody awful life, that we are none of us responsible for our own lives and actions, but merely in the hands of the gods, that Nature don't care a damn, but looks rather picturesque in not doing so, and that whether you're making love, being hanged, or getting drunk, it's all a futile way of passing the time in the brief period allotted us preceding death. It is all, of course, profoundly true, and bears no actual relation to life whatever. It is merely the portentous dirge of the poet's mind – it being the poet's business to put into words the universal wail of humanity at not being able to get everything it wants exactly when it wants it. Everybody knows, in his heart of hearts that it's a first-rate existence if only one or two things would go right.

However the poet's idea is so consoling and seductive that we all succumb to it, and I have too. Not that I don't think it's a tremendous idea to express, and I'm simply carried away by it. I really believe I'm enjoying writing it, and I think you will like it terribly.

I have developed a lot of new theories about writing and style, the latter having acquired a weird penchant for short sentences – not staccato – but a little shorter and crisper even than can be observed in the last chapter of the first book of 2d Coloured – the best thing I ever wrote, I still maintain, at least in the serious line. Also I never now try to get effects, except in comic writing. My maxim is to *see*, relate what you see, and your effects will come. Vision and imagination are the things, and they arise from stored observation. There are no capital letters in the new book, I work a great deal with the dash and colon, and am not afraid of awkward rhythms. If your vision and feeling are clear, they will transcend mere prose. Also I work with short chapters of about five pages each, one after another – no sections. Sometimes I do a whole one in a day. I am far from being through yet, but my navigation is finished and I am riding home on the waves of the story. I hope to be done shortly after Christmas.[27]

III

The Midnight Bell has generally been talked of as Hamilton's most straightforwardly autobiographical novel. His brother stated insistently that it was 'the story of his enslavement to Lily, tailored to the needs of fiction and form', and, more drastically still, that its leading character, Bob, '*was* Hamilton, given a few superficial characteristics belonging to a different class.'[28]

It may be that, writing after Hamilton's death, Bruce had his own reasons for making, even in the midst of praise, the limiting comment that his brother was simply transcribing his experience. Almost fifteen years later, in 1942, Hamilton wrote a severely critical letter to Bruce about his cricket novel, *Pro*:

Have you not a little too much *enjoyed* yourself while writing this book? Am I right in saying that you let yourself go, and enjoyed yourself enormously? My criticism is that you have let personal things and memories – childhood, Brighton, cricket grounds – Barbados – personal happenings – that you have written down these things without really and painfully trying (as an artist must) to convey them vividly to a reader who has no such personal memories.[29]

There is nothing intrinsically of value, or even of interest, in a novelist transcribing his own experience, and there is certainly no duty whatever of accuracy or fairness. One striking quality of *The Midnight Bell*, which sets it sharply above Hamilton's previous novels, is that there is nothing in the novel that is there only because it happened to him. Looking back on it years after its first publication, Michael Sadleir was sensitive to this new authority of tone and narrative: '*Midnight B* I am halfway through. So far it seems to be faultless – gone all limpid and self-reliant – no straining after effect, no youthful exuberance.'[30] The significance of the novel's relationship to the recent disturbances in Hamilton's life is not that he reproduced them in his novel, but that he subtly remade them and imposed a pattern on them for his own purposes. The most obvious example we have of what Michael Holroyd has described as 'almost a transcription'[31] is Hamilton's use of a letter he received from Lily in the Spring of 1928. The original is followed by Hamilton's fictionalized version:

Mrs Conerlly

7 Bentinck Terrace

St John's Wood

Dearest Patrick,

You must excuse me for writing this in pencil but we havent a pen in the house and I am in a hurry to mail this to you. Well dear I suppose by this time you are finished with me and you do not wish to see me again but you must quite understand after being with someone ill one gets very tired and I asked the maid in the house if she would call me at four and she left it until five so you can quite see by the time I was washed and dressed it was nearly six so I thought you wouldnt wait until then so I did not come down and Patrick I havent had anything to eat all day not even a cup of tea so you can see how I feel dearest. I will leave it to you after reading this letter to see if you still want me and if you do meet me on Thursday at 5.30 same time in Rayners and I shall not fail you this time we can spend a little longer together then dear. You can phone me up before to tell me of if you like dear. Well dear I trust you will excuse me again for the pencil and not coming I remain

One who

loves you

Lily. XXXX

XXXX[32]

In *The Midnight Bell*, Jenny has failed to turn up for an appointment, once again, and on the following day a letter arrives at the pub where Bob works:

It was on cheap, ruled paper, from a Woolworth's writing block, and it was written in pencil. The handwriting was rounded, stupid, but conscientious. The 'i's were dotted with a jab and a twirl:

'Dear Bob

'No doubt by now you are through with me as I did not turn up today but Bob it was not my fault dear. You must excuse pensil as I have no pen Well dear you must understand it was not my fault as I was out all that night before and did not get in till half past 4 in the morning and overslept myself untill it was too late to meet you And I have not had anything to eat all day dear as I have no money.

'Well Bob it was not my fault and if you are not through with me perhaps you will meet me on Friday Bob will you I will be at the Green man at 3 and hope you come along there I will be there erlier if you like I hope you will let me hear.

95

'Please excuse pensil and not turning up

yours truly

Jenny Maple'[33]

At first glance these two letters seem strikingly similar. But in reworking Lily's original, Hamilton has systematically removed its ambiguities which would have made it harder for the reader to assess. It is made consistently less affectionate: Dearest becomes dear, One who loves you becomes yours truly, the X's are omitted. Everything that might rouse the reader's sympathy in the original is either left out or given a cynical twist. Thus in Hamilton's version, there is no mention of looking after a sick person, which is replaced by the whiningly self-exculpatory 'it was not my fault'. Finally, though judgement about Lily's handwriting is a matter of opinion (a more sympathetic reader might judge it endearingly childlike), the 'i's' are certainly not vulgarly 'dotted with a jab and a twirl'.

It is undeniable that Bob's initial characterization as a sailor born in the United States is perfunctory and unconvincing. Yet, though he shares his author's sensibility, and doubtless a good deal of his motivation in falling for a prostitute, what are most significant are the differences. At the centre of the story is Bob's eighty pounds, his life savings, which we see poured away on Lily with accelerating speed. Bob has no supportive family. His aspiration to be a writer is implausible and portrayed as hopeless.

Bob repeats Hamilton's experiences, most notably the tea with the three prostitutes at their rooms in Bolsover Street, but he responds entirely differently. The account in the novel is similar to that in the letter quoted above. Priscilla becomes Prunella and the syphilis that 'was in the air' is softened to 'disease and delinquency'. But Bob feels sick when Prunella says of him that 'He's one of us'.[34] Hamilton never believed that he was one of them. The excitement he felt, whether there or in a doss house, was that of a writer who knew he was gaining access to a world that was not his and which he could leave in order to write about.

Whatever the squalor and suffering that Hamilton exposed himself to, the objective truth is that it was he and not Lily who ultimately had the power. If she subjected him to torment, it was from a position of weakness. Any money she was able to abstract from him was irrelevant in any but the shortest term. He was passing through a world in which she was condemned to stay.

Once he was free, Hamilton was able to defeat Lily in two ways. The first was in terms of language. He was able to capture her in a book, and he jokingly alludes to this in the novel itself when Jenny recalls that an author had once given her a book:

'Oh, he met me one night, an' took me back to his flat. There wasn't nothing in it. He gave me a drink, an' asked me to tell him my story.'

'Did you?'

'Oh, yes. I told him something. He said I was so young he wanted to know how I got started. Then he gave me his book, and said I'd find myself in it – or somethin' like that. It was only *me*, under another name, he said.'[35]

Whatever else they are as works of art, in Hamilton's private world *The Midnight Bell* and its sequel, *The Siege of Pleasure*, are a grim inversion of Shakespeare's sonnet number 18, 'Shall I compare thee to a summer's day?' in which the beloved gains immortality through the poet's own language:

> So long as men can breathe or eyes can see,
> So long lives this, and this gives life to thee.

In 1928, before she disappeared from sight, presumably to some unhappy fate, Lily may have had her excuses. But not in *The Midnight Bell* where she is transformed and preserved as an emblem of shallow greed and malevolence. Hamilton could re-invent her and then pin her down:

All at once it seemed that he divined her whole character. She had never once been nice to him – throughout. She had never kept her appointments, unless it had suited her: she had fooled him about her husband, and in every other way: and in their meetings she had tolerated him just so long as he flattered her, and no longer. At the slightest criticism of herself she had been ready to dispense with him. Only when he had given her money had she briefly sweetened and softened towards him, and he had been giving her money all along. She had 'played him up' throughout – that was all.[36]

The second way to defeat her was, after it was all over, to follow the advice of his friends, to dispel the myth of her unattainability which was entirely of his making, to take her on her own terms, give her money and have full sexual intercourse with her, which, by his own account, he later did – 'not very successfully', he told Bruce.[37]

All this had nothing to do with the novel itself, which still stands as a formidable achievement. The subjects and settings of the book had been of immense interest to Hamilton, in various ways, yet the book is marvellously detached. The denizens of pub life, of whom he was now one, are mercilessly explored.

Men! They thrust their hats back on their heads; they put their feet firmly on the rail; they looked you straight in the eye; they beat their palms with their fists, and they swilled largely and cried for more. Their arguments were top-heavy with the swagger of their altruism. They appealed passionately to the laws of logic and honesty. Life, just for to-night, was miraculously clarified into simple and dramatic issues. It was the last five minutes of the evening, and they were drunk.[38]

If Jenny is portrayed without sympathy, Hamilton is equally harsh on Bob's transcendent emotion and his motivation for falling love with a prostitute: 'In brief, because he had given ten shillings to a young prostitute without expecting the usual thing in return he was dreadfully conceited. He was so innocent as to believe the transaction was almost unique. He little suspected cunning mankind's general awareness of the charms of chivalry. He was in love with himself.'[39]

For Hamilton it was a personal triumph of abnegation, a confinement to a particular range of moods, a small cast of characters, an economic story, all taking place within a restricted setting, a progress around London – Warren Street, Soho, Doughty Street, the Whitestone Pond in Hampstead, Bolsover Street – that can be traced on a map.

It was generally recognized that Hamilton had reached a new level. Reviewing the book in the *Evening News*,[40] J. B. Priestley acclaimed the fulfilment of the young novelist's promise and added: 'He is one of the few young novelists who has it in him to work well on a big scale.'

This was what Hamilton now planned, but he also had other things on his mind, for between the completion of *The Midnight Bell* and its publication in the middle of June 1929 Hamilton's life had been changed completely.

10

Rope

I

Now approaching thirty, Bruce had finally finished his first novel, a thriller called *Odessa Road*. At the beginning of 1930 he sent the manuscript from Barbados to Hamilton in London to get it typed and, if he thought it was worth it, to send it to Hamilton's own literary agent, Audrey Heath, who presided over A. M. Heath and Company. On 25 April Hamilton sent Bruce a telegram: 'YOUR NOVEL SPLENDID CONVINCED EMINENTLY PUBLISHABLE LETTER YOU POSTED.'[1] The obvious enthusiasm must derive at least in part from the fact that Hamilton's first play, *Rope*, was opening at the Ambassador's Theatre in the West End that very night. Bruce didn't even know that Hamilton was writing a play and Hamilton may have been guiltily conscious that he ought to have given Bruce an opinion of his novel before he heard about it.

To Be Hanged, as Bruce's novel was later to be retitled, is about the attempt of a journalist to clear the name of a friendless Romanian musician who has been convicted of murder and sentenced to death. It is an atmospheric, fairly average thriller that relies far too much on coincidence. Hamilton meticulously steered clear of this in his novels, with the rare exception at the beginning of *Twopence Coloured*. He shows particular skill in choreographing the progress of Bob in *The Midnight Bell* so that the numerous encounters with Jenny never seem gratuitous. Bruce, who wrote thrillers in which the mechanics of plot are necessarily crucial, relied far too heavily on it. He never made the commitment of his career to writing that Hamilton had, nor, perhaps, did he accord it the same level of attention; his work too often bears the traces of haste.

In *To Be Hanged* the initial involvement of the hero, Edward Willis, depends on his having overheard a conversation at a railway station by the actual murderer and his accomplice on the night of the murder, and on his also being a reporter in court for the trial of the wrong man so that he can make the connection. It should be said, though, that this laziness of plotting was not unique to Bruce. In fact, it was almost a professional qualification among many of the most highly praised and successful thriller writers of the era. The plots of books as celebrated as Nicholas Blake's *The Smiler with the Knife*, John Buchan's *The Thirty-Nine Steps* and Eric Ambler's *Epitaph for a Spy* are all set in motion by devices no less absurd than that in *To Be Hanged*.

The novel ends with a stolid summing up of the two villains by the idealized lawyer for the defence, George Borrodaile, reflecting ideas raised in Bruce's correspondence with Hamilton over the previous couple of years:

'The primal fact about Emily, I think,' said Borrodaile, 'is that she was a stupid person. You may call it a moral kink, if you like, but I prefer to look on it as stupidity. Her mind seems to have been on a level with the minds of those people who used to read Nietzsche without being within a measurable distance of comprehending Nietzsche's sublimity, who could see in his writings only an incitement to a dullard to use brute force for personal ends without scruple. Langridge's ideas were altogether too much for her weak intellect. Her personality convinced her emotionally, and not being able to apply the brake of any wisdom, either instinctive or acquired, she would have no compromise. She did not know the doctrine of moderation – that is, moderation in action, however untrammelled the thought, the doctrine which sent Samuel Butler to Communion once every year, which keeps Bernard Shaw out of gaol, which in more fortunate circumstances would have saved Socrates from the hemlock. But that is stupidity, and from stupidity is born the really genuine fanatic.'[2]

As Bruce was about to discover, Hamilton had been thinking along similar lines. Bruce must have been contemplating his return to England in the summer, and the possibility of encountering Hamilton on almost equal terms as a fellow novelist. But this was not to be. Less than a month after the first telegram, at the end of nearly six months in which he had received no letters, a second telegram arrived from Hamilton: 'PLAY ENORMOUS SUCCESS YOUR SCHOOLMASTERING DAYS ARE OVER WRITING WEEKLY HENCEFORWARD'.[3] *Rope* had now been running in the West End for six weeks.

Hamilton was to tell Bruce that *Rope* had been written in a casual manner, on scraps of paper in pubs and Lyons Corner Houses. In reality he had embarked on this first play with a ruthless intelligence and craftsmanship remarkable for a writer who was still just twenty-four. He made full use of his earlier stage experience and his conviction of 'how successful such plays might be if written and presented in a sophisticated way'.[4] And he found a good subject. In his introduction to the first published edition of the text, Hamilton wrote: 'It has been said that I have founded "Rope" on a murder which was committed in America some years ago. But this is not so, since I cannot recall this crime having ever properly reached my consciousness until after "Rope" was written and people began to tell me of it. But then I am not interested in crime.'[5] The final sentence is certainly false. Books about famous trials were, with trashy westerns, always his favourite leisure reading. His contention that he was not influenced by the Leopold and Loeb case is simply not credible. Certainly Bruce, who probably never saw Hamilton's denial, took it for granted as the inspiration.[6]

Nineteen-year-old Nathan Leopold and eighteen-year-old Richard Loeb, friends and lovers, were brilliant students at the University of Chicago. Both became obsessed with Nietzsche's 'Superman' theory, which they applied to themselves. Feeling free from the laws designed for ordinary people, they decided to commit a perfect murder. On 21 May 1924 they kidnapped Bobbie Franks, a friend of Loeb's younger brother. They immediately murdered him, but then attempted to extract a ransom from the boy's parents. The murder was far from perfect. Leopold had dropped his spectacles while disposing of the body, and they were of an unusual design and quickly traced to him. The typewriter on which the ransom note had been typed was found and linked to the boys and they quickly confessed, each blaming the other. They were tried, and after a defence by the celebrated attorney, Clarence Darrow, were found guilty but sentenced to life imprisonment.[7]

Hamilton must have been struck by these two young men of his own age who had shared his own callow enthusiasm for Nietzsche. But the raw material wasn't enough. Sutton Vane's success had taught him that he needed an essentially dramatic idea to make his play work for an audience. The narrow, perverse genius of *Rope* is in its simplicity. At the front and centre of the stage is a chest which, we are soon told, contains the body of a recently murdered young man. Having set up this ghastly tableau, the murderers, and the playwright with them, can play sadistic variations, inviting the boy's father and sister to the flat, taking tea on the chest and so on. Hamilton had found an authentic addition to the repertoire of horror, without the employment of any on-stage violence or technical gimmickry.

Hamilton had satisfyingly employed both his most practical experience and his most abstract philosophical musings, and if the title of the play – so compelling, though he was considering changing it even at a late stage[8] – derives from the theatrical prop used to kill Ronald Kentley, it derives also from a saying of Nietzsche's which occurs near the beginning of *Thus Spake Zarathusthra*: 'Man is a rope, fastened between animal and Superman – a rope over an abyss.'[9]

Rope was immediately recognized by critics and audiences as a step forward. As a critic in the *Nation* put it, 'A murder play without pistols, knives and spooks was a very distinguished relief; also the author was really talking about something the whole time.'[10] Other critics found, and have continued to find, the subject obscene and unacceptable.[11]

Hamilton had already responded to this in his highly defensive preface. Having achieved such a remarkable success, he was then ashamed of having done so. Arthur Calder-Marshall, meeting Hamilton later, after his first marriage, described how this man 'of singular reserve and charm, became positively vehement in repudiation of [*Rope*] as his claim to fame, rather than his novels.'[12] This conviction survived even the excitement of initial triumph. The newly successful West End author began his preface by describing himself as a highbrow novelist and warning the readers of fiction away and insisting that *Rope* 'is a thriller, a thriller all the time, and nothing but a thriller.'[13]

To those who accused him of having written a simple shocker, he offered his agreement: 'in *Rope* I have gone all out to write a horror play and make your flesh creep.'[14] He disdained, of course, the use of Gothic paraphernalia, though he then went on to describe them with a good deal of relish. Perhaps he was nostalgically recalling his own participation in them: 'To me, in the ordinary thriller and Grand Guignolism of this decade, the incessant round of throat-slicings, eye-gougings, thumb-screwings, floggings, burnings, brain-twistings, charred bodies and the like is merely aimless and sickening.'[15] What Hamilton would not accept was any accusation of seriousness: 'But when "Rope" is accused of delving into morbid psychologies and so forth, of being anything but a sheer thriller, of being anything but a De Quinceyish essay in the macabre, I am at a wretched loss.'[16]

Hamilton did not make use of all the lessons he had learned. In *The Midnight Bell* he had established himself as a writer with a superb ear for stylized yet realistic dialogue. In *Rope* he attempted nothing that a West End audience might find difficult to follow and the dialogue is written in a deliberately retrograde style:

GRANILLO: You fully understand, Brandon, what we've done?
BRANDON: Do I know what I've done? . . . Yes. I know quite well what I've done. (*He speaks in a rich, easy, powerful, elated and yet withal slightly defiant voice.*) I have done murder.[17]

Much of the dialogue now seems painfully stilted, and none of the characters is more than sketched in. But this conservatism, in the midst of the play's apparent innovation, was a significant element of its success, and it still reads like a supremely effective dramatic machine, despite its author's mixed feelings.[18] As he put it much later, 'it *is* my view that the play, *dramatically*, is absolutely first class! I underline the word dramatically because ideologically it is, of course, nothing.'[19]

II

Once again, Hamilton's theatrical connections had been a help. When he had finished *Rope*, he showed it to an impressed Lalla who in turn passed it on to the producer, Reginald Denham. The play was first mounted as a Sunday night performance by the Repertory Players on 3 March 1929. By chance the performance was visited by the eighteen-year-old Kenneth Robinson, who would later be a friend of Hamilton's: 'I was enthralled by it and not at all surprised to see that it became a great success.'[20] The West End production was mounted with a new cast just eight weeks later. Denham, encouraged by the playwright, urged the cast to undertake a relatively restrained, low-key style of performance. The actors responded in turn to the technical skill of the play. Brian Aherne, who played the principal murderer, wrote to Hamilton four months after the opening: 'May I say now what a very great pleasure it has been to work in your play? *Real* pleasure.'[21]

Hamilton had now crossed a line in his life. At the beginning of 1929 he was a young novelist seen as promising by a few critics and a small readership numbering a couple of thousand people. He had been basically unknown and obscure. Now he was public figure. He was also earning a lot of money, £30 or £40 a week he reckoned (for comparison, Ella, the barmaid at The Midnight Bell, earns twenty-two shillings[22]), when he wrote to Bruce at the end of May about his 'strange Byronic dream'. It all seemed uncanny, as he reported with boyish excitement:

For it is not only the money – it is *fame*. And by this I do mean a petty notoriety – but the real article – fame! I have done exactly what Noël Coward did with 'The Vortex', I am known, established, pursued. The world, truly, is at my feet. You, reading a few notices over there, cannot possibly imagine what has happened.[23]

The opening of *Rope* was followed almost immediately by the publication of *The Midnight Bell*, so that within a month, Hamilton attained fame, wealth and also the literary reputation that he had always craved. On the one hand he was being acclaimed by J. B. Priestley as one of the few serious young novelists in Britain; on the other, the performance rights of *Rope* were being sold in America, Germany, Austria and France.

He now faced new demands on his time. Reginald Denham, to whom he had dedicated the text of *Rope*, whisked him off to Italy for a holiday. It was very nice, Hamilton reported to Michael Sadleir, 'apart from a little slightly boring cathedral-raving-about, church-sitting-in, Last-Supper-looking-at, and picture-gallery-mumbling-through.' But then, as he said perceptively of himself, 'I was never very good at beauty.'[24]

Hamilton was eager to write his sequel to *The Midnight Bell* but the newly discovered hot property was prevailed on to attempt another play. He sat in a hotel room in Brighton, he wrote out a list of characters, he wrote a description of the scenery, he drew a plan of the stage, but he couldn't think of a play. It was 'great fun but totally meaningless'.[25] Six weeks later he reported to Bruce that he was still trying to get a play done, but nothing was completed.

When Bruce was about to board the boat to what he still regarded as home, he received a telegram from Hamilton: 'UNSPEAKABLE LONG-ING QUICK QUICK HOLSTEIN'.[26] Both brothers were looking forward to the reunion with keen anticipation. Hamilton had accompanied reports of his own dazzling success with increasingly fervent encouragements to his brother. He had praised Bruce's novel. He had insisted that the success was a windfall that would benefit them both: 'Remember that we have come into our estate.' It was the reward for their mutual devotion to the cause of art, made when they were teenagers. Hamilton also promised that they would live together – after Bruce had made a token visit to their parents.[27] Then, as Bruce's arrival became imminent, Hamilton grew more confident of his ability to help his older brother directly and sent him a telegram promising he could secure him 'an absolutely first-class job'.[28]

Hamilton's extravagant promise of an escape from schoolmastering filled Bruce with a sense of 'exaltation', as much for his own potential prospects, as well as his brother's actual success.[29] In September the long-awaited reunion occurred and Bruce was well placed to observe the changes that three years had worked on his younger brother. Though Hamilton was still only twenty-five, and though in photographs of the time he still looks like a sixth-former, Bruce judged that he had aged considerably. His hair was thinner and Bruce considered that he was now starting to show signs of his anxieties and of his drinking.[30]

It must also have been at this moment that Bruce was first made fully conscious of the gap that had opened between them. He was returning to Britain, still with no fixed idea of his future. His brother was one of the most successful authors in the country, and he looked the part. He was scornful of the vulgar dress adopted by the theatrical profession. Before his own success he had written an almost gratuitously savage protrait of a visitor to the Midnight Bell public house:

He was tall, with a bowler hat, yellow gloves, and a silver-knobbed black stick. He wore an expensive, shapely grey overcoat – rather too shapely: and he had large, handsome features – rather too large and handsome. His eyes were blue and fine. His voice was rich, deep, patrician – authentically beautiful. With all this there was an elusive shabbiness and meretriciousness about the man. In a word – an actor.[31]

The supremely self-conscious Hamilton had dressed himself more like a successful stockbroker than a playwright. But the guise was so studiously assumed, and so perfect in every detail, that it still had an air of theatricality. He was dressed in a hand-made, black pinstriped suit, a black felt hat, highly polished black shoes, all perfectly complemented by expensive and elegant accessories. In Bruce's slightly grudging eyes, Hamilton was 'too splendid', as if he were using his money and success to assert an identity.[32] To Hamilton, Bruce seemed depressed, frustrated, conscious of his failure.[33]

Despite their differences, the two immediately settled down as friends and drinking companions and began to spend time together. In October Hamilton wrote to Bruce, asking him to book rooms for them in Hove where they could both work, alluding to the contemporary song, 'You Were Meant for Me', which had featured in no fewer than three films that year: 'If the landlady doesn't like the idea of me, just tell her that Nature made me and when she was *done*, I was all the sweet things under the *sun*, and I expect she'll come round.'[34] The stay in Hove was a success and Hamilton was able to report to his mother that 'Bruce is a different creature – perfectly fit, really woken up, and his old self again.'[35] Three weeks later there was another welcome development when Faber and Faber accepted Bruce's novel for publication, offering an advance of £30, and planning to publish it in the following spring. Despite its flaws, *To Be Hanged* was considered a promising first novel and both his publishers and his agent, Audrey Heath, were excited about Bruce's prospects. They privately agreed that they would 'put him on the map'.[36]

A triumphant Bruce asked Faber to send a copy of the novel to his godfather, Sir Arthur Conan Doyle. He was in declining health and would die later in 1930, but the old man was still punctilious with his correspondence and Bruce received a prompt reply: 'Your publisher said that I was your godfather, but I am ashamed to say that I have forgotten all about that transaction and remember no more of the incident than you do.'[37] He had enjoyed the opening of the novel but he was ultimately disappointed: 'The weak point is the explanation at the end. It demands a good deal from the reader's credulity . . .'[38]

III

Hamilton's success coincided with a period of upheaval for the rest of his family. Sutton Vane had failed to achieve another success after *Outward Bound* and his marriage to Lalla grew increasingly troubled. When she encountered him at a London railway station 'wearing dark glasses and in the company of a young woman with whom he was plainly on intimate terms',[39] she insisted on a divorce – against the entreaties both of Vane and of Hamilton, whom Vane enlisted to plead on his behalf. The two brothers were always to see the divorce as a disastrous mistake on Lalla's part, removing a prop that had stabilized two lives. Vane spent the rest of his life sinking gradually into failure and then near-destitution. When Bruce returned from Barbados he found Lalla living alone in a pleasant flat off the Old Brompton Road in Kensington, but there were already ominous signs. She was enmeshed in a hopeless love affair, her acting career had come to a standstill and she was drinking heavily. Until her early forties she was constantly writing plays, some of which were briefly staged, but none was enough of a success to earn her any significant financial reward and none of them has been published. From now on Hamilton would repay the considerable debt he owed her by struggling with the escalating problems that would gradually destroy her. Bruce privately considered that her failures with men derived from her being too sexually demanding, in contrast with his mother, whom he had long surmised to be sexually frigid.[40]

Bernard, weakened by his stroke, his literary career finished, was gradually subsiding. By the middle of 1929, Hamilton, referring to him in jocular fashion as 'Pop', reported that he was 'very harmless nowadays'.[41] In the summer Bernard took Lalla out to dinner at the Trocadero in central London. A managerial request that Bernard extinguish his pipe provoked him into ranting against the 'damned Jews' who owned the establishment and he was ignominiously ejected on to the pavement. According to Bruce, this painful incident 'finished his vitality'.[42] By the beginning of 1930, the sixty-six-year-old Bernard was not leaving the house, nor even getting out of his stained dressing gown. He veered between depressed inertia and ineffectual pottering with a projected work on the queens of England. It became apparent that he needed full-time care and he moved first to a retirement home for ex-officers in Westbourne Terrace. A few months later, when the home was suddenly closed down, this lifelong opponent of religious institutions moved into one, a Catholic old people's home in Ealing, in the far west of London, where one of his sole remaining pleasures was to attend services in the chapel.

For the first time Ellen took full control of Bernard's financial affairs and discovered that his fortune was gone amid a mass of debts. The house in Brighton had to be sold at a loss in the terrible post-crash depression of 1930 in order to pay them off. But she had some of her own money and neither she nor, still less, her children, ever suffered any hardship as a result. On 31 July 1930 the family received word that Bernard was dying. Only Hamilton reached the deathbed in time, and was able to hold his father's hand as he died. If nothing else, the stubborn refusal of Hamilton and Bruce to mourn Bernard showed the hold he still had over them. After the funeral, the family gathered at Lalla's flat. When Ellen cried, Hamilton rebuked her: 'It was what she had been longing for, why pretend otherwise? Now at last she was in a position to be completely happy.'[43]

Ellen moved to Hove, temporarily, to live with her sister, and Bruce now faced the question of what he was to do. Hamilton's optimistic plans for their future proved difficult to fulfil in practice. He offered Bruce a room at his flat in New Cavendish Street, but Hamilton was moving in very different circles. Charles Mackehenie was abroad, pursuing his diplomatic career, and Hamilton had a number of professional and friendly contacts in the publishing and theatrical worlds to maintain, which involved a good deal of drinking. Bruce found the idea of being a lodger on the edge of this existence intolerable, and he was even less inclined to seek subsidy from his younger brother, in the way that Hamilton had been subsidized by the family five years earlier. Hamilton himself was torn over his relationship with Bruce. He wanted Bruce to be there, but resolutely kept him apart from his own friends. This was a source of great pain to Bruce:

It would be an exaggeration to say that he kept me altogether out of these relationships. Charles proved to be a notable exception. And the exclusion was never absolute. But the meetings I had with his later, usually more eminent, cronies were, I had to accept it, often the product of accident and thereafter subject to excessive limitations; I would often be almost shooed off if any overlapping seemed imminent. It was not I believe that he thought me unworthy of such company and unable to hold my own in it – though it is true that my moderate means usually made me something of an odd man out. I was always very willing to like these new people, and to the best of my understanding was usually, so far as very limited contacts allowed, liked by them. Nevertheless, with each new friend or set of friends Patrick fell into different habits, often indeed a private language . . .[44]

Like his father, Hamilton re-invented himself for different friends, and it may have been that these metamorphoses were impossible under his older brother's observation. Bruce rented a flat in Shepherd's Bush, where he could write and plan his future, though he continued to see Hamilton regularly,

Hamilton himself was leading the life of a successful young writer, seeing agents, producers and publishers. The literary agents, Patience Ross and Audrey Heath, the producer, Reginald Denham, and of course Michael Sadleir were all friends in varying degrees, as well as professional associates. But for the first time since he had committed himself full-time to *Monday Morning*, he was having trouble in writing. After failed attempts at new plays, he finally managed to produce *John Brown's Body* and this, like *Rope*, was given a Sunday night performance.[45] The strain of emulating his theatrical debut showed what was a lacklustre variation on his previous success. Roger Aschenstein, a great scientist and a good man, kills a man who has broken into his flat and threatened him. In the following hours he makes frenzied attempts to conceal the murder, but at the play's climax commits suicide, contentedly, when his feckless son tells him that he will reform, resume his studies and complete his father's magnum opus. *John Brown's Body* rehearses the ingredients of *Rope* – murder, genius, the concealment of a body, the relationship between father and son – but exchanges the brutal dramatic effectiveness for an unconvicing sentimentality. Patrick's reputation counted for nothing. The reception of the play was unfavourable and it was never produced again. He was also making slow progress on his new novel, provisionally titled *A Glass of Port*.

Among the distractions keeping Hamilton from his long-term projects were the small items of journalism that he was now, as a celebrity, commissioned to write. When the *Radio Times* wanted an article about the developing new medium of radio drama, they approached Hamilton to write a lighthearted item about actors. He wrote with affectionate disillusionment about actors' tendency to romanticize the profession they knew to be 'the most sordid, the most tyrannical, the slackest in the world', and yet:

There is a Certain something, they will tell you . . . You deferentially inquire what this may be? A Certain Curious Something, they add – an Indefinable Something . . . Somehow, whatever you may have suffered at the hands of the theatre, there is Something . . . It appears that there is a Certain Something about the smell of the greasepaint. There is something about the sight of the floats. There is something about the look of a dressing room. There is something about the make-up, the back-stage passages, the rehearsals, the draughts, the trains, the very discomforts, tribulations, and exasperations of it all.[46]

Hamilton approached other commissions more seriously. In March 1930 he provided the sixth contribution to a series entitled 'What I Expect of Life' that was being run by the *Evening World*. He began by articulating what was always to be his general romantic optimism, which would take a variety of forms, and his personal pessimism. To the question of what he expected of his own life personally he answered, 'Absolutely nothing whatever'; and to the question of what he expected from Life, 'All the wonder and power and beauty that infinity contains.' Readers of a series that was designed to elicit rousing advice and easy optimism may have been surprised by Hamilton's grim account of what might have seemed an enviable success:

As for the spectacle of my own life, taken by itself, I can think of no spectacle more inadequate, troubled and ridiculous. In my personal life I am, like everyone else, a superb egoist, and, like everyone else, I know I am condemned to final exasperation and discontent. I have often in this world obtained what I wanted, but I have never so far wanted what I have obtained – and I have long given up the quest.

I know that there are some people who still cannot get it out of their heads that happiness somewhere exists – a thing achievable but for the incessant frustrations wrought by a hostile and mischievous circumstance – but that is no longer my own line of thought. I regard happiness, like pain and excitement, as a mere momentary and fortuitous occurrence, and I know that life is a great deal simpler when it is thrown out of your calculations.[47]

Hamilton's pessimism could be seen as an extreme response to his father's apparently buoyant positivism. Hamilton's feeble, defeated heroes are almost comically the opposite of Bernard's history-altering men of action. Yet the two views are best seen as complementary rather than contradictory. In his moments of personal crisis, Bernard's view of the emptiness of his own life was even more paralysing than Hamilton's, and he shared the view of the powerlessness of the ordinary person. This was why he saw the necessity for Supermen to appear in history at crucial points in order to raise man from one level to another. Hamilton's sense of the ineffectuality of ordinary activity brought him round to embrace views not too distant from those calls that Bernard had regularly issued for a man of destiny with the will to act:

I think it is muddle-headed to argue whether any good will ever come of this world. We are in the childish habit of regarding good as a phenomenon which will or will not occur. The briefest analysis will reveal that it is nothing of the sort. The truth is that no good will ever be done until somebody *does* it (the realisation of this profundity is the secret of the success of such people as Mussolini and Lenin), and it is in the hands of anybody so inclined to do what he is fitted to do towards bringing about what he desires.[48]

Then, for the only time in his life, Hamilton expressed a tremulous hope that his private activities might actually contribute to his vast, political – if it can yet be called political – aim:

I like to regard [authorship] as an undertaking, rather – a corporate body working together in secret – in an open secret. A corporate body for the dissemination of what Matthew Arnold calls 'sweetness and light' in the darkness and anger of civilisation. It often seems that by such disseminations alone may the impersonal aims I have spoken of be achieved.

This may, of course, be a pure fancy on my part. It is a fancy which can only exist in one who expects infinite things from life, and I do not know how many authors do this. At any rate it is my own personal salvation.[49]

Whatever his private moods, as a drinking companion Hamilton was amusing and thoroughly good company. When the American journalist, Florence Milner of *The Boston Evening Transcript*, interviewed Hamilton as an example of precocious success, she found a likeable, charming young man who had 'remained modest and unspoiled'. He talked about his early life in 'a perfectly frank manner', though he was occasionally amused by his old poetic ambitions.

When he came to see me in London, my first thought was: 'How like you are to the best type of serious-minded Harvard student!' Not the dull grind who never looks over his glasses – young Hamilton wears glasses – or over the top of his book at the real world, and who sees nothing between its covers but the dry bones of learning. On the contrary he is like the alert, eager kind, conscious of a real world around him and eager to see it as it really is. Patrick Hamilton is sensitive to life, every phase of it, deeply interested in human beings, in what the world does to them, and in their reaction to all and various conditions which they encounter.[50]

11

Marriage and
The Siege of Pleasure

In the first week of August 1930, Hamilton wrote a letter to his mother:

I am writing this to tell you that I have at last done what you, in your wickedness, have known all the time I probably would do – *married*!

My sweet one – I thought it best not to tell you about this until it was a *fait accompli* – as it could only fill you, and every one, with distress and doubt for me. But I am terribly happy and *madly* in love, and I swear you will eventually be glad.

Sweet one – this is why I have been a little *distrait* lately – and I want to write and tell you that no woman on earth can come between me and my love and adoration of yourself. My love for you has been going on for twenty six years, and will never, never abate. I shall never wander away, or regard you as any thing but the first and loveliest woman on earth. I mean this, my own.

I will try to get down to Brighton as quickly as possible, and tell you all about it. It has all been such fun. I am *incredibly* happy – touch wood.[1]

In correspondence with his mother Hamilton generally fell into the tone of her fiction and, while writing this momentous letter, he may have been struck by its similarity with the opening of her first novel, in which Mrs Carstairs writes her diary on the day she has entered into a marriage for chillingly rational motives.

Hamilton had recently met Loïs Martin at a party given by J. B. Priestley at his house in Well Walk, Hampstead. Photographs show her to be handsome, even striking. She was cultured, accomplished, sensible and, at twenty-nine, three years older than Hamilton. He was immediately attracted to her, and they became friends. She had just ended an unhappy relationship and she made it immediately clear that she was interested in nothing between friendship and marriage.

Loïs's practical efficiency over her emotional affairs may well have impressed Hamilton, so similar to the way he hoped to make the best of his own complications. He agreed to marry Loïs in exchange for an informal marriage agreement. Outside his immediate obligations to her, he would be free to see his friends and family, alone and whenever he wanted. He now had the tantalizing prospect of a life perfectly arranged to suit the compartments of his own mind. The efficient Loïs would provide a setting in which he could once more work, and – attractive but not impossibly so, respected but not idealized – she would also be the willing sexual partner he had been seeking for so long. Meanwhile as far as his drinking friends were concerned he would still be a bachelor, and he could see Lalla, Bruce and his mother just as in the old days in Chiswick. The attractions for Loïs are not so obvious, but Hamilton was charming, presentable, successful, well-off, with the prospect of becoming more so, and at worst she would be left to run her own life, so long as she was willing to run his as well.[2]

It was irresistible and they were quickly married, on 6 August 1930, at Brentford registry office in West London. The proceedings were so hasty that, though Lalla was a witness, Bruce didn't even meet Loïs until after the marriage, when they were nervously introduced at the couple's flat in Upper Berkeley Street. This newly acquired accommodation left Hamilton even more centrally placed in the West End of London than before.

After the marriage Hamilton and Loïs went to Brittany for a fortnight's honeymoon, where they experienced a failure that almost put an immediate end to the marriage. Bruce was always uneasily protective about Patrick in matters of sex. He praised Brian Aherne's performance in *Rope*, for example, saying that 'His powerful masculinity was needful, for with a weaker Brandon *Rope* is, rather curiously, apt to seem like a play about homosexuals.'[3] This is an extraordinary comment about a play based on a murder committed by two homosexuals. Not only that, but when, in the mid-fifties, Bruce informed Hamilton that he might be appearing in an amateur production of *Rope* as Rupert, the man who uncovers the murder, Hamilton observed that the 'only snag is that the part is really cut out for a pansy.'[4] *Rope* reads today as an intensely homosexual play (an aspect that is brought out even more strongly in Alfred Hitchcock's film version). There is no evidence of any homosexual side to Hamilton after his schooldays, but Bruce had various fears about his brother's sex life and these were not allayed by Hamilton's frank description of his honeymoon. In Bruce's somewhat enigmatic words:

Patrick discovered that he was quite unable to manage a satisfactory sexual relation with Loïs. It was a matter neither of frigidity on her part nor impotence on his own, but of one of those psychological incompatibilities that have wrecked or embittered so many marriages. It might easily have done so now, for frustration and mortification produced quarrels that were made more painful because Patrick, perhaps excusably, for a time continued to drink heavily.[5]

The 'frustration and mortification' attributed to Hamilton's inability is presumably a coded reference to premature ejaculation. Once more Hamilton had got what he wanted but was then unable to enjoy what he had got. For a time he talked of arranging a divorce as soon as was possible. In the end, they settled, *faute de mieux*, on a companionable, platonic relationship. Hamilton achieved no sexual satisfaction from the marriage. What Loïs thought is not recorded.

When Hamilton returned from his honeymoon he was in the state from which his marriage had been designed to protect him. He was distraught and drinking heavily. Tensions even began to appear in his relationship with his brother and in the course of one argument he told him, devastatingly, that he was not interested in Bruce's writing. On the very same day he wrote a remorseful letter expressing his implausible trust that Bruce had not been hurt by his outburst:

It is not true in any sense really, and the statement was only made in an endeavour to combat the dishonesty and tortuousness with which you have rightly been accusing me lately.

How could I not be interested in your work – seeing that I love you as no one else?[6]

The dispute may have been resolved, but Bruce did not show his second novel to Hamilton, even though he was deeply depressed about its quality and doubtful about his future as a writer. In November he submitted it to Faber, nervously offering two alternative titles, *Man-hunt* or *Hue and Cry*.

It is the story of Tom, a minor footballer in a lowly provincial team, who, after a bad game and a drunken evening, murders the football club chairman, who has been victimizing him. The bulk of the book shows Tom's attempt to escape. He reaches London where he has sex with a prostitute, stays with a seductive older woman and, at the end of his tether on a Shepherd's Bush pavement, encounters a friendly writer entering his flat: 'The young man – it was a young man, wearing tortoiseshell-rimmed glasses and there was something vaguely familiar in his appearance – paused on the threshold, his latch-key in his hand.'[7] The phrase 'vaguely familiar' is a very private joke because to Hamilton, Lalla and only half a dozen others it would have been obvious that the writer in tortoiseshell-rimmed glasses, wearing a dressing gown and working at a typewriter in Shepherd's Bush was Bruce himself. In the end, somewhat shockingly, 'Bruce' helps Tom flee the country, but then what is most striking about the novel is its politics, more obtrusively radical than anything of which Hamilton would yet have been capable. The murder victim is a fascist, and the two characters (apart from the writer) who consciously help Tom are an 'extreme socialist'[8] and a disgraced ex-policeman who has been converted from 'bright respectful Toryhood' to a 'rancorous Radicalism'.[9]

Frank Morley at Faber and Faber initially showed some enthusiasm but a month later, after 'much discussion', the firm decided to turn it down. Morley wrote a kind and encouraging letter suggesting that Bruce leave *Hue and Cry* for the time being and let him see another, more conventional work that Bruce was writing: 'I have a feeling that your gifts are for the novel proper,' Morley commented.[10]

Bruce was bitterly upset. In his haste to reply he misdated his letter, copying it off Morley's letter of rejection. He turned down Morley's suggestion with subdued bitterness: 'So that's that! I thought on the whole you would come to the conclusion that "Hue and Cry" was not worth while. Still, I'm sure you'll understand that after all that blood and sweat, and also in view of my financial position, I did not care to let the book go entirely.'[11] In the short term, at least, Bruce's decision was correct. Collins accepted the novel and it was published, in the Crime Club series, in the same year. Hamilton read the book when it came out and accorded it warmly limited praise, as a 'magnificent failure'. Bruce, he suggested, had been 'lured by the fatal attractions of "the great idea" and found yourself in a predicament' from which he could escape only by genius or 'descent to complete ordinariness and flatness – "detective-ness" and "thrillerness" in the simplest form.'[12] The message was clear. Bruce's second novel had not fulfilled the limited promise of his first. Bruce would later regret that he had spurned Frank Morley's advice, and left a firm who 'were willing to help me to build a reputation.'[13]

II

Late in 1930 Loïs demonstrated her serviceability. She found a cottage in the small north Norfolk village of Overy Staithe. It was simple, indeed primitive – no running water, 'no lavatory indoors, nor much in the way of utensils to eat with,' Hamilton warned Bruce.[14] It was painfully cold in winter. But this secluded habitation, with its views down to the marshy coastline and the North Sea beyond, was, in its austere way, beautiful. For Hamilton, this 'sombre flatness'[15] would remain his ideal landscape.

Loïs started to do the cottage up and Hamilton, for the first time in over two years, got down to work with his accustomed diligence. By March 1931 he was able to assure Martha Smith that he had 'broken the back of the novel' that was still called *A Glass of Port* and that the book would be delivered in September. He was now back on schedule. By July he was able to report to Michael Sadleir that the first rough draft of the novel was finished and that it would take six weeks to revise. What mattered to him above all else – his career as a novelist – had been resumed:

It is a kind of companion book to *The Midnight Bell* – dealing *un*sympathetically (as in the M.B.) with an earlier Jenny as a servant girl, and describing a prodigious 'night out' she has as such, and I want to call it

> THE SIEGE OF PLEASURE

Do you like this as a title? I do – and I do hope you will let met call it it. I think it is better than 'A Glass of Port', which we spoke of before.

Then next I want to do one on Ella, and so conclude a London pub-and-streets trilogy – as anticipated.[16]

Now, and for some years in the future, the Great Wen, as he almost invariably referred to London (quoting William Cobbett) in his jocose epistolary style, was a place for escaping to in order to do business, have meetings, borrow books from the London Library (which he had joined in March and celebrated with a long poem addressed to Michael Sadleir in his customary adroit rhyming couplets) and, above all, to meet friends and to get drunk. With satisfaction, Hamilton would report to Martha Smith in letter after letter that there was no news, except perhaps an item or two of village gossip. Overy Staithe was his refuge, a small community, mainly of labourers, ideal for the isolation in which he could best write. He felt a sense of security, and with Loïs he attained a degree of domestic contentment. Bruce in his turn had communicated to Hamilton severe anxieties about his own future. Now they pledged themselves to a form of joint stoicism. In the early summer of 1931 Hamilton wrote Bruce a reflective letter on the subject:

I believe that this moment is the gravest and most portentous in both our lives. After a nerve-wracking, ill-adjusted, wretched early youth, we at last know the ropes. I think we should bless our past miseries, as they have reversed the process common to men in general. The more I read the more I am impressed by the wild and lovely happiness which has been the outstanding feature of the youngest days of most men – from Keats and Wordsworth to Gladstone. Then the sourness and horror has come. Well, we have got all our sourness over at the beginning, we have already battled with and been tortured by the monsters – we know what to expect from them, where we are with them, and how to evade and live tolerably in their company. Hereafter let us see if we can be *Statesmen* in the dubious and shifting policies of Life. The days of floundering and uncritically experiencing are over: now is our chance to take charge of ourselves, and with what gifts God has granted us we should be able to give a not ignoble performance, in our alloted role outside the light of fame.[17]

There were some temporary dislocations. Lalla was now becoming seriously unstable, and Hamilton travelled to London to help her 'out of one of the worst scrapes she has ever been in.' A troublesome man was the immediate occasion of the crisis, but the problem was increasingly becoming his sister's mental state: 'The difficulty of coping with her has been even greater than the difficulty of coping with her mess.'[18] Meanwhile a drinking bout by Hamilton had to be handled by the long-suffering Loïs, who became discontented. Hamilton complained that he was 'being bounced from one neurotic woman to another.' But he didn't let it discompose him, or his preparation of *The Siege of Pleasure* for the typist: 'I have got my harmony at last, and don't believe I shall ever lose it.'[19]

Late in the summer of 1931 Bruce came to Overy Staithe for a long stay, renting an adjacent cottage. This proved to be one of the happiest times they were ever to spend together. They worked in the morning and then went for long walks. They ate lunch – Bradenham ham followed by Stilton with Bath Oliver biscuits. They read in front of the fire. Tea followed, another walk, a light supper, and then the radio or games. Many of the activities were a deliberate recapturing of their early childhood, kicking a small rubber ball about on their walks, playing tiddlywinks in the evening.

Bruce still expressed anxieties about the future, but Hamilton was in a position to be blandly imperturbable. To Bruce he could 'only recommend the qualities of firmness and patience – particularly patience.'[20] While Bruce took what comfort he could from this advice, *The Siege of Pleasure*, delivered in the summer, received a largely favourable response from Constable and Hamilton immediately began work on the third work of the trilogy, reporting to Martha that he had 'survived that awful blank period'.[21] The rest of the year passed smoothly as Hamilton divided his attention between his two novels in their different stages of preparation. In November he returned the proofs of *The Siege of Pleasure*, having added a dedication, 'For Loïs'. 'I am doing well in Norfolk this time,' he told Sadleir, 'and the Ella book at the moment is behaving most pleasantly.'[22]

He was feeling confident. In December he turned down an offer from Samuel French for all rights to *Rope*, reasoning that 'the performances might dribble on for years and years and make a great deal more.'[23] Just before Christmas, to his delight, the dustjacket of *The Siege of Pleasure* arrived, a reminder of his return to writing fiction and a promise of all that was auspicious about 1932.

III

When Hamilton first conceived the idea of a novel 'about both servants *and* harlots (possibly the slow transformation of the one into the other)', he was contemplating a 'kind of Mrs Warren's Profession brought up to date', an exposé of the economic exploitation of working-class women.[24]

When Hamilton turned the idea into *The Siege of Pleasure* the result was entirely different. In personal terms, which are irrelevant to an assessment of the novel's merits, it was the second part of his private psychological revenge against Lily Connolly. Having remade her character and placed it in the first novel, Hamilton now denies her her own past and motivation and supplies his own retributive version. In private, Hamilton had called Lily the 'mad harlot from Ipswich',[25] but the Jenny we see in *The Siege of Pleasure* is not irrational nor a victim of economic circumstances nor a free spirit rationally choosing a means of earning a living.

The novel – though in scale and theme scarcely more than a short story – is as vividly, pungently redolent of its time as a newsreel. Hamilton's evocation of the process by which Jenny accepts a glass of port on the mention of a possible job which is never heard of again, flirts, becomes intoxicated, goes for a drunken car ride, abandons her employment as a domestic servant and takes her first step towards prostitution as a substitute, is such a technical *tour de force*, so beyond anything Hamilton had previously achieved, that the reader may not at first perceive that as an examination of prostitution, the story is closer, both in style and moral judgement, to Hogarth's *Rake's Progress* or a Victorian narrative painting than to *Mrs Warren's Profession*.

The structure of the story itself could easily be rendered pictorially. Jenny, a prostitute in a hotel room with a repulsive customer, recalls her fall – 'All through a Glass of Port', which could be the title of the sequence, as it was the original title of the novel.[26] Jenny accepts the glass of port from the worthless Andy. Jenny on a wild car ride. Jenny in the pub on the following morning accepting a whisky and money from the dissolute gentleman. And the final moralistic twist, Jenny back in the hotel room discovers that her repulsive customer is Andy.

Hamilton had already invented Lily as a literary character before he met her. In *Craven House* Mr Spicer's secret mistress, Catherine Tillotson, sends him a letter strikingly similar in its grammar and spelling to those Hamilton would shortly receive from Lily. Catherine's friend has told her that if you wish me to go into rooms where we can Be quiet with each other you must give me something regular as a lady cannot manage to subcist on a little preasant now and again when she is a lady and not like others And Mr. Kelly has said again he will take me to New York only last night soon if he gets his deal through as he expects and that will Be nice So if you will write me please to above address by the return and say what you intend by me And if you can afford something weakly like it will Be nice, as we could have very pleasant times together and it would Be pleaseant and I will for the present sign myself

> Your little companion,
> CATHERINE TILLOTSON[27]

Lily appeared in Hamilton's life like an embodiment of his fictional creation, so when he turned her back into literature and invented a past for her, it must have seemed natural to turn to the postscript of the above letter: 'P.S. After I saw you last night I met two boys who took me out to Richmond in their car it was so nice I am a little bloto tonight as I write as they have all been giveing me more than is good.'[28]

It must be remembered that the principal difference between the Hamilton who planned *The Siege of Pleasure* and the Hamilton who wrote it is that in the interval he had become closely acquainted with a number of prostitutes. The idea that prostitutes are doing a job like anyone else, or alternatively that they are helpless victims, is portrayed as self-serving bourgeois smugness in *The Midnight Bell*. For example:

> 'What's wrong with 'em?' asked Bob.
> 'What's *wrong* with 'em?' said Ella. 'The *creatures*.'
> 'Ladies must live,' hazarded Bob, a little securely.
> 'Don't you tell *me*,' said Ella, and left him.[29]

In *The Siege of Pleasure* Hamilton repeatedly lays the responsibility on the individual: 'It is doubtful whether Jenny could be said to be the owner either of a character or conscience.'[30] Hamilton's pessimism about life at the individual level leads him into a curious conservatism. As Jenny becomes uncontrollably drunk she also becomes truculently rebellious towards the two old women who employ her: 'She was as good as them any day. She betted Andy had got as much money as them any day, and what mattered in these days save money? What were class distinctions nowadays? Relics of the past. She'd show 'em. She'd show everybody.'[31]

This bitterly ironic outburst could have been written by Bernard, if he had had the talent, as a lofty rebuke to servant girls with ideas beyond their station. At the end, Hamilton is complicatedly torn about what his fable means:

Probably there was never any doubt of Jenny's social destiny, but can it not at least be said that that glass of port unlocked her destiny? Her ignorance, her shallowness, her scheming self-absorption, her vanity, her callousness, her unscrupulousness – all these qualities – in combination with her extreme prettiness and her utter lack of harmony with her environment – were merely waiting and accumulating in heavy suspense in the realms of respectability to be plunged down into the realms where they rightly belonged: and a single storm, lasting no longer than six hours achieved this.[32]

But Jenny never benefits from any of her betrayals and thefts. Hamilton's fictional world renders her helpless in the face of temptations and rewards that are illusions. The idea that something could be done by an individual, or an organization, to save women like Jenny, to reform them, was sentimental nonsense. Hamilton was no Fabian. Everything would have to be remade. A larger, and more powerful, philosophical system would be needed, one that did not rely on the efforts of ordinary individuals.

12

Accident

I

The new year of 1932 began with the excitement of a public controversy. A version of *Rope* with Ernest Milton in his original role was to be broadcast in January by BBC radio and the *Daily Herald* immediately began a campaign against it, denouncing the Corporation for 'morbidity' and 'sensationalism'. They were joined by the *Morning Post* and then, as Hamilton reported to Bruce with some satisfaction, the British Empire Union accused him of 'polluting the ether'.[1] The BBC held firm and the play was broadcast with great success, stimulating Hamilton's first interest in the possibilities of the medium.[2]

Anticipating a visit to London to celebrate his pleasure over the dustjacket of *The Siege of Pleasure*, Hamilton wrote a letter to Martha Smith with a slightly ominous tone:

Is there any possibility of wrapper squealing when I see you. I shall certainly see to it that I am in town when the little one sees light.

I also find 1932 bearing an uncanny resemblance to 1931, and even my sides are not splitting in quite the usual manner at the 100% all-laughing mirthquake which life undoubtedly is. Do I detect in your letter the distant hoot and rumble of an approaching bus?[3]

Later in the month Hamilton and Loïs went to stay with Lalla in her flat in the Earl's Court Road. On a Sunday evening they went for a walk in the streets nearby, where Hamilton was hit and almost killed by a car. The circumstances of the accident can still plainly be seen. In poor light, an extremely inattentive motorist driving along Lexham Gardens might cross the large and busy Earl's Court Road in the belief that Logan Place on the other side was a direct continuation. In fact the roads are slightly askew, with Logan Place, from the point of view of the driver from Lexham Gardens, moved slightly to the left. Thus, the young man who was driving correctly on the left-hand side of Lexham Gardens plunged across Earl's Court Road without stopping and suddenly found himself not just on the right-hand side of Logan Place but up on the pavement. For Hamilton, with a speeding car on one side and a high wall on the other, there was no escape. He was hit and carried along on top of the car before being thrown off.[4]

Hamilton was taken to the nearby St Mary Abbots Hospital. His left leg and arm were so severely broken that the bone was projecting through the skin. Both bones in the wrist were broken and he suffered a number of severe flesh wounds. His nose was virtually ripped off. For a week, he was in a critical condition. After that, depressed and in great pain, he had to endure a long, slow process of recuperation, with the help of the doctor, Major Sinclair, who had been first on the scene and later, at Hamilton's request, became the doctor in charge of the case.[5] Hamilton spent three months in hospital, in plaster and in traction, devotedly nursed by Loïs. This care had a decisive effect on their marriage. In its early years Hamilton had spoken frequently of divorce as a possibility. 'I'm stuck with Loïs now.' he used to say, not unaffectionately, to Bruce after the acccident.[6] When his condition had improved sufficiently he was moved to a nursing home at 99 Cromwell Road, where he still required extensive treatment, such as on one occasion the agonizing draining of 'septic matter' generated by an attempt to insert a metal plate into the arm. He was virtually unable to read and had no imminent prospect of writing.

A quarter of a century later, when Hamilton was recovering from a mental crisis as serious, in its way, as his car accident, he recalled the moment of his recovery, '*Bruce*'s coming to see me, at No 99 years ago, and my suddenly telling him I was better!'[7] The medical treatment was a success, though many of the effects were permanent. In the recollection of Kenneth Robinson, who got to know Hamilton at the end of the 1930s, Hamilton never spoke about the accident in his presence but 'The facial scars were noticeable without being too obtrusive, though I think he was very self-conscious about them. One was aware of the partial loss of use of his left arm.'[8] The broken leg healed well enough and Hamilton was later to be able to resume the energetic walking that was his principal form of exercise. His damaged left arm did not prevent him taking up golf. But Hamilton, who had been sensitive enough about his appearance before the accident, was always to be self-conscious about the clearly evident scars on his face. All the available photographs of Hamilton dating from after 1931 have been heavily touched up along the nose, where the scar was most disfiguring, and in future years he would refer to himself jokingly as a cripple.[9]

The accident had other effects also, as J. B. Priestley noted three years later:

If he has not yet had the very big public he deserves, I think this is because the motor-car that knocked him down in January 1932, seriously injuring him so that he could not work for two years, chose its moment to strike with diabolical precision. At that time his public was rapidly growing; the reviewers were waiting to praise the final novel of his trilogy; and he himself was obviously in a fine creative vein, a young artist quickly maturing. Few novelists can have had a more bitter stroke of bad luck.[10]

Hamilton was not entirely idle for the rest of the year. Robert Milton, who had directed the 1930 film version of Sutton Vane's *Outward Bound* (starring Leslie Howard and Douglas Fairbanks Jnr), had offered Hamilton a £70 advance to turn *The Midnight Bell* into a play, which was tentatively planned to open in April 1933.

At the beginning of that year, Hamilton, now largely recovered, and Loïs moved to the Wells Hotel in Hampstead, just a few yards from the house where they had first met. Also staying there was another young writer, Arthur Calder-Marshall. Sitting one evening in the bar of the hotel, though it was actually more of a public house, Calder-Marshall 'paid no attention to the entry of a young man, who came in and sat down unobtrusively at the other end of the bar. A glance at him revealed to my keen new novelist's eye that he was some commonplace office worker, the sort of chap you'd pick out for a police identification parade, if it weren't for the fact that he had a deep unsightly scar running down his forehead and the length of his nose.'[11] Like other friends, Calder-Marshall noticed Hamilton's habit of sitting 'for a whole evening in the bar listening apparently enthralled to the most inane pub conversation',[12] a promising sign that he was starting to think of writing fiction once more.

Early in the year there had been a court case in which Hamilton sought damages for the accident and the result was never in doubt. He was awarded £6,000, an amount that Hamilton gleefully and almost disbelievingly received early in March: 'I got it in two cheques – imagine mildly handing in *four* figure cheques to the bank – and it seems to be there all right.'[13]

Hamilton stayed in London for a while, working with Robert Milton on *The Midnight Bell*, but, though the production seemed always about to begin, it all came to nothing. Then he and Loïs set off on a holiday in Greece and Italy. His messages showed that his spirits were returning: 'Athens a bore – Parthenon a bore – Praxiteles a bore – Corinth, Epidaurus, Scinium, Marathon, all bores – *club* bores.'[14] He expanded on this judgment in his next letter: 'I now think the *world* is very much *over-rated*. I somehow expected much *more* from its famous beauty spots. For sheer *beauty* I've seen things lovelier in England than I've ever seen since I've been travelling.'[15]

Bruce's life had been transformed by Hamilton's accident. He had moved across London from Shepherd's Bush in order to be closer, he had spent extended periods of time attending on him and his own writing had been interrupted almost as much as Hamilton's. He had now finished a new novel, *The Spring Term*, and it was due to be published later in the year by Methuen, having been turned down by two other publishers. But he couldn't rely on this to earn him money and he now had to decide what he was going to do. He had always been more politically committed than his younger brother, and he felt an increasing interest in the Soviet Union. So with a mixture of motives, partly professional hopes of a vague kind, partly curiosity, he determined to learn the language and visit the country. He picked up some Russian by staying with an émigré family in Paris and then, in September 1932, sailed for Leningrad.

As a seventeen year old, Bruce had been discomfited when he met Hamilton, after a gap of six months, and discovered that he had developed a passionate interest in poetry. As he put it, 'I had always been the "literary one"; and I did not at first relish having my nose put out of joint by a brother more then three years my junior.'[16] Now history was to repeat itself, with an element of farce, to cite the new object of Hamilton's adoration.[17] An expedition of the sort Bruce was attempting held no attractions for Hamilton, but he could trump his older brother in another way. By the time Bruce arrived in the Soviet Union, Hamilton had become a Marxist. Before the end of September he wrote to Bruce almost guiltily defending his new belief:

This thing *means* something to me. It is not a *game* – like all my other romps – it is my *vocation* – however humble the part I play. It is not only my *religion* – it is my *hobby* – the *details interest* me – in the same way that stamps interest a philatelist. For this reason I am in a position to *master* it – as I mastered novel writing. . . .

I am, of course, Marx mad at the moment – regarding Lenin as the sort of Luther in the Marxist Reformation.[18]

His commitment to master Marxism, as he had mastered novel-writing, must have been felt by Bruce, who considered himself a long way from mastering novel-writing, as a low blow. And while Bruce was struggling in the Soviet Union to little avail, Hamilton was working his way through Karl Marx's *Capital*. '*What* a book!' he proclaimed enthusiastically.[19]

Hamilton was now engaged in a wide range of activities. Only rarely in the rest of his life, and then only for restricted periods, would he make the total commitment of his time and energy to fiction that he had in the years up to the composition of *Rope*. The reading of *Capital* had exposed the shortcomings of Hamilton's truncated education, and he set about attempting to teach himself some geography and mathematics. He also bought a parrot. When this proved to be a poor talker, Loïs had to return to London with it to secure a more loquacious specimen to which Hamilton became, for a time, greatly attached. This Hamilton christened Quarles, in tribute to Michael Sadleir, and as a tribute to the General Secretary of the British Communist Party, taught it to say 'Pretty Pollitt'.[20] He and Loïs also began to make the house more comfortable. They obtained a wireless, hired a piano and Hamilton attempted to rent a room 'in one of the railway carriages down the lane – where I can work by myself.'[21]

All of which was slowing the progress of Hamilton's new novel, provisionally titled *Time, Gentlemen, Please*, 'rather as a gentle reproach and warning to modern civilization, than as rendering the familiar pub-cry.' It was to be the final part of the trilogy provisionally titled *The Last Days of London*: 'and that will be that – and the end and expression of the first phase of my intellectual existence. Not very bright, so far, I am afraid – but all in the way of learning, and, if fate is willing, I am still well ahead of time. What news of *your* novel? – the long pause after the proofs, I presume.'[22]

II

The Spring Term was Bruce's first attempt at a straightforward literary novel. It dramatized his own experiences of teaching at a preparatory school before attending university in London. Though competent enough, the story of Frank's term at a school, which ends by his exposing the appalling mismanagement of the headmaster, reads like an unhappy conflation of Evelyn Waugh's *Decline and Fall* (which had been published five years earlier) and Dotheboys Hall in *Nicholas Nickleby*. Bruce imprudently refers to the latter in the text when he superfluously informs the reader that the headmaster is 'Squeers over again'.

Hamilton was able to place his fears right at the centre of his books. Bruce seems to have felt an inhibition that prevented this. Instead, the most vivid, powerful episodes of his books tend to occur almost irrelevantly at their edges. *The Spring Term* – dedicated 'To My Mother' – begins with, in the lightest of disguises as the hero's father, a savage portrait of Bernard as he was at the end of his life:

He was not a colonel, really. The courtesy title only represented the old man's wistful ideal. He was not a colonel; he was not anything. He had been brought up to a hope of great possessions, had been disappointed, but had obstinately lived a life of laziness on a steadily diminishing income. He had never done any work; there was no achievement on which he could look back with pride. But he came from a cadet branch of a great house, and by this he felt himself justified.

Frank looked at his father; at his scraggy throat, his weak chin, his drooping, dirty yellow moustache, his bleared, pink-rimmed eyes, with their familiar expression of resentful anger. Dried slabs of greasy food discoloured the lapels of his ancient Norfolk jacket. Even by the electric light it was apparent that his neck was unwashed; and his nose needed wiping. A disgusting figure! Yet he was Frank's father, and Frank knew that many of the Colonel's characteristics were latent within himself.[23]

Hamilton and Bruce's fears about their father increasingly concerned not so much anything he had done to them, which, even by their own embittered accounts, amounted to little more than strict questioning on their reading when they were children.[24] They were worried that they might be like him. In Bruce this manifested itself as an anxiety that his career might amount to nothing but a series of failed endeavours, and, unlike his father, he had no fortune to live off. When Bruce was away, Hamilton could once more talk of their joint plans, and this governed his response to *The Spring Term*, which he praised with warm equivocation as '*a fine piece of work*. You would have no difficulty in maintaining this standard, and so becoming a fine novelist, and I hope (but know) that the extremely warm press which I feel you are bound to receive, will not lure you into becoming anything of the sort!'[25]

What must have been more puzzling still was Hamilton's suggestion that they could now write together. Hamilton claimed to have a specific '*simple* and *popular* book in mind' which would suit them perfectly: 'Do you realise that our respective talents are now *blending* into each other in a rather extraordinary way – you with your vastly increased literary power – me with my new passion for facts and study.'[26] Meanwhile, Hamilton wondered if Bruce could obtain for him a 'death-mask or life-mask or something' of Lenin for his study. Bruce responded enthusiastically to the idea of collaboration, and Hamilton now spoke optimistically about their future: '*Extraordinary* vistas are opening up, as you say – and all through *your* enterprise in making this trip and opening my eyes to the light.'[27] This was as far as this work, drawing on Hamilton's scholarship and Bruce's literary ability, ever got, and Hamilton's excitement was tempered by the news that their mother was ill. At first he was relatively encouraging, but a fortnight later he reported that she needed an operation for cataracts in order to save her sight, but was in such 'an appalling state of nerves, sleeplessness and depression' that she was not yet in a fit state to have it.[28] Bruce immediately returned from the Soviet Union and the family celebrated Christmas together at Lalla's flat in Willow Road, facing the western edge of Hampstead Heath.

Ellen Hamilton had always made it clear to her children that she had no intention of suffering the decline into helplessness she had seen her husband undergo. Now she faced a prospect of blindness and disabling illness. Early in January 1934, while she was staying at Lalla's flat in Hampstead, she left a note on her door, like the ones Hamilton used to leave her, saying she had taken a sleeping pill and asking not to be disturbed in the morning. Lalla realized what was happening and sent the following telegram to Bruce, Hamilton and Loïs, who were all together at Overy Staithe: 'COME IMMEDIATELY MUMMIE VERY ILL LALA' (the spelling is accurate). They arrived at Willow Road after midnight.

Bruce was to write that they were 'a family closely united in love and understanding'.[29] These qualities never found better expression than on that night when they allowed their mother to choose to die with dignity and courage. The following day at noon, Lalla entered the room and found Ellen in a coma. A suicide note had been left. She died on the following day. The children's abetting of their mother's suicide entailed some risk (unlike attempted suicide, it remains a crime to this day), but the investigators were sympathetic. The coroner's verdict was suicide as a result of temporary insanity. She was buried in Highgate Cemetery, where one of her neighbours is Karl Marx.

13

The Plains of Cement

I

Hamilton was still pursuing his interest in Marxism. He began to subscribe to a host of left-wing periodicals, telling Bruce cheerfully that he had 'found some form of adult replica of the weekly bliss of the "Magnet" or "Gem".'[1] He was also, finally, making serious progress with the new novel. In October he had told Michael Sadleir that it would take five months to finish it: 'I know you must think me awfully lazy and dithering, but one must remember that the accident did completely do me in, and I really wanted the long holiday and period of relaxation before starting again. But now I am truly back on the job.'[2] Sadleir informed him that there were already two books with Hamilton's original title, *Time, Gentlemen, Please*, so a month later Hamilton had a new suggestion, *The Black Dispenser*.

By early 1934, Hamilton was able to assure Bruce that he had adopted a strict routine, 'the same every day. *Work*, walk, lunch, sleep, *Work*, beer, supper, *Read*.'[3] Now he thought of the title *All Out*. When Constable amended this to *All Out, Please*, he objected that

I have lost the double meaning I intended and it scarcely has any application to the book, which is wandering away more and more from the pub itself as I write.

If making a change is going to be a lot of bother I suppose this wouldn't matter, and would like to leave the matter entirely in your hands, but if this is not so I have the following suggestions:–

THE PLAINS OF CEMENT

or

THERE ARE WHEELS WITHIN WHEELS

The first I like, and the second would suit the book wonderfully. In fact I like them both really. There is also:

THE RAIN ON THE ROOF

which I thought of today.

I wish you would choose between them, or ALL OUT, PLEASE if necessary.[4]

Hamilton's thirtieth birthday passed almost unnoticed as he assured Michael Sadleir and Martha Smith, using their characteristically jokey language, that he was 'Doubleyouking [that is, working] at a furious pace' even though he had been delayed six weeks by 'his mother's illness etc', as he put it stoically.[5] By May the book was delivered. Michael Sadleir pronounced it 'a gem' and there was no more trouble, except for a dustjacket whose original version, it was agreed, portrayed a scene that looked more like Peckham than Tottenham Court Road.

Hamilton himself daringly and beautifully summarized the story of *The Plains of Cement* in its closing pages through the sad consciousness of its heroine, Ella, the barmaid of the Midnight Bell:

And, indeed, what had taken place in those dull months? Nothing, really, whatever – nothing out of the common lot of any girl in London, if you came to think about it. She had had an elderly admirer, (what girl has not been in such a dilemma at some time or another?) about whom she had not been able fully to make up her mind. Nothing in that. A connection of hers had been ill – a stepfather whom she disliked, and there had been domestic troubles. Nothing in that. She had been depressed by the fogs and the cold – who had not? – who had not? She had looked for another job, but it hadn't come to anything – an ordinary enough occurrence. She had had what the gentlemen in the bar would have called a slight 'crush' on the waiter. But that was not the first time a girl had had a 'crush' on a man she worked with. You soon get over that. No – seen from an outsider's point of view she was lucky if she had nothing more to grumble about, and the gentlemen committed no error in tact in joking with her and teasing her just as usual.[6]

The Plains of Cement was Hamilton's best book so far, his funniest and most moving, the first to use the full range of his talents. Though nearly

132

twice as long, the book is even less eventful than its predecessor, a story of things failing to happen, or simply fizzling out. *The Midnight Bell* ends with a slightly forced assertion of Bob's vitality, when he decides to go to sea, thus removing him from anything that could be imagined in the world of that book. *The Plains of Cement* ends more tellingly with the desolate but stoical Ella placing at least some value on her self by rejecting the grotesque Mr Eccles.

Eccles is wonderfully portrayed as monstrously unlikeable without ever being reduced to a villain. From his first appearance he is alive with Hamilton's imaginative hatred, subordinated, at first to his new hat: 'You could see that it cost him sharp torture even to put it on his head, where he could not see it, and it had to take its chance.'[7] The vividness of Hamilton's language here is directed less at its own Dickensian involutions than at an attentiveness to detail. When Eccles searches for his card, 'he bent his head down, not unlike a parrot diving into its feathers, to rummage more deeply'.[8]

Eccles's courtship of Ella is a comic horror story, from when she first senses that he is observing her over the bar: 'She had the knowledge as someone sightless might have the knowledge of being in a Turkish Bath.'[9] But the relationship receives its fullest and most eloquent expression in the dialogue, unwinding in repetitions, clichés and misunderstandings, with a virtuosity far beyond anything Hamilton would ever attempt in his work for the stage. The book is impossible to quote from representatively because the exchanges repeat and accumulate like minimalist music over pages, occasionally with the counterpoint of Ella's irritation with Eccles's extended tooth, or his umbrella, grudgingly held over her at an angle so that it strikes her head every half dozen paces 'with a sort of methodical springy poke'.[10]

Hamilton is occasionally accused of misogynism, largely, it seems because he has monstrous female as well as male characters. What is more interesting is that the characters to whom he gives his fullest imaginative sympathy are, without exception, female. A flaw in the presentation of Bob as a hero was that he had to be portrayed as something other than what he was. If the name Ella is reminiscent of Cinderella, then she is a Cinderella who does not transcend her circumstances. Twelve years later George Orwell would write *Politics and the English Language*, an influential attack on clichéd and pretentious use of English.[11] One of the reasons why Patrick Hamilton is a better novelist than Orwell is his sense that the job of a writer was not just to purify the language but to find the poetry in the language that people use. Hamilton's portrayal of Ella is an anticipation and rebuttal of Orwell's disdain: 'The banality of the expressions she employed in voicing her thoughts was no criterion of those thoughts' real shrewdness or aptness. Infinitely stale and hackneyed idioms she certainly used, but this was merely because, having access to the wisdom of the ages, she used the expressions sanctified by the ages.'[12]

The Plains of Cement starts to show the traces of Hamilton's Marxism, though it might be more precise to say that it was Hamilton's own imaginative sense of a deracinated city, a culture unable to fulfil the human needs of a large proportion of its citizens, that made a millenarian political philosophy attractive to him. The importance of the following passage can be judged by the fact that it supplied the title of the novel and also his original title for the trilogy as a whole:

And in the murky dusk of evening, it was a turbulent and terrifying spectacle which met her eyes and smote her ears. She had never seen so many desperate buses, and blocked cars, and swarming people, in her life. In all the teeming, roaring, grinding, belching, hooting, anxious-faced world of cement and wheels around her it really seemed as though things had gone too far. It seemed as though some climax had just been reached, that civilization was riding for a fall, that these days were certainly the last days of London, and that other dusks must soon gleam upon the broken chaos which must replace it.[13]

The Plains of Cement completes a trilogy of very different books. The second book precedes the first, which it explains, and the third occurs roughly simultaneously with the first, though it is typical of Hamilton's resolutely unobtrusive craftsmanship that he eschews any complicated or tricksy cross references between the two. Though Hamilton was frequently eager to talk about the books in large sociological terms, their real virtue is their particularity: Bob's masochistic passion, Jenny's self-destructive urge for gratification, Ella's stoicism, are not representative of social injustice, or any other generality.

Immediately after the publication of *The Plains of Cement*, Constable decided to issue the trilogy in a single volume and Hamilton once more faced the problem of a title which would bind the disparate stories together. Since the characters were most obviously united by their setting, some urban imagery seemed most promising. Hamilton suggested *West One* or *Seven Millions and Three*, and Michael Sadleir responded with *Off Tottenham Court Road*,[14] which Hamilton pronounced 'awful': 'First of all it sounds just like a guide book (and a very dull one at that), and then I think it's dreadfully commonplace, drab and uninspired in every other way.'[15] For his part, Sadleir resolutely resisted *Seven Millions and Three* which he had thought 'was a sketch of the title rather than the finished one – particularly as we are not quite certain that the population is seven million or indeed to which boundary of London the figure is to be taken.'[16] He could have added that in *The Plains of Cement* the population of the capital is given as six million.[17] In some desperation he had canvassed around the Constable office for suggestions, which included: 'London and Three', 'A Pint of Bitter', 'White Port', and 'Port and Lemonade'. Hamilton's final title, a comic distortion of Jules Verne, *Twenty Thousand Streets Under the Sky*, was, it seems, only chosen at the last minute.

The volume was accompanied by J. B. Priestley's introduction. It is enthusiastic and occasionally perceptive, but in general new works of fiction are better off without an analysis shackled to them, determining the way in which they should be read. For his own reasons Priestley was too willing to portray Hamilton sentimentally, as a realist, concerned with evoking our sympathy for certain categories of people. Priestley also criticizes Hamilton for excessive use of capital letters in a comic context, failing to see that Hamilton had refined their use in *The Plains of Cement*. In the following passage, Mr Eccles has been boasting of having money during the course of his unpleasant flirting with Ella: 'There was something so eccentric, so uncalled-for, so ponderous and inelegant in Mr. Eccles' allusion to what he had put by, that she had not the slightest doubt that he was doing what was known as Getting it In. Or Letting her Know. And that meant Advances again.'[18] Capitalizing these phrases seems a reasonable enough way of evoking the coarse, cartoonish form of Eccles's manner. Putting them in quotation marks, would be too pedantic and disdainful, and less funny.

A crueller response would be to cite J. B. Priestley's later novel, *Three Men in New Suits* (first published in 1945), which begins with a scene in a pub that is little more than an exercise in Hamilton pastiche by a writer who entirely lacks Hamilton's ear or his sense of the byzantine hidden workings of such an institution. Unlike Hamilton, Priestley really is more interested in types than individuals, in issues rather than idiosyncracies, and the result is a book as flat as its title.

II

Hamilton wrote of his villain, and oblique self-portrait, Ernest Ralph Gorse: 'Too much thought is bad for the soul, for art, and for crime. It is also a sign of middle age, and Gorse was one who had to pay for the precocity of his youth in the most distasteful coin of premature middle age.'[19] When Hamilton was just thirty, at an age when other writers are still just beginning their careers, he had a consciousness of a long career behind him and he began to live the life of a man ten or twenty years older. The domestic details were the preserve of Loïs and their landlady in Overy Staithe, Mrs Bird. He worked, walked, played golf, drank, endeavoured to get Lalla out of scrapes and visited London. He continued to study Marxism, and its manifestation in Soviet Russia. He even planned to write a book about Marx, but he never sought an active political role in the way that Bruce was doing, and attempts to encourage him to get involved, were a failure. Bruce was sure that 'unconsciously he did not care about my giving too much of myself to anyone but himself.'[20] During this period, Charles Mackehenie was based in Paris and invited his old friend to visit him. Hamilton's perpetual reply was 'I don't like abroad' and 'London is my village'.[21]

He had found an equilibrium, and he was unhappy with anything that might unsettle it. His frequent suggestions to Bruce were well meant, but also designed to keep him on hand, as the last member of the family with whom he could maintain a relationship on equal terms. When Bruce confided in him that he was attracted to Josefina Mackehenie, the sister of Maruja, Hamilton responded with the intemperance of man who didn't want the relationship with his separate groups of friends to be complicated by inter-marriage:

With regard to the Mackehenies, on ripe consideration, I am inclined to think you would be well advised to make no further effort. Take the word of a ten year old campaigner in that direction that they are – though a *fascinating*, agreeable, amusing, and extremely *friendly* family – in the long run utterly self-absorbed and *unreliable* in a peculiarly deceptive and elusive way which only makes itself clear in a succession of facts rising up above appearances in the course of years.[22]

The girls were worse still, '*stupid* and *immature* – in fact I should say *backward*', and Hamilton's conclusion was uncompromising: 'I should advise you quickly to let the relationship drop or wither. Certainly don't make advances to [Josefina] – at least I *now* feel that quite strongly at the moment.'[23]

Although, when Bruce was away, Hamilton had a habit of proposing schemes involving collaboration and co-habitation, when they were back together the schemes never quite worked out. According to Hamilton, the trouble was that they were 'so *paralytically* close to each other in all matters that the *minutest* divergence has the appearance of being a stupendous gulf, particularly under the magnifying influence of beer – the neurotics' microscope.'[24]

Bruce was influenced by Hamilton's injunction concerning the temptations of Josefina, as he so often was by his brother's advice. In any case, this was a semi-illicit attraction because Bruce was at the time, informally at least, engaged to a woman he had met in Barbados, a painter called Aileen Laurie, who had accompanied him on his return to England to study at the Royal College of Art. When he married her, on 29 December 1934, it was like an act of defiance. Hamilton was displeased, not only because he wished to keep Bruce to himself, but because he disliked Aileen. In Bruce's curious words, Hamilton had 'established in his mind an irrevocable though only partly justified prejudice against her.'[25] Insofar as their close relationship continued, it was as before, the two of them together, occasionally with Loïs on hand, Aileen hardly ever.

Bruce was divided in his response to Hamilton's disapproval of his married state. In future years, Hamilton would speak openly about his own marital discontents, sometimes cruelly disparaging Loïs, but Bruce always refused to reciprocate with similar confidences about his own private life. Yet in still more important matters Bruce remained doggedly, almost pathologically, under Hamilton's influence. In the first years of their marriage, Aileen wished to have children but, because of financial worries 'plus I am afraid the influence of earnest entreaties from Patrick that I should not expose myself to the risk of utter loss of independence',[26] Bruce insisted on the use of contraception and, when Aileen accidentally became pregnant, on an abortion.[27] As so often in his life, Bruce sees himself as having made the wrong initial decision, often under the influence of Hamilton, after which it was too late to put matters right. When they afterwards tried to have a child, it proved impossible.

Bruce and Aileen lived at first in Pimlico in central London, then in the summer of 1935 moved to a cottage in Dorset that Bruce had bought. Hamilton visited once, for a few days. Reciprocal invitations to Norfolk were always extended to Bruce alone: 'Perhaps I should have stood on my dignity, and refused to go by myself. But I was not prepared to forsake all others, virtually to give up Patrick to save Aileen some mortification.'[28]

14

Money with Menaces
and *Gaslight*

I

The publication of *Twenty Thousand Streets Under the Sky* had been, as Hamilton had foreseen, like a door shutting on a period of his life. He had reached a crisis in his fiction career, and for the rest of 1935 he felt paralysed. He had used up his experiences and for the first time nothing new had occurred in his life that could form material for a novel. In fact, his life was now specifically designed to avoid the conflicts and stresses that had inspired his best work. His hobbies rattled around in the space left by his failure to write. There were occasional drinking binges and some serious bouts of depression. Shortly before Christmas he admitted to a 'hideous disinclination towards work. It's no use – these periods will come over one, and one can only wait patiently till they pass. I feel sure I'll get a break soon.'[1]

The break came from an unexpected source. Val Gielgud, the brother of John and the pioneering Head of Drama at BBC radio, had been an admirer and ally of Hamilton's ever since the broadcast of *Rope* in 1932. In February 1936 he wrote to Hamilton wondering if he would be interested in attempting an original radio play: 'a psychological thriller along the lines of "Rope" would be grand'.[2]

It was the perfect moment, for both men. Val Gielgud needed to show that a successful playwright would produce original work for the new medium. Hamilton may have felt that, for the moment, he lacked the resources to write a novel, but radio drama, a form still in its infancy and of which little would be expected, he could approach, as he had the theatre, in the spirit of a technical exercise. When Val Gielgud wrote a laudatory, almost obsequious, preface to the printed version of Hamilton's first two radio plays, he stressed that a radio play needs all the virtues of a stage play, but there were other demands also. The characters must be clearly defined, and the plot must be straightforward. The audience would be far more general than for the theatre, let alone the novel. On the other hand, there was the possibility of a mobility of action that was more comparable with the cinema than the theatre. In Gielgud's view, Hamilton's attempt showed how well he had 'studied the specialised problems and exercised his natural ingenuity in their solution.'[3]

To an even greater extent than with *Rope, Money with Menaces* is a skilful dramatic machine. Andrew Carruthers, a businessman, is phoned by a man who claims to have kidnapped his daughter. He is made to proceed round a circuitous route, to take a thousand pounds from his bank, receiving various calls from the blackmailer along the way. In the end it turns out that the daughter has not been kidnapped and that the blackmailer (who has not actually received the money) is punishing Carruthers for having bullied him at school.

The play is gripping from moment to moment, makes skilful use of the medium and is monumentally implausible, particularly in its assumption that when Carruthers is making so many phone calls he would not have made an extra one to check if his daughter really had been seized. The blackmailer's final revelation may be the closest we have to a description of Hamilton's own sufferings at Colet Court at the start of puberty. It marks the first appearance in Hamilton's work of the notion that the criminal, especially the con-man, is like the artist because both seek to gain power over the world:

I have not only revenged myself personally on you, for making me suffer cruelties and indignities which it is not seemly, in the name of humanity, that one human being should suffer at another's hands: I have also, just for once, symbolically taken revenge for all those who were like me against all those who were like you – revenge for all the little boys, in all the schools, who have ever lain awake in terror, or cried themselves to sleep in the dark of dormitories . . . all right, Carruthers, that will be all, as you used to say to me.[4]

In November, Hamilton was approached by Alfred Hitchcock to see if he had any interest in writing a film script for him. Their paths would cross repeatedly for the next twelve years leading to their finally working together, with strangely unhappy results. It is scarcely surprising that Hitchcock would have been attracted to Hamilton's world, since they shared not just the craftsmanlike interest in suspense so brilliantly stretched out for a whole evening in *Rope* but the view of the relationship between men and women as an area of torment and humiliation. Hamilton's response was perfunctory, offering Hitchcock a synopsis of *Money with Menaces*, and he rightly anticipated that nothing would come of it.[5]

When the play was broadcast, on 4 January 1937, Hamilton considered it 'foully produced and acted' and was amazed to find it 'a smash hit! – the greater part of the press saying that it was a model for all future wireless plays, and making a most unexpected fuss about it.'[6]

II

During Hamilton's period of inactivity, Bruce had been very busy indeed, and in 1936 and early 1937 two novels came out in quick succession. Both were clear advances on anything he had written before. *Middle Class Murder* is a sombre and gripping thriller. The leading character, Tim Kennedy, is a dentist and a psychopath: 'He was an egotist in the most absolute sense; he had no real belief in the existence of any sensations, emotions, or thoughts, which he did not feel in his own organs, his own nerves, his own mind. He regarded the world as a medium for the exercise of his personality and the fulfilment of his desires.'[7] He decides to murder his wife, who has ceased to attract him after a road accident has left her permanently disfigured. He finally commits the murder, but is destroyed by his blackmailing servant. It is a savagely bleak tale, unrelieved by the grim comedy that mitigates Hamilton's darker conceptions, and this may have prevented it achieving the success which, for the first time, a book of Bruce's deserved.

Hamilton was greatly impressed by it. He later praised Bruce's creation of the cheerfully wicked blackmailer: 'you have a particularly fine gift for portraying the horrible evil of a certain type of semi-proletarian, semi-petit- (very petit) bourgeois character.'[8] But he was to pay a more sincere compliment by drawing on it for his treatment of the villains in *Gaslight* and *The West Pier*.

There are hints of Bruce's political affiliations. Virtually the only sympathetic character in the novel is Lawrence Cox, headmaster of the local co-educational school 'who had been to Soviet Russia and liked it'.[9] At a tennis party, Kennedy wanders around listening to the conversation and hears an exchange between Cox and General Doughty, a 'Die-Hard Tory', about the famine that had been deliberately manufactured by Stalin (though this was disputed at the time): ' "Dying like flies, dropping down in the streets, cannibalism too. And the only decent farmers shot out of hand." "I tell you again you're wrong about the Kulaks, General. It's not that they're good farmers, they're speculators." '[10]

Any ambiguity about Bruce's view of this debate was resolved by his next book, one of the most remarkable left-wing novels to be written in England during the thirties. In his memoir of his brother, Bruce lays great stress on Hamilton's Marxism but places little emphasis on his own. In practice, Hamilton's politics, though fervently embraced, were never much more than a private hobby. Bruce was an activist. *The Brighton Murder Trial: Rex v. Rhodes* is presented as merely edited by Bruce Hamilton, thirteen years in the future (in 1950), and is written in the form of the trial reports that both brothers always loved. By that time, Britain has been subsumed into Soviet Europe. Bruce tells us that a history of the revolution is still to be written, so 'In the circumstances no apology need be offered for publishing the details of a tragedy which may now seem very small beer, but which may finally be found to have significance as one of the most perfect specimens of the operation of bourgeois justice in the period of decline – the trial for murder of James Bradlaugh Rhodes.'[11] This trial, dating from the pre-revolutionary days back in the thirties, is of historical importance because 'It was the first occasion in England on which a clear-cut issue, of whether a man did or did not commit homicide, was permitted, with a disarming frankness, to be judged in the light of the political sympathies of the ordinary middle-class jury.'[12]

The novel is, in fact, intended as an ironic reversal of the observations then being published of the Moscow show trials, which had been taking place for several years. In case there were any doubt about this, or about where Bruce's sympathies lay, one of the dedicatees of the book is the left-wing lawyer, Dudley Collard, who was one of the more egregious apologists for Stalin's terror. At the time Bruce was writing the book, Collard was in Moscow observing the entirely fraudulent trial of Zinoviev for treason. His reports on the proceedings in the *Daily Herald* were so favourable to the prosecution that they were reproduced in *Pravda*.[13] He also wrote to the *New Statesman*, 'dismissing theories of threats, drugs, torture and promises as ridiculous.'[14]

The book consists of ingeniously constructed court transcripts, which show the trial of a decent Communist worker who is ultimately found guilty of murder and hanged, although he has plainly been framed. Under cross-examination, however, he has time to defend the use of state terror by Stalin:

I should say millions was a gross exaggeration.

You regard these executions with equanimity? – There is no comparison between steps, however ruthless, taken by a state to protect itself and private murder.

You don't object to wholesale murders, but you draw the line at private murder? – I do not accept the phrase of 'wholesale murder'.[15]

And he also denies the charge that 'The Communist Party of Great Britain takes its orders from Moscow, does it not?'[16]

The scarcely implicit argument of this novel is that it is not the Soviet Union but England, a country 'under Capitalist dictatorship'[17], whose courts are truly corrupt. At the end we are told, in reassuring terms, of the fate of one of the dishonest witnesses for the prosecution: 'Two years ago, Sawyer, after a long and conspicuously fair trial at the First People's Court at the Old Bailey, was shot.'[18] Bruce once made the extraordinary charge that his brother might, 'given the opportunity have become a persecutor'. He believed he could trace Hamilton's implicit psycho-pathic tendency 'in the lines of his beautifully shaped mouth'.[19] Speculation of this kind is pointless. All that can be said for sure is that at least Hamilton, whatever his political affiliations, never went as far as to defend mass-murder in print.

The Brighton Murder Trial: Rex v. Rhodes is of some historical interest, and cleverly constructed, but apart from its culpable blindness to reality, it just isn't good enough. For G. W. Stonier in the *New Statesman* it was 'well done, but rather bland in its message' and the transcript of the trial 'convincing enough but hardly exciting'. Other critics were more sympathetic. One lawyer wrote a laudatory review arguing that the jury's verdict of guilty was correct – on the evidence presented to them.[20] Hamilton, though, was thoroughly enthusiastic about the novel,

which is magnificent, my dear boy, and on which I congratulate you from the *bottom of my heart*. . . . I am now definitely of the opinion that *Middle Class Murder* was your best till then, and then this comes along and caps it.

In fact, Bruce Hamiltons are about the only thing I can read nowadays – these two books having been the only ones which have given me that warm, excited feeling in this last year.[21]

Bruce had written a political novel set in an imaginary world. Hamilton now began to think along the same lines.

III

By 1937 Hamilton's austere, isolated residence in Overy Staithe was no longer fulfilling its function. He became increasingly unhappy, his drinking bouts were more frequent. During one of his visits to London, he met and fell in love with the young Irish actress, Geraldine Fitzgerald, who was about to leave Britain for a moderately successful career in Hollywood. The affair, if it can be called that, followed what was now a pattern. Fitzgerald herself was baffled by the excessive, idealized expression of Hamilton's regard. There was never any question of a sexual relationship, or of Hamilton leaving Loïs for her. Loïs played what was, in Bruce's words, 'her usual part, patient, kind, and sadly tolerant'.[22] The only result was that Hamilton drank more self-destructively for a time. He was not managing to write anything of consequence.

In the autumn both brothers made long trips with their wives, almost as an expression of dissatisfaction with the state of their lives. Bruce returned for an extended holiday with Aileen to her native Barbados. Hamilton made the only visit of his life to the United States. He may have arranged some minor business meetings but there could have been nothing important enough to justify the trip. *Rope* was in the past and *Gaslight* still in the future. He needed to get away, even if this meant he had to travel in order to do it: 'Oh my God how I hate ships! The stuffiness of the cabin, the noise of the water swishing by, the noise of the electric fan, the filthy *smells* everywhere, the throbbing, the intolerable *boredom*. Never again.'[23] Yet the purgatorial journey proved worthwhile: 'There is no doubt America is an experience like no other – there is an air of a sort of *party* going on all the time – a party in which everybody's just beginning to get a bit tight and things are going with a bang.'[24] Hamilton reported to Bruce his enthusiasm for New York City. He was sober, going every day for a two-hour walk in Central Park, and he was getting some work done. He had 'high hopes that this trip is going to shake me out of my rut and start afresh'.[25] He had an amiable, valedictory dinner with the recent American immigrant, Geraldine Fitzgerald, and also saw Charles Mackehenie. The trip was a success, as he was to recall: 'I had a marvellous time there – that is, as soon as I had made up my mind to take things easily and not let it get on top of me!'[26]

Then, on their way back to England, he and Loïs had a less successful sojourn with Bruce and Aileen in Barbados. According to Bruce, this was because Hamilton, who disliked even British summers, had ignored his advice and arrived during the hottest period of the year. The women, it seems, were also to blame: 'Each suspicious wife was too conscious of the other's foibles. But neither made any difficulty about our getting together by ourselves.'[27]

For Loïs, the benefits of the holiday must have been mixed. But Hamilton had been restored. He returned to England with a determination to change his life. At the beginning of 1938 they left Overy Staithe and moved temporarily to Oxford, 'determined not to sink back into the Norfolk rut',[28] and they began to look for somewhere new to live. Within a few months Loïs had found a pleasant flat in Henley, just a couple of minutes' walk from the Thames, which runs through the town centre. It is a prosperous, highly respectable small town to the west of London, for which Hamilton never developed much affection. But it was quiet, with easy access to London by train.

At the same time, Hamilton was writing once more with confidence in all three of the genres in which he had found success.

IV

The trip to America had restored the impulse to write without providing Hamilton with any new material. From now on, in general, he would have to look elsewhere than his own immediate experience. He had promised Val Gielgud a radio play, and for *To the Public Danger*, a moralistic tale about drinking and driving, he adapted the drunken escapade from *The Siege of Pleasure*. Two men get drunk in a pub with a working-class girl, Nan, and her boyfriend, Fred. Then they all drive away recklessly. As in *The Siege of Pleasure*, they seem to hit a man on a bicycle. Fred, who is disapproving, insists on leaving the car and going to report the incident. The others drive off and are killed when the car leaves the road. Then, as with *Money with Menaces*, there is a bathetic twist when we learn that the car had not in fact struck a body but a sack of potatoes draped over a bicycle leaning on a fence. 'If only they had gone back to see!' comments the coroner, in a long, platitudinous speech which Hamilton was asked to add to the final text in order to provide a more explicit moral for road users.[29]

To the Public Danger is far from an impressive work of literature, but it does show Hamilton's remarkable sense of form and technique. The didactic morality is trite in the extreme, but the piece is skilfully paced. The whole play is a crescendo, first of drunkenness, then of speed, culminating in the final crash. During the course of the play, the dialogue degenerates from a tipsy flirtatiousness into yells and screams and a final smash. Like its predecessor, the play attracted considerable attention, both favourable and hostile. In this case, Hamilton received hostile letters from what is now called the Road Lobby, people who felt the play unfairly maligned the road user.

It wasn't only his own past work that Hamilton drew on. The crowning irony of *Gaslight*, the play he was now writing, is that unknowingly the villain has all along been in possession of the diamonds for which he has been searching. It was, one imagines, with a further sense of irony that Hamilton found the most eery dramatic device for that play almost thrown away in a peripheral episode in an earlier book by his own brother. In Bruce's first novel, *To Be Hanged*, the hero is questioning a woman about one of her lodgers. While Mickey, the wrongly convicted musician, was playing at the local cinema, Emily was, the woman says, sneaking out:

'Well, you might go up to the King's Arms and ask her what she was up to of an evening, when he was fiddling away up at the pictures. She thought she was mighty smart, slipping away quietly when I was washing up in the scullery. But I always knew when she'd gone, because the gas in the kitchen went up brighter when she turned it out in the sitting-room. And she didn't go up to bed, neither, unless she undressed in the dark, because it would have gone down again when she turned the light on upstairs. . . .'[30]

Hamilton told Bruce that he proposed to make use of this idea and Bruce cheerfully agreed, insisting that he had no copyright on it.

In *Rope* two murderers invite friends and relatives of the corpse to eat supper off the chest in which it is contained. In *Gaslight* a man brings a new wife to live in the small house in which, many years before, he has cut another woman's throat. In this setting, he attempts, with a series of tricks, to convince his wife that she is going mad. Meanwhile he leaves the house each night and, unknown to her, returns through the attic to the upper floor to search for the hidden jewels for which the murder was committed. As he lights the gas, the light in her room sinks. What was a clever, incidental detail for Bruce, becomes a central motif of madness and horror for Hamilton.

The first half of the first scene of *Gaslight* is the best drama Hamilton ever wrote, as Mr Massingham needles his wife with the implacability Bruce had described in his own wife-murderer two years earlier:

He was never importunate, never angry, never upset. On matters affecting his immediate desires he was indifferent to arguments, impervious to snubs, and impossible to withstand. 'Please do this little thing for me,' he would say, by voice or expression, and in the end you would come to think that you were in the way, that you had been ungentle and unaccommodating. He would accept your surrender with graciousness and tact. You could not help liking him.[31]

Hamilton had previously been praised for horror that didn't rely on props or trick effects. *Gaslight* starts even more effectively. We begin the play believing we are witnessing a drama about a woman going mad. When we discover we are wrong we have to reconsider all we have seen. We are watching a psychopath at work, and he is manifesting his evil, not with physical torture but with squabbles about putting coal on the fire, an apparently misplaced picture and grocer's bill.

Though the play is subtitled 'a Victorian thriller in three acts', this first scene bears few traces of pastiche. Then the play changes, and becomes far more of an orthodox melodrama, with the appearance of the avuncular and reassuring Sergeant Rough, a somewhat perfunctory version of Sergeant Cuff, the detective in Wilkie Collins' *The Moonstone*. The disturbing themes that the play first touched on – of a woman's attraction to a man who is trying to destroy her – are dispensed with in favour of the simple, though still exciting plot to catch Mr Manningham.

Hamilton took a far greater professional pride in *Gaslight* than he had in *Rope* and he was delighted when Bruce first read it and agreed:

Without being a great work of art, I do think *G.L.* has a sort of *genuineness* in its very *bogusness* – it is sincere 'good fun' 'theatre' – a sort of dramatic '*pastiche*' of Wilkie Collins or Gaboriau – and as such a complete whole and entirely brought off. I don't have the same feeling of *shame* as I have always had in 'Rope'.[32]

And, years later, he concurred with Bruce in ranking the plays lower than the novels,

but I think you use the wrong word when you call them 'insincere'. To call, say, *Gaslight*, insincere, is, I think, as wrong as to call *The Speckled Band* by Conan Doyle insincere. Neither are *meant* to be sincere, if you see what I mean. They are just meant to entertain in an exhilarating way. By the way, it is worth noting that your godfather took as poor opinion of his Sherlock H. stories as your brother does of his plays.

That is why I still think it possible to be sincerely 'insincere' and do not propose *totally* to abandon the theatre.[33]

Gaslight opened on 5 December 1938 in Richmond and then transferred early the following year to the Apollo Theatre in the West End, where it ran for four months.

15

Impromptu in Moribundia

I

Towards the end of his life, the American critic, Lionel Trilling, meditated on what in the 1930s had drawn so many people to support a system that even at that time should have been seen, as it was by others, as a moral and political catastrophe:

I speak of the commitment that a large segment of the intelligentsia of the West gave to the degraded version of Marxism known as Stalinism. No one, of course, called himself a Stalinist; it was the pejorative designation used by those members of the class of advanced intellectuals who were its opponents. At its center was the belief that the Soviet Union had resolved all social and political contradictions and was well on the way toward realizing the highest possibilities of human life. The facts which refuted this certitude were not hard to come by but the wish to ignore them was resolute, which is to say that the position of the Stalinist intellectuals of the West was not, in any true conception of politics, a political position at all but, rather, the expression of a settled disgust with politics, or at least with what politics entails of contingency, vigilance, and effort. In an imposed monolithic government they saw the promise of rest from the particular acts of will which are needed to meet the many, often clashing requirements of democratic society. The Stalinists of the West were not commonly revolutionaries, they were what used to be called fellow-travellers but they cherished the idea of revolution as the final, all-embracing act of will which would forever end the exertions of our individual wills. Failing the immediate actuality of revolution, their animus against individual will expressed itself in moral and cultural attitudes which devalued all the gratuitous manifestations of feeling, of thought, and of art, of all such energies of the human spirit as are marked by spontaneity, complexity, and variety.[1]

This is both right and inadequate, since a defining characteristic of this political movement was its dangerous aestheticism, the degree to which it expressed itself in artistic form. Hamilton's view of what was wrong with human relations in English society was not something that could be corrected by wage-bargaining or legislation. Much of the Marxism of the intelligentsia was actually an aesthetic attitude, an apocalyptic despair that required an apocalyptic solution. The enticement of Soviet communism was not that it disregarded the artistic spirit, but that it gave it a quite new, central importance. In Britain there was a tradition of sneering at artists who associated their cause with that of the proletariat. In August 1934, the first All-Union Congress of Soviet Writers took place, as if its members were workers like any other. By the following year, the already well publicized proceedings had been translated and published in Britain.

The conclusions of the conference had been decided in advance by Stalin. All the motions were passed unanimously by the six hundred delegates, without even a single abstention.[2] Previously the Soviet revolution had been associated with progressive art but this was now decisively condemned and replaced with a new idea, defined at the conference by Andrei Zhdanov:

Comrade Stalin has called our writers the engineers of human souls. What does this mean? What obligations does this title impose on you? It means firstly that you must know life in order to depict it faithfully in artistic productions, to depict it not scholastically, not in a dead fashion, not simply as 'objective fact', but to depict reality in its revolutionary development. At the same time the faithfulness and the historical concreteness of the artistic depiction must be combined with the task of the ideological refashioning and education of labouring people in the spirit of socialism. Such a method of artistic literature and literary criticism is what we call the method of Socialist Realism.[3]

In Britain the message was taken up with remarkable speed. The young art historian, Anthony Blunt, who by then was in the pay of the Soviet secret services, wrote that under socialism the artist 'will take a clearly defined place in the organisation of society as an intellectual worker with a definite function.'[4] The critic, Philip Henderson, could begin a survey of the novel for a mainstream publisher stating that he had 'dealt with the novel primarily as a form of social activity, rather than as an isolated art form obeying its own laws' and by social activity he meant 'the struggle of capital and labour, the class-struggle, which, in the last resort, is the struggle between fascism and communism.'[5] The more openly commit-ted Ralph Fox, who was to be killed in the Spanish Civil War, asked for a 'new realism' which, paradoxically, meant not a description of what society was like, not 'man at hopeless war with a society he cannot fit into as an individual, but man in action to change his conditions, to master life, man in harmony with the course of history and able to become the lord of his own destiny. This means that the heroic must come back to the novel, and with the heroic its epic character.'[6]

The Soviet system was so interested in its writers that it was able to enforce the adoption of Stalin's new aesthetic principle. In fact, it has been estimated that of the 700 writers who attended the First Congress of the Union of Soviet Writers in 1934, only 50 survived to attend the second in 1954.[7] Of the five principal speakers at the conference, four were murdered within five years of the Congress.[8]

In Britain, no such compulsive force could be exerted. To Hamilton, increasingly a keen student of Stalinist thought during the thirties, the call for a new heroism in literature must have been eerily reminiscent of his father's artistic creed, and indeed of the fascistic kitsch of Bernard's fiction. When, in 1939, Hamilton sent Bruce a copy of a speech by Stalin, it was his fatherly qualities that he stressed:

I don't imagine you will have seen this, and it is *magnificent*. Written in that lucid, dignified, semi-paternal style of his, it is the most refreshing and reassuring thing in the world. I am happy to say I have never had any doubts of this great man, and this should shame anyone who had during the Trotskyist business. As the years go on I get more and more respect for him as having original genius instead of being a mere Lenin-follower.[9]

Everything that his own father had never been. But Hamilton's very incapacity for seeing life in heroic terms was one of the principal reasons for Marxism's attraction and he could never have considered himself capable of attempting such a theme.

Nevertheless, the Marxist discussion of art did have a traceable influence. It connected the consciousness of artists to material historical forces. Marx had discovered the laws of history and they were now being embodied in the political forces at work in the Soviet Union. If writers could take up this challenge, then Shelley's dictum that poets were the unacknowledged legislators of the world would finally come true. Some of the finest poems of the decade wrestle with the idea of the mind manifesting itself in history, imaginative ideas being made material. Already in 1933, Louis MacNeice wittily subverted the notion in his short poem, 'To a Communist':

> Your thoughts make shapes like snow
> The gawky earth grows breasts,
> Snow's unity engrosses
> Particular pettiness of stones and grasses.
> But before you proclaim the millennium my dear,
> Consult the barometer –
> This poise is perfect but maintained
> For one day only.[10]

In April 1937 W. H. Auden picked up and developed his friend's image in his complex, ambiguous political poem, 'Spain':

> On that tableland scored by rivers
> Our thoughts have bodies; the menacing shapes of our fever
>
> Are precise and alive . . .
>
> Madrid is the heart. Our moments of tenderness blossom
> As the ambulance and the sandbag;
> Our hours of friendship into a people's army.[11]

II

Hamilton probably never read Auden's poem, though he was following the Spanish Civil War keenly, and rebuked Bruce for his pessimism.[12] He even contemplated going on a walking holiday there with Charles Mackehenie.[13] But when he came to write his only political novel, his epigraph, a quotation from a popular science book, *The Mysterious*

Universe by Sir James Jeans, shows that he was exploring the same area as MacNeice and Auden:

the universe begins to look more like a great thought than like a great machine. Mind no longer appears as an accidental intruder in the realm of matter; we are beginning to suspect that we ought rather to hail it as the creator and governor of the realm of matter . . .

In August 1938 he signed the contract for the novel that was originally called *Assignment in Moribundia* but was retitled *Impromptu in Moribundia*. Quite different from anything else Hamilton ever published, this is a Wellsian, Swiftian fantasy about a journey to another planet which is a parodic, fantastic version of our own, 'in which the ideals and ideas of our world, the striving and subconscious wishes of our time, the fictions and figments of our imagination, are calm cold actualities.'[14]

The nameless hero – Hamilton's only first-person narrator – uses an 'Asteradio' to travel millions of miles to the world of Moribundia. This is a place where the myths and ideologies of our own world are literally, though surreally, true. He arrives to see the symbolic cricket game in Henry Newbolt's imperialist poem, 'Vitaï Lampada', being ritually enacted. He travels to Nwotsemaht (Thamestown, i.e. London) on a bus the conductor of which is a redfaced exponent of the fabled cockney humour.

Between Raglafart Erauqs and the River Semaht, he takes up residence in a hotel, The Moribundian, which gives him the chance to make his observations. The most obvious characteristic is that people communicate using speech balloons, as in press advertisements, about the benefits of consumer products such as Smoothall soap, Slooshall washing powder, No-ra-zor-o.

He meets and becomes attracted to Anne and they begin a form of affair which culminates in a sexually unsatisfying, indeed unconsummated, trip to Seabrightsone. The narrator also spends some time with the Jugginses who embody the bourgeois myths about the working class. They are lazy, rich, keep coal in the bath. He becomes ill, which gives him the leisure to make an examination of Moribundian literature.

Ultimately the narrator encounters the Little Man, the ordinary person praised for his stolid good sense but here portrayed in a group as a malevolent band of dwarfs imposing a punitive orthodoxy. These are revered on Moribundia but the narrator falls foul of them, is pursued by them and only just makes his escape back to Earth.

Impromptu in Moribundia is so misconceived, in general and in detail, as to be almost beyond criticism. Reviewing Philip Henderson's *The Novel Today*, George Orwell wrote: 'The basic trouble with all orthodox Marxists is that, possessing a system which appears to explain everything, they never bother to discover what is going on inside other people's heads.'[15] This perfectly diagnoses what is wrong with *Impromptu in Moribundia*. Throughout, Hamilton deprives himself of his greatest gift, which is his eye for what life is like *beneath* people's facile illusions and myths. He is a master of the particular who has shackled himself to a story about generalities. Worst of all, it is dull and relentlessly unfunny. There is, for example, the hero's first sight of Moribundia. A stanza from Sir Henry Newbolt's exhoratory poem, which in Hamilton's time was learned by every schoolboy, is used as the novel's second epigraph:

> There's a breathless hush in the Close to-night –
> Ten to make and the match to win –
> A bumping pitch and a blinding light,
> An hour to play and the last man in.
> And it's not for the sake of a ribboned coat,
> Or the selfish hope of a season's fame,
> But his Captain's hand on his shoulder smote –
> 'Play up! play up! and play the game!'

The narrator arrives in Moribundia to find this very game in progress. He describes the scene as the cricketer leaves the field:

I stress the selflessness, for it was obviously not for the thought of any fame he might win that season amongst his schoolfellows, nor was it for any hope of getting a permanent place in the first eleven and so having the privilege of wearing a blazer (a curious ribboned affair – rather exotic, I thought) like his Captain's – that this boy meant to go in and win. No, it was because his Captain had hit him upon the shoulder and told him to play up, and to play the game.[16]

Comic material that might pall in a thousand-word *jeu d'esprit* is here stretched out for a 289-page novel, along with far too many examples demonstrating Hamilton's belief, previously only tested in his first novel, that spelling words backwards is inherently funny. Hence Yrneh Tlobwen, Nacirema, *Ehtteivosnoinu*, Scitcelaid and so on and on. Given that Michael Sadleir would later cruelly criticize one of Hamilton's best novels, it is barely credible that he would allow his friend to publish this mistake.

Nevertheless the book does have the interest of being the only open expression of Hamilton's political and aesthetic views. His Gulliver notes ingenuously: 'As we know, the labouring man in our own world, believing, rightly or wrongly, that wealth is somehow caused and created by labour, his own labour, is liable to suppose that he should have a due "share" of that which he has created, and to make trouble if he feels he is getting something less than that share.'[17] He quotes the absurd Moribundian view that the country called *Ehtteivosnoinu*

was a place of punishment of the *Tsixram*'s evil, that is to say, a pandemonium wherein his notions and practices reached their logical and terrible conclusion. Chaos, starvation, greed, famine, tyranny and a horrible uniformity in the lives of the masses were, as far as I could gather, the prevailing conditions. In addition to this, I understood, everybody was compelled to wear the same clothes and nobody was allowed to laugh.[18]

His view of his British contemporaries could have been dictated by Zhdanov. Shaw and Wells (to dispense with the backward spelling) are tolerated by the authorities because they knew that 'there was nowhere any deep-seated change lurking behind the highly-readable polemics of these two, and that time would expose the unreality and irrelevance of their teachings'[19] and Wells is further denounced for criticizing the Soviet Union.[20] Eliot, Joyce, Huxley, Lawrence, Sitwell, Graves, Sassoon might seem to be rebels but are 'for the most part hopelessly and morbidly turned in upon themselves, and sterile in consequence.'[21] The sexual metaphor is developed as the narrator argues that 'art, literature and poetry in Moribundia take on a more and more painfully subjective aspect, more and more the character of meaningless masturbation, there being no future which they can fertilize.'[22]

Finally, there is the portrait of the ordinary man:

I saw cupidity, ignorance, complacence, meanness, ugliness, short-sightedness, cowardice, credulity, hysteria and, when the occasion called for it, as it did now, cruelty and blood-thirstiness. I saw the shrewd and despicable cash basis underlying that idiotic patriotism, and a deathly fear and hatred of innovation, of an overturning of their system, behind all their nauseating idealistic postures and utterances.[23]

Admirers of Hamilton, like his brother Bruce and J. B. Priestley, have both deprecated and trivialized the influence of his Marxism as, at best, filling Hamilton's desperate need for a reassuring structure. One of the few commentators who have spoken up for him is Claud Cockburn, himself an influential communist: 'It is never explained just how a philosophy of endless change, endless struggle, endless search for solutions to endlessly evolving new confrontations could be considered as any kind of escape to any kind of security.'[24] There is no doubt that Cockburn's description of Hamilton's Marxism applies to *Impromptu in Moribundia*, in which Moribundia represents decayed stasis, while the Soviet Union embodies dynamic change. On the other hand, Claud Cockburn, writing in the early 1980s when there was no longer any excuse for ignorance, was mischievously ignoring the real question about Hamilton's Stalinism: that it involved the fervent defence of a system that was committing atrocities which rendered the objections to his own society – to which he gave so much space in *Impromptu in Moribundia* – trivial by comparison. He disbelieves the true accounts of what was occurring in Stalin's Soviet Union, and denounces those who criticize it. Yet this is beside the point. In later years, Hamilton was to say that his favourite quotation was a statement by the nineteenth-century scientist, Thomas Huxley: 'The player on the other side is hidden from us. We know that his play is always fair, just and patient. But also we know, to our cost, that he never overlooks a mistake or makes the smallest allowance for ignorance.'[25] Hamilton took a high Victorian, mechanistic view of the world, to which he gave a pessimistic, retributive slant of its own, and it was this, previously intuitive vision, that his Marxism codified. Stalin's Soviet Union was at the fixed point of Hamilton's philosophical universe, essentially an idea, by which everything else should be assessed. The commitment, once made, was not something that could be thrown into doubt by reports from ideological enemies or even by what he saw as renegade Marxists. It was only to be expected that Stalin would be criticized and denounced, just as Christ had been. All the more reason to keep the faith.

On its publication in February 1939 the reviews of *Impromptu in Moribundia* were surprisingly favourable. According to Lettice Cooper in *Time and Tide*:

Where Mr Hamilton is pointed and penetrating is in his exposure of those comfortable notions which English people draw over themselves like warm blankets to keep out the cold wind of inevitable change. Moribundia is the country of those about to die because its inhabitants resist the flow of and movement of life. In fact this is a good Marxist pamphlet in a light and readable form.[26]

More shaming still for Hamilton, he received praise, albeit in an anonymous short review, from 'that Trotskyite rag', *The New Statesman*, which considered it 'not only extremely amusing but an excellent piece of social satire. . . . Mr Hamilton is able to make some excellent jokes and some shrewd Marxian criticism.'[27]

In April, Bruce wrote Hamilton a letter from Barbados mistakenly commiserating on the failure of *Gaslight* and congratulating him on the success of *Impromptu in Moribundia*. Hamilton hastily assured him that it was the other way round. *Gaslight* had got a 'grand press' and 'could really be called a "success" without kidding oneself – as good as *Rope* anyway. *M.*, on the other hand, isn't selling at all.'[28] Hamilton's exhilaration at the success of *Gaslight* was entirely differ- ent to the quite unexpected triumph of *Rope*. A second time was more satisfying than a first, which could be viewed as mere chance, and he was delighted with the praise of theatrical stars such as Noël Coward, Ivor Novello and the successful playwright, James Bridie. He con- fessed that

all these things happening at the same time have give me an enormous fillip, and for the first time in years I really feel like doing some work. I certainly think that with this sudden burst I am now what you might call 'known' by reading and theatre-going people – in fact I think I could very nearly say, paraphrasing Keats, 'I think I shall be among the English writers while I live.'[29]

III

The last novel by Bruce before the war blended his new, overtly radical politics, with the conventional thriller form that he seemed to have left behind. *Traitor's Way*, published in 1938, is the story of Noel Mason, a young fellow-traveller, who receives a long prison sentence for striking the policeman who has killed Noel's communist friend at an anti-fascist demonstration. He escapes from prison and steals a car in which he finds, as luck would have it, a secret treaty between the British fascist movement against which he had been demonstrating and the Third Reich.

Noel must evade capture – and the bulk of the book is dismayingly similar to his earlier tale of a man on the run, *Hue and Cry* – and deliver the treaty to Colonel Raymond, a Labour leader admired by Mason for 'his utter devotion to the cause of peace, and his unremitting opposition, in general and in detail, to the many recent compromises the Government had made with the Fascist powers.'[30] There is a final twist when Mason arrives at Raymond's house. Not only has Raymond moved but, by evil chance, the house is now rented by the very fascist leader who has made the treaty with the Nazis. Fortunately all comes right at the end and on the final page Colonel Raymond is able to conclude: 'Peace is safe, at least for the time being, and maybe for a generation; for there are signs that Fascism may not be able to survive this blow.'[31]

This lazy, lacklustre thriller did nothing for Bruce's fortunes. He was now approaching forty, none of his books had made much money, and he decided that he would have to make some commitment to a career outside literature. While he was in Barbados, he was offered the chance of taking up his job once more as a schoolmaster. Though this would give him security, Bruce was reluctant to accept. He returned to England 'to see if I could rustle up a job more closely allied to my hopes and expectations',[32] though he was far from clear what these expectations were.

Bruce contacted publishers, newspapers, magazines, film studios, the BBC, but he received no immediate offers. Looking back, he believed that he would have been able to find something if he had persevered, and at the time this was the firm view of Hamilton, who urgently opposed the idea of returning to the old job in Barbados. He argued that Bruce ought not tamely to recapitulate a period of his life that he hadn't much enjoyed the first time round, and he offered to support Bruce and Aileen (who had returned from Barbados to join him) in England while he searched for something to do. This was a generous offer, made even before *Gaslight* had opened, let alone achieved the later American success that would make Hamilton financially secure once more. But Bruce considered it morally impossible for him to accept this, partly because he planned that any prosperity would enable Aileen and him to have children, thus, as he saw it, defying Patrick.[33] He accepted the Barbados offer.

The two brothers knew that this would be a decisively long parting, and there was also, despite the hopeful conclusion of Bruce's novel, a more ominous sense of approaching war. In the final weeks before Bruce left, the two brothers took two holidays together reflecting two sides of their relationship. They visited a professional golf championship in Oxhey in Hertfordshire. Then, in Bruce's newly acquired Morris Eight, they spent a week driving around Kent and Sussex, visiting places with which their family had been associated, including Waldershare, near Canterbury, where their father had been born. Their consumption of alcohol was relatively temperate, by Hamilton's standards: nothing but four or five double whiskies each evening.

In September 1938, Bruce and Aileen boarded the steamer for Barbados.

16

The War and
Hangover Square

I

With Bruce back in Barbados, the brothers' relationship quickly reverted to concerns of ten years previously. Hamilton immediately began to worry on his brother's behalf about what he would do when he was finished with Barbados: 'I don't really feel (I may be wrong) that you would ever want to sink into a pension-taking rut!' Bruce had been complaining once more about his inability to get down to any sustained writing and Hamilton advised that he take up once more his long-contemplated historical novel 'like knitting' and '*some such thing* might ease your writer's conscience, for the time being, and finally produce something of real worth and weight.'[1] He promised to do his best to get a theatrical version of *Middle Class Murder* adapted by Lalla, put on at Richmond, where *Gaslight* had first been staged, but, rightly as it turned out, he was pessimistic.

Lalla was having recurrent problems and Hamilton spoke of being fatalistic about her but this was becoming a good year. The success of *Gaslight* was cumulative. The French rights had been sold and, with a war in prospect, Hamilton decided to make the best of it and accept an English offer for a film version. Meanwhile he was being 'absolutely wonderful' on the 'drinking situation'. He restricted himself to the drinking regime they had kept to on their holiday and the occasional binge. More important, he felt, 'I *always* have a meal in the evening, and this regime, kept up over a long period, is really beginning to tell advantageously on me as a whole.'[2] He was sure there would be a war soon and looked forward to it.

So positive was Hamilton's feeling and such was the renewed affection for the theatre caused by the success of *Gaslight* that he made the bizarre decision to accept the job of theatre critic at the eccentrically left-wing journal, *Time and Tide*, a position for which he was singularly ill-suited. He regretted the acceptance, almost as soon as he had made it, describing the activity to Bruce as 'peculiarly degrading in a subtle way.'[3] Not only that, it required constant travelling from Henley.

Twopence Coloured proved that he had forthright and entertaining views about the medium, but he found himself unable to write in such a way as a critic. His first review was of *Bridge Head*, a sombre play about a land commissioner in the West of Ireland. *Time and Tide*'s sub-editors implicity showed their opinion of their new drama critic's first review with their almost parodically unsparkling headline, 'Social Conditions in West Ireland'. Hamilton's numbly expressed praise for the play's social realism can have done little for the Westminister Theatre's box-office receipts:

Quite apart form its sincerity and cleverness, it would be impossible not to welcome a play of this kind, if only because of its rare yet immediately recognizable merit of being about 'something'. It is not, that is to say, a play about idiosyncracies and happenings observed in a social vacuum; it is first and foremost a picture of certain concrete social conditions, and of the relation of these conditions to the individual, and of their effect upon him. Individuality and characterization is not, of course, lost in such a treatment; it is, on the other hand, enriched and doubled in interest.[4]

By the time he wrote his second column, a fortnight later, his patience and sympathy were evidently wearing thin. Reviewing a comedy and a serious drama, he dismissed the first as 'one of those far too familiar muddles in which, along with avowedly superficial comedy in which actors are simply trying to get laughs or good lines, assaults are made upon our sentiments, and attempts are made at reality.'[5] And of the second:

Though bearing every evidence of an intelligent and discerning mind behind the writing, and so tempting one to overpraise, this play fails to hold the interest in the theatre because there is nothing of the theatre about it . . . we feel all the time that it should be read at home, not acted in public . . . in place of action all we get is one verbose person walking away so that another may immediately enter and be verbose. One is less impressed by the anguish of the characters portrayed when one reflects upon the extent to which their large incomes must assist them in supporting it.[6]

No third column appeared. He cited a dispute with the magazine's owner as an excuse for devoting his energies to issues that were speedily becoming more serious. The following year *Time and Tide* employed George Orwell, who enjoyed the post no more than Hamilton had.[7]

For many Communist Party members, the signing of the Nazi-Soviet Pact on 23 August 1939 was a tragedy, even though its most sinister clause, the division of Poland between the two countries, was still a secret. Many left the party, or, if not members, dissociated themselves from it. Those who remained performed extraordinary and ignominious convolutions to justify their continued support. The invasion of Finland by the Soviet Army on 30 November made things even worse.

Almost alone, Hamilton – who was not even a party member – was entirely unperturbed. The beginning of the war came as a relief of tension, even if it did mean that during the day 'Henley High Street is like Chiswick High Road, owing to London evacuees all speaking Cockney.'[8] When Bruce asked how he was feeling about the German-Soviet pact, he replied firmly, with multiple underlinings, '*exactly the same as I always did in every respect and concerning every country!*'[9] He insisted that nothing had come as a surprise, including the invasion of Finland, which was beginning on that very day and about which he was and always would be entirely unsentimental: 'To this I stick through thick and thin – Hitler's power is on the *decline*, however long he may take in going. The arrangement he made with Russia was a terrible *symptom of weakness* from which there is no sort of recovery in the long run.'[10]

Behind Hamilton's most powerful work had always been an inchoate sense, the more powerful for being undefined, that these were the last terrible days before an apocalypse came to sweep the detritus of the deracinated, urban society away. Now he felt, with both excitement and fear, that it had come. Writing to Bruce on the final day of 1939, looking out of his window at a snow-covered, silent Henley, he expressed, perhaps for the only time in his life, views that happened to coincide with the mass of the British people:

I am sometimes inclined to get depressed about everything, but then I remind myself that we always *knew* this was going to happen – tried to get the best out of life until it *did* happen – and that it's absurd to grumble now it's come. I always knew that the 2nd World War would be the end of life as we knew it, and, alas, I still think so. But a better world will come out of it all right and if you and I aren't starved or bumped off by some explosive, we'll live to see it. But all this we know.[11]

But that old depraved world that the war had killed off was, as he knew, his own imaginative territory and early in the new year he began a novel set in its dying days. Right from the start he saw it as a thriller and that it would be called *Hangover Square*, derived from a joke he had made to Bruce when walking across Hanover Square in central London in the previous year.[12] By June he was working hard on it and hoping to finish it by the middle of July,[13] but the novel was to prove much harder to complete.

Hamilton was now starting to lead a different sort of existence, with different possibilities. Through the success of *Gaslight*, he had become a close friend of the theatrical producer Bill Linnit, a handsome, witty, cynical, very successful man, who as Hamilton explained to Bruce, exercised 'very much the same sort of fascination over me that Charles [Mackehenie] used to exercise.'[14] In tones of almost childlike awe, he described a weekend in which he had accompanied Bill in his Rolls-Royce down to Bournemouth for the opening of a show, during which they had 'mingled with the 40 women' in the cast. They had returned and stayed at the Savoy Hotel, all interspersed with a lot of golf, 'with *caddies*!' It was wartime and Hamilton was living better than ever before: 'It was all absolutely crazy, and although I was living like a multi-millionaire I hardly spent a penny! The general effect was good, as when I got back I started writing quite hard and quite well and still am.'[15] Gradually, though, Hamilton stopped trying to describe to Bruce the other lives he was leading with different people, referring instead occasionally to 'extraordinarily interesting' times where he had been meeting 'extraordinarily interesting people' but tantalizingly promising to tell him when they next met, by the West Pier, as they used to say in a recurring joke.[16]

In the first years of the war, Hamilton felt reawoken by 'a sense of *interest* and *excitement* which keeps one going – aeroplanes, tanks and troops going through the streets – there is a sort of nightmare *stimulation* of the faculties. What I am trying to say is that one is not (as one would have imagined) in a blue funk and miserable: one is, at present at any rate, quite composed and just about as happy or miserable as one always was.'[17] He reacted tetchily when Bruce accused him by letter of being 'like a philosopher in a dark room looking for a black hat that wasn't there.' On the contrary, he insisted, he was fit and well, and keeping up with current affairs through newspapers and regular visits to friends and to London. On one visit to 'the front line' during the Blitz he 'was made a little sick by the wreckage – Oxford Street, Lewis's gone, Peter Robinson with huge chunks of white pillars lying in Oxford Circus (as though Samson had been having a go at it) – a ghastly playing-card subsidence of three or four floors on top of the Langham, a huge building completely gutted in Gt Portland Street.' He wasn't exactly happy but he wasn't stale.[18]

Was it not really Bruce who was depressed, stuck out in Barbados, cut off from the communal intensity of life in Britain? Hamilton made a variety of wild suggestions that can have been of little help to his brother. He could give up schoolmastering, return by boat to Britain ('People *do* seem to go across the Atlantic still'), he could move to another island, or to South America. 'You *are* a writer and not a schoolmaster,' Hamilton wrote encouragingly.[19]

His life was full of distractions. On the day of Belgium's surrender, he was in London watching a private screening of the film version of *Gaslight*, starring Anton Walbrook and directed by Thorold Dickinson, that drew the warmest praise Hamilton would ever give to a film adaptation on one of his works: 'The story was *incredibly* ballsed up and ruined, but actually the production and technique was excellent and Anton Walbrook gave a really first class performance. On the whole, the whole thing wasn't too bad.'[20] He complained to Martha Smith of suffering from 'a thing called OCCUPATIONAL NEURITIS!' and he was contemplating finishing *Hangover Square* by dictating it to Loïs,[21] which presented certain problems since, unlike any other member of the Hamilton family, she was engaged in war work, driving an ambulance for the ARP. Apart from this, Loïs led a lonely life, as Hamilton spent an increasing proportion of his time in London. Bruce surmised guardedly that 'her war experiences must have been relatively lacking in the factitious stimuli of excitement, danger – and hard liquor; and been a great deal more bleak than [Patrick's] own.' Nevertheless, with an optimism that had a certain factitiousness of its own, he pronounced himself 'quite sure that she engaged in active and useful employment which filled her solitary hours.'[22]

By early 1941, the exhilaration of war was wearing off. There was no prospect of bombs in Henley, so the main trouble was not the danger 'but the bloody *inconvenience* and *boredom* – the restrictions, the black-out, the travelling, petrol, parking and telephone difficulties.' Worse still were the stories of the 'bomb braggarts', boasting of their proximity to danger.[23] The frustration at least goaded Hamilton into finishing his novel. The method he adopted was that he 'stayed in bed all day and drank a great deal of whisky in the evenings'.[24] By March he could report that *Hangover Square* was finished and delivered:

It is a long book (over 100,000 [words]) and, you will be pleased to hear, *extremely* good! It's unambitious, a sort of 'thriller', but I have a feeling that, in its own *métier*, it's the best thing I've ever written!

This is most satisfactory, as the effort to concentrate and write a long book in wartime has been *prodigious* – and I have lost that awful feeling of waste which has been on me so long.[25]

II

Hangover Square, Hamilton's most intense and powerful novel, is almost a retelling of the story of *The Midnight Bell*. Bob, the twenty-five-year-old barman, created by the twenty-five-year-old Hamilton, has become thirty-four-year-old George Harvey Bone, at a time, Christmas 1938, when Hamilton was thirty-four. Jenny Maple has become Netta Longdon. And the money that is systematically to be plundered by the woman has inflated from Bob's eighty pounds to George's three hundred in War Loan and seventy-eight pounds twelve shillings and threepence in cash.

Yet, unlike Bruce's recent rehearsal of an earlier idea, *Traitor's Way*, there is no sense of mere repetition because Hamilton has transformed the story by pushing it to an extreme. The result is less like a novel than an extended poem of humiliation. Hamilton emphasizes this with his repeated quotations throughout the book from Milton's epic of passive suffering, *Samson Agonistes*. Even *The Midnight Bell* was far from being a realistic rendering of Hamilton's own experiences, as his artistic impulse steered him away from his own prior intention to achieve a sociological examination of the world in which he had moved. *Hangover Square* is still further from being a picture of social life, except in its more circumstantial aspects. It is more profitably seen as a near-expressionist version of Hamilton's own fear, presented in the form of a novel, whose most realistic aspects are those where the world had changed to fit the author's already existing paranoia. The sense of vague impending apocalypse in *Twenty Thousand Streets Under the Sky* has now been replaced by the rumblings of imminent war. The unfocused perception of evil is now embodied by thuggish fascists.

The hero, George Harvey Bone, is a pathological symbol of Hamilton's hopeless form of passive, idealizing love and there is no suspense about his treatment at the hands of the woman he masochistically adores: 'Having disgraced himself, having put himself beyond the pale, by being distractedly in love with her without inspiring an atom of affection in return, he could no longer expect the normal amenities of intercourse.'[26] The only suspense in *Hangover Square* is as to the means with which each dose of torment will be meted out to George, who has taken Hamilton's romantic pessimism almost to the point of martyrdom: 'He saw he could never be happy, that only disaster lay ahead. But he would have had his moment, a few days, a brief spell of bliss – the fulfilment, the justification of his long trial.'[27]

The most extraordinary creation in the book is Netta Longdon. In her previous incarnation, as Jenny Maple, she was a small, pretty creature stirred by an impulse of petty, temporary self-gratification. Netta is given a plethora of evil motives and characteristics, as if she contained everything that Hamilton hated. She is impersonal like a fish, 'something seen floating in a tank, brooding, self-absorbed, frigid, moving solemnly forward to its object or veering sideways without fully conscious motivation.'[28] She veers between indifference to George and hatred of him, provoking a compulsion to destroy him because, unlike her and her friends, 'he was not totally ineffectual'.[29] Hamilton depersonalizes her further still, as her name suggests. She is the woman who traps men, 'He was netted in hate just as he was netted in love',[30] and with her strange second name she suggests the cursed, depraved capital itself, London, 'the crouching monster' as he was to call it on the first page of *The Slaves of Solitude*.

The extent to which he turned her into everything he hated and feared is shown by a savage private joke in the novel. George lodges in the fictional Fauconberg Hotel, Fauconberg Square, the same place Anthony Forster stayed in *Monday Morning*. This is actually Earl's Court Square, as is demonstrated when George leaves it in order to walk to Netta's flat. He turns left into Earl's Court Road, walks past Earl's Court Station and approaches Cromwell Road from the south. 'He crossed over Cromwell Road, and looked up to see if there was a light in her flat.'[31] A simple retracing of George's footsteps, or a glance at the map, will show that his walk has brought him to the junction of Earl's Court Road and Logan Place, the scene of Hamilton's accident. He placed her at the spot where his arm was paralysed, his leg permanently damaged and his nose ripped off.

The novel is animated by Hamilton's hatred but this is also the source of its most damaging flaw. *The Midnight Bell* cleverly tails off when we expect a violent showdown between Bob and Jenny, though at the beginning of *The Siege of Pleasure* Jenny is still anxious to get off the street lest she should encounter him. *Hangover Square* announces from the beginning that it is heading towards a violent climax. After the ghastly *tour de force* of humiliation in Brighton which culminates in Netta and her two companions leaving George with the hotel bill, he is finally roused to anger: 'They were a dirty lot, and Netta was the dirtiest. He felt he would like to beat her up, do her some physical damage, smash her face and tell her to go to hell. He could understand men wanting to hit women.'[32] It is a terrifying, exhilarating passage in which Hamilton enlists the reader in a desire that Netta be punished. But Hamilton raises this subject of violent frustration only to evade it by creating the clumsy, unnecessary and unconvincing device of George's split-personality, a literary mechanism rather than a medical condition.[33] Much in the way that Hamilton compartmentalized his own life in order to simplify it, so George's invented psychological condition fudges the crucial moral and aesthetic challenge of the book, which is to justify the final terrible murder at the end, especially since Hamilton takes great trouble to link the final catastrophe with the outbreak of the Second World War. George murders the fascist as Britain finally gives up its policy of appeasing fascism. Just at the moment when Hamilton seems to be fusing his private and public concerns, he withdraws.

Constable were delighted with *Hangover Square* and Michael Sadleir considered it his best novel.[34] By the autumn Hamilton could report a reception such as none of his books had previously seen. James Agate had trumpeted in his column in the *Daily Express* that 'This magnificent thriller is the best study of a trull since Shakespeare's Cressida. . . . Don't gulp this. Ration yourself to fifty pages a day and make it last the week.' It was to this recommendation that Hamilton attributed a sudden increase in the book's sales, and the success almost took Hamilton by surprise: 'Oddly enough, I did not intend it to be a good book, writing it almost for "fun"; but it did get hold of me in a remarkable way, and the leading character, George Harvey Bone, is, I think, quite a *creation* – and I'm not sure that it's not my best.'[35]

III

Hamilton's delivery of the manuscript of *Hangover Square* and his thirty-seventh birthday coincided with the alarming prospect of military service, for which Hamilton was technically eligible (the age limit was forty-one). In the First World War Bernard's father had enlisted and manoeuvred himself as close to the front as possible, but neither of his sons had any military ambitions. When Bruce briefly considered returning to Britain the following year, it was only on the condition that Hamilton could secure him a job that would avoid his being conscripted on arrival.[36] In Hamilton's case this proved not to be a problem, since he had a medical examination which passed him as a lowly grade three, classifying him as entirely unsuitable for any form of combat: 'This, I take it, lets me out of it for the time being, though whether one is used in some sedentary form or another sooner or later I don't know.'[37]

Four months later Hamilton was summoned to an interview with a Henley bureaucrat who asked him what his occupation was:

I said a writer, and he replied that if I could write a good hand I might be very useful. Extremely farcical, but as it looked as though I might have to spend the rest of the war licking stamps and addressing envelopes in Reading, I wisely pulled some strings. Got Bill Linnit to talk to Basil Dean who saw me and gave me a job on Ensa! I don't have to do very much at present (I write the chat linking up the songs in Ensa broadcast half hours) but it means going to London a lot.[38]

The Entertainments National Service Association did not enjoy a particularly high reputation during the war (it was popularly known as Every Night Something Awful) and Hamilton showed his view of it in *The Slaves of Solitude* when he derisively placed it last in a series of terms whose meaning the heroine, Miss Roach, does not understand, after WREN and WAAF (two of the women's services) and the NAAFI (the Navy, Army and Air Force Institutes which run canteens, stores and so on for the service personnel). Hamilton's relations with Basil Dean, who was a powerful figure in the British film and theatre world, were poor and his actual work was less satisfying than anything he had done since his days in melodrama when he was a teenager.

Hamilton was not at the centre of historical events. If the war against fascism was to be followed, as he hoped (at least in an abstract sense), by the collapse of capitalism, then Hamilton's position would be that of a distant observer from the vantage point of a genteel suburban town, which he occasionally left for games of golf with Bill Linnit, lunches at the fashionable Ivy restaurant, off Cambridge Circus, with Michael Sadleir, and the occasional drinking binge. He complained about a 'horrible sense of being shut outside the room during the bloody birth and climax of history'[39] but on the whole he decided that he had to cut himself off from what was happening or go mad. Almost in disbelief he saw that the apocalypse had occurred, yet the old society which he had pronounced dead in *Hangover Square* was doggedly persisting:

One goes up to town and wades through glass-strewn streets and rubble-blocked ways and still-smoking buildings to one's destination, wondering whether it will still be there – and the phones being out of order causes incredible anxiety generally. But again it is *astonishing* how quickly the town pulls round, and establishes a new *modus vivendi* in a few days. People of course are 'wonderful'. What one can put up with when one has to![40]

Life in the many mansions of Hamilton's life was satisfactory, as Hamilton jocularly complained to Bruce, who must have had difficulty mustering much sympathy, 'such a rackety life nowadays – in so many different sets – all apart and yet having to be attended to – the Michaels, the Cockburns, the Linnits – including one or two Amours (light-hearted, non-George Boney ones, but taking up a lot of time.)'[41]

These amours were a product of Hamilton's filial relationship to his golfing friend, Bill Linnit, who appears lightly disguised as the handsome, cynical, womanizing theatrical agent, Eddie Carstairs, in *Hangover Square*. Eddie is Hamilton and George's opposite: 'He didn't look as though he was particularly interested in women; or rather he looked as though he was on the whole too successful with women to be particularly interested in them.'[42] Eddie's philosophy is one that Hamilton had never previously been able to accept in theory, let alone put into practice:

'There's only one thing that's any good with a certain type of woman, you know,' went on Eddie. 'Ask her for what you want, ask her whether she means to give it to you, and if she doesn't, throw her out of the window.'

They all three laughed at this, because, among other things, he did not use those exact words, but more vulgar, vivid and racy ones.[43]

These scenes where George Bone meets the successful theatrical people in Brighton embody Hamilton's own duality, as an insider who felt that he was an outsider. In his own life, the author of *Hangover Square* was more at home with the successes that dazzle George than with the Earl's Court failures which torment him. Back at the time of his obsession with Lily Connolly, Hamilton's friends were urging him simply to pay her money, possess her and forget her, if not in those exact words, as Hamilton would say. The only surviving accounts of Hamilton's sexual activities, such as they were, are those by Bruce and these must be treated with caution since the brothers' discussions on the subject consisted largely of mutual commiseration. For many years Bruce was paralyzed by the anxiety that he was 'uniquely unattractive to women'[44] and Hamilton insisted to his older brother that he was 'every bit as bad'.[45] Bruce reports that, due to the lack of a sexual relation with Loïs, Hamilton had 'as before [his marriage], to go with tarts; not however very frequently and usually when tight.'[46] One of them, according to Bruce, had been of great help to him as a 'steady'; she was not only attractive, but nice-natured, amusing, intelligent, imaginative, and happily willing to indulge the idiosyncratic deviations from absolute normality that Hamilton shared with almost every normal man (though few admit it) and which with him was a mild form of masochism. This intermittent relationship lasted for many years. But it could never be fully satisfactory in averting reactions producing a sense of delinquency and shame.[47]

Now, it seems, under Bill's tutelage Hamilton was able to engage in some more straightforward, brief affairs. As Bruce noted approvingly: 'There was one girl whom Hamilton knew and was attracted by, and with whom, taking advice from his mentor, he managed to spend a night that gave him great pleasure, no reaction, and no shame – and what was better still, no emotional commitment.'[48] Bill Linnit's supposed wisdom in sexual matters seems to have amounted to little more than the unremarkable old theatre and film world tradition of preying on young actresses who frequently felt, or knew, themselves to be in a position that prevented their saying no to those with power in the profession. Yet even under Linnit's influence, Hamilton seems to have obtained little significant sexual satisfaction.

His principal new friend referred to above was Claud Cockburn, the iconoclastic journalist, author of the subversive subscription periodical, *The Week*, and probably the wittiest communist in Britain. For several years he and Hamilton were close companions, and each was of use to the other. Cockburn was an intermediary between Hamilton and the Communist Party, with whom Hamilton always had distant and awkward relations. Accounts of Hamilton based solely on Cockburn's testimony must always be regarded with grave suspicion, since he was celebrated as an embellisher or even an inventor of good stories, but he claims to have defended Hamilton when he was accused of being a fascist because of the uncanny accuracy of his portrait of Peter in *Hangover Square*, supposedly denoting an intimacy with the Blackshirt movement.[49] He also provided virtually the only personification of a communist – a drinker, storyteller; upper-class renegade – that appealed to Hamilton.

For his part, Hamilton could help the notoriously indigent and improvident Cockburn. He arranged for Constable to commission Cockburn to write his memoirs, he lent him money, and he even put him up when Cockburn was bombed out during the war. Above all, he was, as Hamilton described him when he first mentioned his name to Bruce, 'a *grand* drinking companion with a sense of humour the nearest thing to our own that I have ever met.'[50] The friendship coincided with, if it did not provoke, a new and higher level in Hamilton's drinking. And along with this he still met Martha Smith and Michael Sadleir in Gordon's Wine House, near the Constable offices, where he drank sherry.[51]

By the autumn of 1941, the production of *Gaslight* was confirmed for New York under the dull new title, *Angel Street*. Hamilton was cautiously hopeful: 'It would be nice if it was a success and made some money – but one can't feel very excited because the Americans have such funny ideas and one suspects they are going to put it on all wrong. However, one never knows.'[52]

The production, which starred Vincent Price, perfectly cast as Mr Manningham, could not have opened at a worse time, two days before Pearl Harbour, and initial box-office receipts were poor. But it recovered. Mrs Roosevelt, the wife of the President, came to see it and it turned into a major success, achieving 1,295 performances, the longest run by a foreign drama in Broadway history.

The success may have been in part a result of at least one of the dreaded American ideas. One perceptive audience member, David O. Selznick, the producer of the screen versions of *Rebecca* and *Gone with the Wind*, recalled

the moment which, more than everything else in the play combined, made *Angel Street* such a sensational success in New York – that in which the detective left his hat. This was perhaps the most widely discussed moment in the history of melodrama in this generation of theater. I saw the play in New York, and never before have I witnessed anything in the theater remotely approaching the effectiveness of this particular scene. The audience was so terrified that part of it literally stood to its feet and screamed, with at least a third of the audience screaming at the stage, 'The hat! The hat!' When the detective returned for the hat, I cannot describe the audience's relief and pleasure. I think it would be worth almost anything to buy this particular moment from the owners of the play.[53]

This *coup de théâtre* is not in Hamilton's text, where Inspector Rough doesn't even wear a hat, but an inventive piece of stage business inserted in the Broadway production. The money came to him just the same. Even before the play had opened in America, Hamilton was aware of a shift in his fortunes:

Oddly enough, in this war, I have been astonishingly successful – have taken a sort of dialectical leap into a much higher plane of success. They seem to read my books and put on my plays everywhere! – the BBC never put on anything else! – but of course one can hardly respond to this sort of thing under these ghastly conditions – and it is such an utterly *different* sort of success to the one I planned for myself. However, one day one may shape it into the right mould.[54]

17

The Duke in Darkness

I

Hamilton was convinced that *Hangover Square* had been relatively easy to write because he had started it as a straightforward, unpretentious thriller. Almost as soon as he had finished it, he decided to attempt another popular form, 'a sort of high-brow "Cloak and Sword" – just as *Rope* and *Gaslight* were "high-brow" thrillers.'[1] Within a couple of months he had decided on an '*historical* melodrama! – about an imaginary imprisoned Duke in France of latter 16th century – Henry, Guise, Navarre period. What a nerve! I doubt very much whether it'll come off but I'll try and finish it, as I've got to write a play. There is, by the way, a lot of money still to be made in the provinces.'[2]

From early adolescence, when the literary Bruce had been supplanted by his younger brother, Hamilton had consistently triumphed over his own brother on his own territory. When he loudly proclaimed that he was writing *Hangover Square* as a straightforward thriller, he was once more appropriating a genre in which Bruce had specialized, and with his Midas touch he had achieved a success Bruce must have viewed with mixed feelings. Hamilton had been encouraging Bruce in his ambition to tackle an historical theme for many years, but now he decided to attempt it himself. The story of his new play, *The Duke in Darkness*, derived from an idea he had first put to Bruce back in 1928. Hamilton had suggested a play about Napoleon in exile on St Helena:

We might do it together. How about calling it
LONGWOOD
A Comedy.
and do it in the Uncle Vanya manner, with those terrible, and infinitely laughable and pathetic nerve storms with Gourgaud. Gourgaud, who weeps, and raves, and is soothed, and called a 'baby' by his master, whom he at last discovers is an 'Egoist' (a little late in the day!). And the mildew and the rats and the storms and the Governor. Tell me what you think of this. We really might take it up together as a hobby and make something great of it.[3]

Hamilton felt more admiring about Napoleon than this would suggest. In his previous letter to Bruce he had gone so far as to describe Napoleon, in terms reminiscent of his father, as 'the greatest man that ever lived'.[4]

Hamilton changed the setting to sixteenth-century France, Gourgaud became Gribaud but his character, 'dark, wiry, quick-moving, pale, passionate, and feverish'[5] is the same. Napoleon had become the Duke of Laterraine, imprisoned for fifteen years in one room, against the wishes of the common people who support him. And an idea originally conceived as comic had become a suspense melodrama. In executing his plan, Hamilton had not finally decided whether the play should depend on a compelling idea, as with his two previous successes, or whether it should simply be a full-blooded drama, and he included the ingredients of both. For five years the Duke has feigned blindness, in order to reduce the vigilance of his guards, and there are some tense manoeuvrings as an antagonist attempts to test its authenticity. And then, finally, in order to escape, and help his country, the Duke must sacrifice his old friend, Gribaud, who has gone mad and is now a liability to the cause.

Bill Linnit was enthusiastic and he approached Milton Rosmer who had made such a success of Rough in *Gaslight*. Though impressed, Rosmer was doubtful of his own ability to play the lead, or to find good enough actors for the other main roles: 'As a conventional play it is so unusual that one hesitates to guess what its appeal might be.'[6] This may just have been his polite way of saying that he didn't believe the play had commercial possibilities. Whatever his views, Rosmer was contracted elsewhere but the play soon attracted the keen interest of Michael Redgrave, who directed the production and took the bravura role of

Gribaud as well. (The Duke was played by Leslie Banks, who would be the Chorus in Laurence Olivier's film of *Henry V* in 1944.) Hamilton was delighted and later looked back affectionately on his relationship with Redgrave:

I think M. R. was the most intelligent actor I ever met. . . . I have many happy memories of the days when he and I were working together. He could drink square with me – and that is saying a lot – and he *did* drink square with me! We used to 'tire the sun with talking and send him drinking down the sky'. Also he was a Bolshie of just about my weight – and I'm sure he still is.

I shall always remember him telling me (oddly enough in dead sobriety, while having tea at a hotel in Leeds) that the business of a *producer* (I think you know he produced, as well as acting in, 'The D. in D.') was to bring out the *intentions of the author*. This is a most unusual attitude for a producer to take – amongst actors it is practically unknown. Actors and producers generally think that authors don't properly understand the business – and, of course, they are more often than not *right*.[7]

Redgrave's enthusiasm and his respect for the author were not accompanied by commercial success. The play opened in September 1942 at the Lyceum Theatre, Edinburgh, and then on 8 October at the St James's Theatre, London. But after a mixed press, 'some rave, some ferociously anti', it ran for just two months. Three years later Michael Redgrave would give one of his greatest performances in a strikingly similar role, as a possessed ventriloquist in the film, *Dead of Night*.

In retrospect, at least, it is clear enough why *The Duke in Darkness* failed, and why it has rarely been revived. It lacks the sheer mechanical tension that make *Rope* and *Gaslight* so irresistible, whatever their limitations. The two killers in the first and Mr Massingham in the second are both perverse, psychopathic artists, manipulating their dupes, and the action of each has a terrifying clarity. But Hamilton never found a good enough reason for the Duke to feign blindness, it doesn't justify itself in dramatic terms, and it becomes a tiresome encumbrance rather than a source of increasing tension. The same can be said for the factitious moral dilemma concerning the murder of Gribaud.

The young poet, Arnold Rattenbury, who was working for the communist literary periodical, *Our Time*, met Hamilton while he was writing *The Duke in Darkness*, 'usually drugged and always propped up in bed when I called on him as messenger-boy from the office. . . . Given his condition when I saw him, and my unimportance, he said very little I can remember – except once. I had mumbled something about my sense of wonder at his play. "So you noticed?" he said, straining forward from the pillows, "There, the Duke's speech, at the top of the page – there – it's a paraphrase of Lenin's *One Step Forward, Two Steps Back*," and then sank down again into stupor.'[8]

For the first time in his theatrical career, Hamilton had felt constrained by his need to make a public, political statement. There is nothing necessarily wrong with polemic, or anything else, in art. But the speeches in *The Duke in Darkness* are written by Hamilton in his perfunctory, public-spirited Ensa mood:

DUKE: No. Listen to me. I can see these things. I have had time, in my long, long darkness behind these walls, to see these things. Just as I can see a board of chess, and the whole game to the end. And at the end, the game belongs to the people. You can work yourself into every kind of rage – you can suppress and dominate and torture them, as you do, in their hundreds and hundreds of thousands – for years. And after you, for years, or hundreds of years, there will be those to follow you, as dark or darker than you, to carry on your work. But still, this will not destroy the people. This will make them learn and live the more. You are condemned, however long and cruelly the battle is waged. And then the people will be all the world, and the world all the people – and the world will be its fair self, not the wild arena of slaughter, devilry, and misery it is now.[9]

The Duke in Darkness, with its jejune ideas shackled to the medieval mummery of its setting and language, bears a disconcerting resemblance to the fiction of Bernard Hamilton. The opening of the play, in particular, is strikingly reminiscent of the passage in *Coronation* quoted above, page 17). There were good personal reasons why Hamilton couldn't be a writer of cheery propaganda.

II

Early in 1940, Hamilton had received a surprising and gratifying letter from Michael Sadleir, who had been re-reading his early novels. He was particularly struck by *Craven House*. He had some objections to the early pages but then concluded: 'The book is grand entertainment. If only it was simpler at the beginning! I suppose it's hopeless to expect you to go over it for a new edition? It ought to be a standard thing of its kind; but many readers must have been baffled by the involutions and ironies and parentheses of those early chapters.'[10] Hamilton was understandably grateful for this, 'just at this time, when I am at last writing a book and thinking of myself as a writer again, it gave me an enormous fillip.' He expressed interest in revising *Craven House* but he was unable to undertake it for some time, any more than he could fulfil Val Gielgud's hopeful commission for him to 'write a similar play [to *To the Public Danger*] with the man who refuses to recognize the blackout as the villain of the piece as opposed to the drunkard in charge of a car.'[11]

Two years later, in the wake of *Hangover Square*'s success, Sadleir wrote again, having now re-read *Craven House* 'really carefully' and with even more enthusiasm.[12] Hamilton took up the task and scrutinized his now sixteen-year-old novel. He did some pruning. In particular, the jocose chapter headings were cut back almost entirely. The original heading of chapter four, book one, reads: 'Pities a Little Girl: wonders at sundry Tribal Beliefs: is Reticent about a Tramp: deprecates a Little Boy's treatment of a Little Girl, and describes, in General, a Sunday at Craven House, before the War.' This is replaced in the revised version by 'Sunday at Craven House'.

Authorial revision performed in later years is generally either trivial or damaging. Most of Hamilton's revisions are of the first kind. In 1926 he had written:

It is Elsie's moment. She wears more than a queenly and self-reliant look now. She is a queen entire. And lifting her figure even higher than queens are supposed to, and wearing a little dim smile that all the more charming queens must have worn, she delivers herself of her last remark on the matter.[13]

Re-reading this in 1942, he did little more than fidget with the text:

It is Elsie's moment. She wears more than a queenly and self-reliant look now. She is a queen entire. And lifting her figure even higher than a queen might have to, and wearing a little dim smile that all the more charming queens might have worn, she delivers herself of her last remark on the matter.[14]

1 & 2 Bernard Hamilton and Ellen Hamilton at about the time of their marriage.

3 Patrick's birthplace: Dale House, Hassocks.

4 Ellen Hamilton with her youngest son, Patrick. 5 Bruce, Lalla and six-year-old Patrick.

6 The successful young author Patrick Hamilton, photographed in 1931. 7 Patrick Hamilton's adoring brother, Bruce, at a similar age. They would always look strikingly alike.

8 The young actress Diana Hamilton, *née* Helen Hamilton, known to her family as Lalla.
9 Lalla's husband, Vane Sutton Vane, whose play, *Outward Bound*, brought an unaccustomed taste of success to the Hamilton family.

10 The bookmark of Patrick Hamilton's father, the motif of which was later adapted for the ring fraudulently worn by the confidence trickster, Ernest Ralph Gorse, in *The West Pier*.
11 Hamilton's first wife, Loïs.

12 & 13 Hamilton's two closest friends, Charles Mackehenie and Michael Sadleir.

14 Lalla, the never-more-than-moderately-successful West End actress.

15 The original production of *Rope* at the Ambassadors Theatre in 1929.
Ernest Milton is on the right.

16 A revival of *Rope* by the Barbados Players Green Room Theatre Club in 1955.
Bruce Hamilton is at the centre, standing with a cane; Aileen Hamilton is seated at far left.

17 The climactic scene of *Gaslight* in its original production at the Richmond Theatre, 1938.

18 Hamilton's second wife, Lady Ursula. 19 Patrick Hamilton at forty-six in a photograph
that, in his own words, makes him look 'jolly handsome'.

20 & 21 Bruce and Lalla Hamilton in middle age.

22 A unique photograph of Hamilton in an affable mood. The retouching to disguise the scar on his nose is plainly visible.

23 Patrick Hamilton at the height of his success, photographed in his rooms at Albany by Bill Brandt during the Second World War.

The heavier cuts fall on the sentimental final love scene. From the following passage in the original version, for example, Hamilton cut the final four words:

'I think you would be making a mistake,' says Elsie.

Which throws Master Wildman into more dazzled ecstasies. 'A Mistake! She thinks he would be Making a Mistake! A Mistake! A Mistake! Oh, you glorious ridiculousness.'[15]

The general effect of the changes would be undetectable to anybody who didn't have the two texts side by side. The re-issue had two more important results. It brought a good novel back before the public, where it was praised once more by James Agate and swiftly sold out its print run (but could not be reprinted because of wartime paper restrictions). It also restored the closeted world of Craven House itself to Hamilton's imagination. The influence may already be seen in *The Duke in Darkness*, with its idea of confinement and ultimate escape. But Hamilton was also starting to think of a new novel.

This was held up because he was frantically busy, largely with his expanding business and social life. There was some war work. In the middle of 1942 he became adviser for plays with the Soviet embassy, 'which means play-reading and more work and darting about'.[16] There were also two hiccups in his dealings with Bruce. He was unable to find a suitable job for him, but cheerfully suggested once more a return to writing: 'There is a terrific boom in books nowadays (as there is also in the theatre) incredible as it may seem.'[17] Six months later, when he received Bruce's cricket novel, *Pro: An English Tragedy*, his response was a masterpiece of faint praise and ambiguous enthusiasm: 'It is more than up to standard and I daresay your best book – I am not quite sure. The whole conception is magnificent – as a conception, I mean – a subject I should have adored to tackle myself if I had the requisite know-ledge . . .'[18] Hamilton criticized Bruce's undisciplined use of autobiographical material and suggested that he had attacked a large subject in too modest a way. And he asked rhetorically, and devastatingly: 'Is the (to me and many others) exquisitely interesting cricket stuff going to fail to interest and to some extent become tedious to the general public?'

Pro, Bruce's best novel, is an authentic curiosity, rather as if a sporting tale for schoolboys were to have been rewritten by Thomas Hardy in the manner of *Jude the Obscure*. Edwin 'Teddy' Lamb attempts to follow in the footsteps of his father, Albert, a famous cricketer. He has moments of success, particularly when he invents a new kind of delivery, 'Q-bowling', but he enters into a disastrous marriage and then is injured on a tour of the West Indies. He loses his money and the injury gradually destroys his career. He takes to drink, falls into destitution and ends, like George Bone, by putting his head in a gas oven.

As a portrait of failure, *Pro* is genuinely harrowing and it is difficult not to read it, at least partially, as an allegory of his own failure to live up to the achievements of his brother. The book's conclusion, as Teddy prepares to kill himself, is both powerful and a sign of artistic failure:

Was it his fault? . . . Had there always been some fundamental weakness about his character? Even in his mood of self-chastisement he was doubtful. Surely he had shown, more than once, determination in conquering obstacle after obstacle, in becoming a professional cricketer at all, in making himself a good bowler by dint of unremitting practice, in contriving his 'Q-bowling', in turning himself into a spin bowler when his 'Q-bowling' was stopped, in successfully working up his batting when his bowling arm let him down. Was that the record of a weakling? At what point in time had the change come, his defences broken down, his will and character been undermined, so that he was left alone and exposed to a wretched old age? Was it perhaps that all men had only a certain reserve of energy and resistance to draw on, and that he had by ill chance and evil circumstances, been compelled to expend his too prodigally? Or had the War, those shiftless dangerous years, unprofitably squandered in the critical prime of his youth, taken its belated toll? Certainly it was then that he had learned to drink, and his generally successful contest against a besetting temptation had only ended in capitulation almost the other day.[19]

Too often Bruce seemed baffled by his characters and their fates, not because of their complexity but rather as if he lacked the literary confidence, or ruthlessness, to mould his characters to a plot, to create an alternative world. Hamilton was often similarly baffled when it came to the events of his own life, but for him literature was a realm of order.

Pro is indeed a tragic tale, totally unrelieved by the terrible comedy Hamilton found even in the darkest extremity. Like George Bone, Teddy is commemorated in death with a bathetic newspaper obituary, but Bruce would never have dared to risk Bone's farcical epitaph, the final lines of *Hangover Square*:

SLAYS TWO

FOUND GASSED

THINKS OF CAT

Tragic also that Bruce's best book should, as Hamilton shrewdly suggested, disqualify itself from the serious attention it deserved. There are aesthetic problems that make sport inescapably difficult to place at the centre of a novel, but there is also the non-aesthetic problem that a large section of the reading public is lost at a stroke.

There was a long delay in obtaining a response from Cresset Press, who had published *Traitor's Way*, but in September 1943 they accepted *Pro* and offered an advance of £50. No publication date was fixed because of limitations on the supply of paper. In the event, it was published after the war, in 1946.

III

Angel Street ran on Broadway right through 1943 and Hamilton was making, in his own words, 'an astounding amount of money'.[20] In the first half of the year Hamilton, uncharacteristically, yielded to the temptation to cash in on its success by writing 'another Victorian thing', eventually called *The Governess*, which showed Inspector Rough in action at an earlier period of his life. Hamilton considered it 'more than up to standard' but the response of those who read it was less favourable. An attempt to persuade John Gielgud to produce it came to nothing.[21]

This was frustrating, but Hamilton had no need of extra money. Almost sheepishly, he told Bruce that he had acquired a set of rooms in Albany, an institution on the north side of Piccadilly best described as a cross between an apartment block and a gentleman's club (those other successful playwrights, J. B. Priestley and Terence Rattigan, also had rooms there): 'This may seem awfully extravagant but I have got in on the cheapest possible terms, and its being so central and quiet is really worth its weight in gold. I have *got* to *have* a place in London nowadays.'[22] This was reasonable enough. Albany was just a few minutes walk from Michael Sadleir and Martha Smith at Constable to the east, and from Bill Linnit at O'Bryen, Linnit and Dunfee to the north. Audrey Heath and Patience Ross at A. M. Heath were just across the road. Hamilton was busier in London than ever, and getting back to Henley in the evening was a chore under wartime conditions.

The acquisition of a flat may have been logical, especially since Hamilton could now readily afford it, but it was also ominous. Since his move to West Kensington when he was nineteen, perhaps even since he boarded at Holland House, the place he had slept in had not been a home but a temporary refuge, to be abandoned in its turn when professional and personal conflicts became intolerable. With the success of his novels, New Cavendish Street was an escape from the family. Overy Staithe was an escape from the social distractions of London. When his work got into a rut, his solution was to flee to Henley. He always saw these rented accommodations as retreats and accorded them little value in their own right. On a later visit to Overy Staithe, Bruce observed Hamilton behaving like 'a fugitive from justice expecting arrest at any moment', appalled by the prospect of meeting anyone he knew. Now he was growing tired of Henley – 'because the people there got on top of me and never let me work', he would later say.[23]

The sequence of evasions had brought him back to his starting point, the West End of London. The flat in Henley was maintained for years to come, but Hamilton now needed a refuge from his refuge. As the widening fissures of the next years were to show, the relationship with Loïs was failing, even in its rigidly constrained, negotiated form. Loïs, on the whole, had stoically accepted an arrangement which, after all, she had entered into with open eyes. She organized, decorated, cooked and was out of the way when Hamilton fell in love. But her very efficiency increasingly counted against her as she became a resented matron whose supervision had to be evaded.

Some years later, Compton Mackenzie would tell Hamilton that the idea of trying to work in London was lunacy: 'London, he said, was a place for business and fun – then you had to retire to the country and get down to it.'[24] Mackenzie kept to this and lived to be eighty-nine. Even at its most successful and assured, Hamilton's life had always been a precarious balance, and he had explored this balance in his fiction. In *Gaslight* Rough describes whisky as being something 'between ambrosia and methylated spirits'.[25] In *Hangover Square* George Bone confesses: 'I hate drinking really.'[26] In *The Slaves of Solitude* the timid Miss Roach is initially liberated by alcohol: 'She felt the drink affecting her potently, but this time the result was not one of making her unhappy, of setting her on edge, but of composing her beautifully, of balancing and refreshing her.'[27] The effects on Hamilton became less controllable, and the balance began to waver. The principal means of restricting his drinking had been to restrict the opportunities to indulge in it. Now he was in London, he drank more heavily, more often and the drinking even spread back to Henley. Hamilton confessed to Bruce that he was now seeing less of Claud Cockburn 'because I *daren't* drink on his scale. Did I tell you of the *spectacular* drunk I had with him down at Henley?'[28]

Hamilton complained of being 'badgered on all sides – theatre people, film people, Ensa, firewatching, lack of help (we have no maid and have to do everything ourselves at Henley now)'. The result of this, and domestic details which he described as not communicable, was that his life had become 'a complete shambles, intellectually and emotionally'. He had been drinking too much and made himself ill.[29]

And the money was still coming. Hamilton was a desirable commodity. In the autumn of 1943, Twentieth-Century Fox offered £1,000 for the film rights to *Hangover Square*. Hamilton was not interested and turned them down. Hollywood has always had a particular respect for people who despise the movies and are not interested in making them. So Fox increased the offer to £2,500 and then to £5,000. Hamilton was still not sure, and he mused about the problem to his brother, who had recently been offered a £50 advance for *Pro*:

What a racket! I don't know whether I should take this or not. The point is that the money I eventually get will be absolutely *negligible* – and I don't want them to make a balls up of the film. If I knew they would do it properly I would let them have it for much less. In the meantime I am trying to sell the idea to Hitchcock (who is over in London and wants me to do something I've refused to do). What a film he could make of it, couldn't he?[30]

Early in 1944 Hamilton accepted Fox's offer, estimating that he would receive no more than £250 of it. Having paid a reasonably large sum, the producers then removed everything except the title, the schizophrenia device and the idea of murder. The period was changed to 1903, Bone became a pianist, composer and mass murderer. And, as James Agate, one of the book's leading admirers, concluded his angry denunciation of the film:

Apart from one tiny shot, no drink is consumed, and everybody in the film might be teetotal. The atmosphere of that kind of saloon bar which reeks of yesterday's fug and fumes is at no time suggested, nor is there any hint anywhere of that hangover which thickens every page of Hamilton's little masterpiece of frowst. In a word, this is the worst betrayal of a first-class novel that I ever remember . . .[31]

Such was the hostile, patriotic reaction on behalf of a betrayed British author that the film's director, John Brahm, felt compelled to mount a defence and he sent a cable to a British newspaper:

In the book the characters, particularly the women, are of a most unsavoury nature, so a nice new girl was added to provide some good element.

The period was changed to 1903 on the grounds that, in modern times, Bone would have been captured after a first murder by modern methods of crime detection, and that multiple slaughter would have been impossible.[32]

This self-inculpating defence demonstrates little more than Brahm's ignorance of the original novel. On its own terms, the film is an atmospheric, impressive thriller, superbly designed and with a fine musical score by Bernard Herrmann. The young V. S. Naipaul saw it in Trinidad, and in a complex way its portrait of London fused with his later reading of the novels. Hamilton was furious even though he must have known that a faithful adaptation of the novel would have been impossible at that time, whoever had undertaken it.

He was no better pleased with the considerably more faithful re-make of *Gaslight* starring Charles Boyer and Ingrid Bergman (and retitled *Murder in Thornton Square*): 'I don't get a *penny* from this – and the film opens in Milan! – Bergman sings four songs in the course of the production! – and the detective *marries* Mrs Manningham!! What a racket! I shall protect myself more carefully in future.'[33] Apart from the shift in the social scale, which, in any case, is not intrusive, the adaptation is faithful to the spirit of the original and is, arguably, an improvement on it. What is most effective in the play, the domestic torture applied by the husband to the wife and her fear that she might be mad, is given more emphasis, and the mechanics of the plot, the husband's motivation, the reason for the detective's involvement, are made much more plausible. The independent producer, David O. Selznick, took an interest in the film because he had lent MGM two of his stars, Ingrid Bergman and Joseph Cotten, and the long letter he wrote to Louis B. Mayer, after seeing a rough-cut, suggesting scenes that ought to be re-shot, is a masterpiece of professional analysis.[34]

The danger of the gloomy early years of the war had excited Hamilton. In the final year, when ultimate victory was just a matter of time, his mood changed: 'I think the war is going to be over fairly soon, and curiously enough the consciousness of this makes it about ten times more difficult to bear than in any other period of it. It is a sort of nightmare within the nightmare.'[35] His mood fluctuated as he swung through periods of heavy drinking and abstinence, social life and isolation, work and paralysis. In the summer of 1944 he was finding his new novel impossible, and he saw no prospect of *The Governess* being staged until after the war. Within a couple of weeks he had cheered up, having resigned at last from Ensa. Shortly after that, a production of *The Governess* was decided on and Flora Robson, then one of the most distinguished actresses in Britain, took the leading role, though the rest of the casting proved difficult. Hamilton complained that actors were 'as scarce as butter and eggs', though Milton Rosmer was available to take his old role as Rough. But the production itself demanded a great deal of travel up to Glasgow where it was opening and this would now take up more of his time and keep him from what Bruce had recently described as his true vocation, novel writing.[36]

It proved to be a peculiarly frustrating distraction. Hamilton spent six moderately promising weeks, travelling in 'hellish conditions', superintending the play's progress through a series of minor theatres. Then, when it ought to have transferred to the West End, there was a problem. As Flora Robson later recalled, 'London plays, even bad ones, had long runs, and we could not get in.'[37] No theatre was available for it, or became available for the rest of 1945. In the end the production never reached the West End stage, nor was the text ever published.

18

The Slaves of Solitude
and Peace

I

For Hamilton the war had lost its dark glamour and had taken on a bustling, tawdry tedium. This was symbolized for him above all by the ubiquitous, noisy presence of American servicemen. In one letter to Bruce, written in a railway compartment full of American soldiers 'screaming the place down', he complained: 'With all the good will in the world, I must say these allies of ours are a dreadful misery socially – they are absolutely everywhere – like locusts – and they are at last getting on everyone's nerves – poor things.'[1]

In conceiving his new novel, which by November 1944 already had its final title, *The Slaves of Solitude*, Hamilton drew on all the experiences of the previous year, except for his success with *Gaslight*. His revision of *Craven House* suggested the idea of a claustrophobic, conflict-ridden dwelling. Henley, dully distant from the danger, provided the setting. The locust-like Americans, feeding off what the locals cannot afford, are in the background. If *Hangover Square* was a pre-apocalypse book, then *The Slaves of Solitude* takes place in the bathetic post-apocalypse period. As with *Hangover Square* it is a mistake to give too much emphasis to the novel as a quasi-journalistic evocation of a period. Hamilton's disingenuous prefatory note asserts that the novel's principal setting, the Rosamund Tea Rooms, 'resembles no boarding house in this town [Henley] or in any other, though it is hoped that it resembles in some features every small establishment of this sort all over the country.'

This may be true of the boarding house's more trivial details, but from

Miss Roach's perspective, Mr Thwaites, the dominant figure staying at the Rosamund Tea Rooms, is 'president in hell'.[2] If *Hangover Square* was a poem of humiliation, then *The Slaves of Solitude* is a poem of fear, and again – and more convincingly than before – Hamilton's imagination fuses his private experience with the dimly perceived world of history outside. In comic, distorted form, the savageries of the war are re-enacted in a provincial boarding house. But the novel is not an allegory. Rather, it is Hamilton's attempt to make a connection between large historical forces, the evil that we read about in the newspapers, and the squabbles and petty struggles that make up quotidian individual existence.

And, as always, when exploring horror Hamilton is at his most personal. When we first see Miss Roach enter the Rosamund Tea Rooms she hides upstairs to avoid the bullying Mr Thwaites but can still hear his voice 'booming nasally, indefatigably, interminably'. As a young man, Hamilton would avoid his father in just the same way. He once reported to Bruce (he was twenty-three at the time):

I am at the moment trapped in my bedroom, our papa having returned from New Zealand and paying his first call here to-day. I can hear him from here, (I'm in our 'Den') occasionally murmuring, elephanting into his room, and having conversations with Mummie.

The gong will ring in half an hour and I shall go down cheerfully and listen to murmurings.[3]

The terrible Thwaites, stupid and crude, is not a straightforward portrait of the far more intelligent and charismatic Bernard, but to portray him at his most appalling, Hamilton draws on his father's idiosyncratic langu-age. Thwaites's use of absurd archaic phraseology is much in the style of Bernard Hamilton. His drunken response to being told to keep quiet, 'By the Lord Hal . . . A Veritable Thrust!', could be a quotation from Bernard's novel about Prince Hal, *Coronation*. And at his very worst, Thwaites is given one of Bernard's own lines. In his late attempt at a memoir, Hamilton recalls an intoxicated Bernard observing the girl behind the cashier at a French restaurant, and speaking in his supposedly French accent, 'looking leeringly at the girl, and intending her to hear, "Ah – but yess – she is a buxom little woman! And she knows it, too!" '[4] Mr Thwaites speaks similarly of Vicki:

'She's a tease all right, isn't she? Yes – she's a tease – isn't she?'

This was bad. Was it possible that two sips of whisky (two inexperienced and enormous sips) had gone to his head?

'Yes,' said Mr. Thwaites, 'she's a vamp all right! She's a tease. And she knows it, too. Doesn't she? What?'[5]

The portrait of the two American officers is skilful, though not entirely escaping the stereotyped portrayal of the subject in the curiously similar *The Way to the Stars*, a movie (written by Hamilton's fellow Albany resident, Terence Rattigan) largely set in a country residential public house, which was released to great acclaim in 1945, when Hamilton was still writing *The Slaves of Solitude*.

But the rendering of the German émigré, Vicki Kugelmann, is one of Hamilton's greatest and most unsettling achievements. He captures her deft but atrocious use of English idioms with the literary equivalent of perfect pitch. Vicki uses her friendship with Miss Roach to commandeer Lieutenant Pike and to invade the Rosamund Tea Rooms but, until a very late stage, the reader cannot be sure exactly what to make of Miss Roach's hatred of her. Is there not some truth in Vicki's repeated accusation that Miss Roach is staid, prim, inhibited? The ambiguity is tellingly maintained even at the violent climax. Miss Roach's fury is finally released when Thwaites suddenly asserts that she has only denounced Vicki because she has been scorned. His statement is ugly, but may also contain an element of truth, that Miss Roach is furious with Vicki because she stole the American away from her. Then, comically and disgustingly, we discover that the accusation concerns not the American but a British adolescent boy in whom Miss Roach has been taking an affectionate, entirely maternal interest.

The achievement of a happy ending for Miss Roach is a dark variation on the climax of *The Plains of Cement*. There Ella has the possibility of inheriting money from her sick father-in-law. She guiltily wishes him dead but he recovers. Her limited, stoical achievement is to reject Mr Eccles. By contrast, Miss Roach's triumph is complete, but achieved through a combination of luck and shocking violence. She defeats Vicki by inheriting money from a providentially dead relative. She defeats Thwaites by striking him with a blow which may be partly responsible for his subsequent death.[6]

Rope was a callow, spuriously moralistic portrayal of two boys killing for kicks. In *Hangover Square* and *The Slaves of Solitude*, Hamilton's two most passive leading characters, George Harvey Bone and Miss Roach, in the end can only define themselves through killing those who claw at them and hold them down. The first instance is tragic, but in the second case Miss Roach fulfils herself, even apparently becoming more physically attractive as a result of finally asserting herself.[7]

Miss Roach's escape from Henley is also Hamilton's. This accounts for the savagery of the portrait of the town when Albert Brent, a piano tuner, suddenly arrives on the scene to provide a neutral view of the boarding house's guests 'in this dead-and-alive dining-room, of this dead-and-alive house, of this dead-and-alive street, of this dead-and-alive little town – in the grey, dead winter of the deadliest part of the most deadly war in history'.[8] The incongruous sentimentality of the final words, one of the book's few wrong notes, as Miss Roach falls asleep, 'God help us, God help all of us, every one, all of us', may be best explained as oblique, deflected self pity.

As soon as Hamilton began the novel he saw it as 'a long and would-be important book',[9] but novels now took him longer to complete. The following September, Hamilton was 'working like mad to finish the book by Christmas'[10] but the periods of intense, effective work were intermittent and it took more than another year to complete. For the final burst, Hamilton adopted his *Hangover Square* regime, sitting in bed and writing there until the early evening, breaking only to be served with meals by Loïs. The book finally appeared in the summer of 1947.

II

In May 1945 the war ended and Hamilton was able to take pleasure in 'a series of little anti-toothaches – the lifting of the black-out, the weather forecasts again, the allusions to cricket in the newspapers, the hope of petrol and a car again, the arrest of prominent Nazis etc.'[11] Hamilton's final summary of the previous six historic years, which he had anticipated for so long, was curiously simple but also heartfelt, using the analogy that for him meant more than any other: 'In fact it was all a very funny business altogether and I don't think I shall ever stop being grateful for its being over – just as I'll never stop being glad I'm not in hospital with my accident.'[12]

Hamilton's life was now superficially as it had been ten or even fifteen years earlier. Only the proportions allocated to the various pursuits were different. Attachments to friends would change. Charles Mackehenie would be replaced by Bill Linnit. Dick Clancy, the son of the man who had secured the compensation for Hamilton's accident, became a particularly close friend when he became a communist, and then a less close friend when his politics changed. Hamilton didn't care about the politics of his club friends, or his publishers, or his agents, but his left-wing friends had to stay left wing. Among his hobbies, golf and, increasingly, chess were becoming important. (The first makes a curious appearance in *Hangover Square*, the second is used clumsily in *The Duke in Darkness*, when the Duke gains an implausible checkmate in four moves.[13])

Most significantly, Hamilton's drinking had become more frequent and a good deal heavier. When Bruce arrived back from Barbados in the middle of 1946, he was shocked most of all by its compulsiveness. He calculated that Hamilton was rarely drinking less than the equivalent of three bottles of whisky a day. The cost of such extreme consumption would now scarcely be a consideration, so much has the real price of alcohol fallen, but in the austerely rationed economy of post-war Britain, which in certain respects was even worse off than it had been during the war, the relevant comparative example of consumption today would be a cocaine habit. A bottle of whisky then cost about twenty-five shillings, but these were hard to come by and most of Hamilton's purchases were either on the black market or at local bars or clubs. Bruce calculated that Hamilton was spending on himself – that is, without counting the money he spent on buying drinks for others – about £6 a day, which adds up to about £2,000 a year.

It is impossible to make precise comparisons, though Hamilton, who usually rented his accommodation, could certainly have bought a large, elegant house in the centre of London for half that amount. At the time that Bruce was making his calculation, the literary magazine *Horizon* published the responses to a questionnaire on 'The Cost of Letters' sent to several writers. To the question, 'How much do you think a writer needs to live on?', George Orwell replied:

At the present purchasing value of money, I think £10 a week after payment of income tax is a minimum for a married man, and perhaps £6 a week for an unmarried man. The *best* income for a writer, I should say – again at the present value of money – is about £1,000 a year. With that he can live in reasonable comfort, free from duns and the necessity to do hack work, without having the feeling that he has definitely moved into the privileged class. I do not think one can with justice expect a writer to do his best on a working-class income.[14]

And in response to a further question, Orwell estimated that 'at most a few hundred people in Great Britain earn their living solely by writing books, and most of those probably writers of detective stories'.[15]

Writers on Patrick Hamilton, beginning with Hamilton himself, feel compelled to provide explanations or motivations for his drinking. Most of these are disputable, but other aspects are not. Whether or not his success caused him to drink more, there is no doubt that without the wealth provided by *Gaslight* Hamilton could not have financed his consumption. Except on rare occasions, his drinking took place within traditional settings, with friends, in clubs and bars, and in the Britain of the late forties, substantial financial reserves were needed for that sort of heavy drinking. He was now spending money faster than he was earning it.

The effect of alcohol on the quality of Hamilton's writing is also a matter of dispute. He did not write while drunk, and generally worked on his books in periods of abstinence, or in the lesser degrees of consumption that Hamilton called abstinence. These periods of abstinence were becoming more widely spaced and, whatever the quality of his work, his writing was slowing down. The health implications were also ominous. During the times when he was drinking, he also smoked heavily and ate little. It was only during this period that Kenneth Robinson, a friendly acquaintance who saw Hamilton irregularly, became conscious of him as a seriously heavy drinker. They met for lunch at the Ivy and Hamilton only picked at his food but drank a great deal, though his companion noted that his tolerance for alcohol was 'quite considerable'.[16] Robinson's perspective is useful as a guide to the control Hamilton maintained over his life. At a time when Bruce considered his brother to be in some distress, Robinson saw a man who was 'an absolutely delightful person, extremely good company'. He was not obtrusively political, and apparently happily married: 'one of my most engaging friends'.[17]

Always, for Hamilton, there was the consciousness of his siblings' lives, running in tandem with his, versions of what he might have been. Bruce was more stable, but was, in the literary terms that meant so much to them both, a failure. When Hamilton urged him, perhaps unrealistically, to give up his teaching and commit everything to the possibility of his writing, he was only echoing what was almost a truism among major writers. In a further answer to the questionnaire quoted above, George Orwell wrote about writers financing themselves with another job, but argued that it must be something non-literary: 'I can just imagine, for instance, a bank clerk or an insurance agent going home and doing serious work in the evenings; whereas the effort is too much to make if one has already squandered one's energies on semi-creative work such as teaching, broadcasting or composing propaganda for bodies such as the British Council.'[18] On the other side, Lalla was an extreme, tragic version of Hamilton's tendency to domestic chaos, dissolution, illness. Her string of disastrous lovers, all loathed by Hamilton and Bruce, had culminated, just before the war, in an almost equally disastrous marriage to Bertie Meyer, a failed theatrical manager, twenty-five years older than she was and an old friend of Bernard's: 'Could there have been here,' Bruce asked, almost unnecessarily, 'more seriously than with Patrick, indeed disastrously, another search for a father figure?'[19] The marriage was no more successful than Bernard and Ellen's. Like Hamilton she drank heavily and suffered from periodic depression. The difference was that Lalla had neither a career nor children to divert her energies.

In October 1945 she was found to have breast cancer and had an immediate mastectomy, one breast entirely removed. By the following month the operation had been pronounced a complete success and, according to Hamilton, her principal concern was 'how to escape from Bertie who, although he had really behaved *excellently* according to his lights through all this, is a menace.'[20]

In the the last days of the war Hamilton had offered prayers to 'the Red Star in the East' that he and Bruce might meet as soon as possible, but when they were finally re-united, in the summer of 1946, the result was not entirely the anticipated success. Bruce was dismayed by Hamilton's complaints about Loïs, and even more by their bitter squabbling when they were together. He was even more concerned by his brother's drinking, by the expense, and the behaviour that accompanied it. In his own description of Hamilton's behaviour during this visit, Bruce implies that his character had been affected for the worse. In Bruce's view, he overtipped waiters and taxi-drivers in an attempt to win their favour, for which they viewed him with almost open contempt. Bruce also felt that Hamilton was needlessly submissive with friends like Bill Linnit and Claud Cockburn.[21] In assessing testimony of this kind, however, some account must be taken of the disparity between the status of the two brothers, which was even greater than on their previous meeting. Hamilton would sometimes – perhaps unthinkingly – make this brutally clear. When the two brothers went with Claud Cockburn to attend the final performance of Hamilton's play, *The Governess*, at the Embassy Theatre, Swiss Cottage, Hamilton took Cockburn, but not Bruce, backstage afterwards to meet the cast. Bruce was deeply hurt.[22]

Bruce was now in his late forties and was returning to Britain principally in order to complete a doctoral thesis on an aspect of Barbadian history. This was of only limited, academic interest, though a passage in the preface gives some sense of the island's attractions for him as compared with the rigidities and confinements of life in England:

There is a prevailing easy-going good nature, a less agreeable side of which is seen in a quite excessive tolerance of small abuses. There is a quick sense of fun, sometimes childish but often quite subtle, and capable of being effectively directed, in true British fashion, against any form of pretentiousness . . . There is a simplicity and restfulness of behaviour which creates a delightfully easy and soothing social atmosphere.[23]

Bruce's life and career were now centred on the island of Barbados. Though he continued to write novels for the whole of his residence there, he never, despite Hamilton's advice, used it as a source of material (apart from an entirely insignificant, and unevocative, few pages in *Pro*). With the exception of his last published book, the milieu of his fiction continued to be a paler version of his brother's, as if in ever more hopeless competition.

Bruce's disapproval of Hamilton's financial expenditure must be seen at least in some measure as the attitude of a poorly paid teacher – in his own words, 'long regarded as "the poor one of the family" '[24] – to a way of life to which he could now scarcely hope to aspire. He was at least partially aware of this conflict and in a journal he kept during 1946, Bruce attempted to paint an objective portrait of Hamilton's failings. He concluded that 'the answer obtained by adding together his drinking, his social preoccupations, his imperfect sincerity, the want of largeness in his existence, and the absence of real liberty and repose, either external or internal, seems to be a great danger of loss of creative power.' The cracks in their relationship devastated Bruce and forced him to reflect on the unforced love that he painfully lacked: 'In my life I have fully received such love only from Mummie and Lalla. . . . To whom have I myself been able to give good and effective love? Fully only to Patrick, I believe – and there I suppose we have represented everybody's tragedy.'[25] Yet Bruce could also pay touching tribute to Hamilton's essential kindness. He describes an occasion when they went to see the great old music-hall comedian, George Robey, now in decline, failing before an audience at the Brighton Hippodrome: 'Patrick, who had met him here and there, went round to his dressing-room. "They don't want me any more," Robey said, but Patrick vehemently denied this, telling him that though of course fashions had changed he was as good as ever, as every discriminating person in the audience knew.'[26] A generous gesture, but Bruce fails to add that Hamilton the novelist made deft use of his own consolation in the climax of *The Slaves of Solitude* where the elderly, retired comedian, Archie Prest, finally gets a role in pantomime because of the wartime shortage of actors and is a glorious success.[27]

19

Rope on Film

I

The saving of the British film industry is a recurrent mirage that always makes a good press story. Early in 1947 there was great excitement at the announcement that Alfred Hitchcock had founded a production company called Transatlantic Pictures Corporation with the British film producer, Sidney Bernstein. A six-stage studio would be built in England and the company would make films on both sides of the Atlantic. (These hopes, as so often before and after, were unfulfilled, and no studio was built.) The shooting of the first, *Under Capricorn*, was delayed by the prior commitments of its star, Ingrid Bergman. So the company fell back on their alternative project, a screen version of *Rope*.

The only surprise is that Hitchcock and Hamilton should not have worked together before. Their careers had moved in parallel, both fusing a form of urban horror with their own personal expression of sexual fear. *Gaslight* in particular expresses the theme of the manipulation or tormenting or murder of an innocent woman by a man that recurred in Hitchcock's later work. It might have been expected that they would collaborate, but although there was every opportunity for them to do so, there were considerable obstacles. Hitchcock approached Hamilton more than once for ideas, but Hamilton had even greater reservations about the cinema as a genre than he had about the theatre. For his part, Hitchcock was so dominant in the creation of his scripts that he never proved able to work with a major writer for any length of time. In fact, it was his specific policy not to do so. He was even more ruthless in his treatment of writers than he was, more publicly, in his treatment of actors. And he particularly distrusted writers who shared his interest in suspense.[1]

In 1942 when Hitchcock was working for David O. Selznick, and fast establishing himself as a major director, he was offered the chance to direct the screen version of *Gaslight*. He turned down the idea, ostensibly because he never wanted to direct another costume picture after his unhappy experiences on *Jamaica Inn* in 1939.[2] An equally important reason must have been that he had effectively made *Gaslight* twice for Selznick already. *Gaslight* was first performed in the same year that Daphne Du Maurier's novel, *Rebecca*, was published and the resemblances between the two are striking. Both are the story of a woman suffering, in different ways, at the hands of a man who has killed a woman before. (The plot had to be changed for the film version but, as Selznick assured Du Maurier, the effect was much the same.[3])

Suspicion, which Hitchcock made in the following year, gave the story another twist. A woman (played by Joan Fontaine, who also starred in *Rebecca*) gradually develops the belief that her husband (played by Cary Grant) is trying to kill her. The original story was of a woman so in love with her husband that she permits him to murder her (though the studio compelled him to change the end so that Grant turns out to be innocent).[4]

Rope was a project Hitchcock had been interested in ever since he had seen the original London production. The rights were acquired by the new company, and Hamilton himself contracted to work on the screenplay. Early in 1947 Hamilton spent three weeks, 'working stupendously', writing a play which he considered to be good. Already in a condition of exhaustion, he began work with Sidney Bernstein on the screen version of *Rope*. Bernstein was a unique figure in the British film industry, owner of the Granada cinema chain but also one of the founders of the London Film Society, the first film society in the world. Hamilton described him as a 'most *delightful* man, but, in his delightful way, a *slave-driver*!' and he considered the four weeks he spent on the film far harder than writing the original play.[5]

While it exhausted him, Hamilton also found the experience exciting. The greatest tribute Hitchcock made to the play was his decision that its adaptation demanded an extreme cinematic technique. The play takes place in real time, with no breaks (the second act begins at the very moment the first act ends). The play is like a theatrical conjuring trick and we must have the chest in view continuously in order to maintain the tension – the audience must always be sure that the body is still there. The film was not only to be Hitchcock's first in colour, but it was to be shot without cuts. He was of course constrained by the length of a reel – ten minutes – but even these changes were disguised by such tricks as blacking out the camera briefly as a character passes in front of it. As Hamilton observed:

This means that you can't switch from one scene to another. The camera, like an invisible man simply walks about the flat (or rather apartment, for it has been translated into American) and sees and hears everything. Never done before, and so, as you can imagine, a difficult job for an inexperienced screen writer.[6]

The strain of this work was so great that Hamilton immediately embarked on a three-week drinking binge. This was concluded only by a severe attack of alcoholic gastritis – an inflammation caused by the toxicity of the alcohol attacking the lining of the stomach – and Hamilton was sent to a nursing home. 'I mean to use this as the starting point for a long, long wagon,' he assured Bruce, 'so have no fears for me.'[7]

As his discontentment began to grow, Hamilton was greatly consoled by the 'rave press for *The Slaves of Solitude* – far and away the best I have ever had for anything in my life.' He was particularly gratified by an enthusiastic letter from his fellow Albany resident, Osbert Sitwell, and they had a cordial meeting. This inspired a rare reciprocal compliment from Hamilton, which was to read the work of another living writer. He reread Sitwell's novel, *After the Bombardment*, and maintained that it and Arnold Bennett's *The Old Wives' Tale* 'are the only two novels (which I have read anyway) which really add up to anything in our time.'[8]

Much of the rest of Hamilton's time was spent waiting. His contract with Hitchcock rendered him liable to be called on for six weeks' work, if necessary in Hollywood, to Hamilton's horror. But the pay was good. He had received £3,000 for the film rights and been guaranteed a further £300 a week for any additional work he did. 'So you see I could well afford the meagre £100 I sent you,' he told Bruce consolingly.[9]

Hamilton compartmentalized his writing, just as he did the other different aspects of his life. His novels were what he unreservedly valued, and what he wished to be judged by. He ranked his plays lower, though he considered them 'sincerely "insincere" '.[10] Whatever enthusiasm may have been aroused by his new experience of writing in collaboration, Hamilton continued to disapprove of the whole cinematic genre: 'Films are fundamentally no good because they are ephemeral, *ephemeral*. You must either write *printed books* or *printed plays*.'[11]

His emergence from the nursing home was followed by 'an absolutely *filthy* period of *depression* and *stagnation*'. The cause, in Hamilton's own view, was idleness 'assisted by the bottle' and one of the hottest summers of the century, to which Hamilton showed his traditional aversion:

As for the idleness – that was caused in four ways (1) Just *idleness* (2) the heat (3) being *still kept waiting about 'Rope'* and unable to settle down to anything (4) being kept waiting about my new play.

The latter is a bit of a tragedy. I had worked *enormously* hard at writing it and really thought I had pulled it off this time, and was really pleased with myself. Showed it to Bill, who hemmed and hawed. Showed it to two others, who also hemmed and hawed. Then the matter was left in abeyance for about 2 months or more (can't go into details – too complicated) and then just recently I spent a week-end with Bill. He said that, completely against his own judgement, he would put the play on in October in London in the swellest manner possible (no try-out, or Embassy nonsense). Believing passionately in the play, I accepted his offer. So I took it out and re-read it. He was right. It simply won't *do* – fundamentally hopeless – though with some rather *super* things in it – which is what makes it so tragic.[12]

About *Rope* he heard nothing, as was so often the experience of Alfred Hitchcock's screenwriters. In the autumn of 1947, Sidney Bernstein deferred to his partner and his collaboration with Hamilton was scrapped. Then, without informing Hamilton, Hitchcock invited Hume Cronyn (who had acted in his recent films, *Shadow of a Doubt* and *Lifeboat*) to prepare a treatment which was completed by December. Then, without telling Cronyn, Hitchcock scrapped the dialogue Cronyn had written and brought in the young playwright, Arthur Laurents, who completed a first draft before Christmas. The dominant influence was Hitchcock, introducing a vein of perverse humour and emphasizing the implicit homosexuality (though it necessarily had to remain a covert theme). Filming began in January 1948 and it was released in America in

August (though it was the following year when it reached Britain and was seen by an appalled Hamilton).[13]

In a mood of defiance (*'Bugger* plays!', he wrote to Bruce), he began what he planned to be a great novel, 'having suddenly been inspired with what I only hope and pray is a formula for this.'[14] He was so serious about his new project that he rationed his meetings with Claud Cockburn to Thursday mornings, and apart from that just 'a few evenings on the black market. And that is all.'[15]

The timing was appropriate, for Hamilton was now entering into the most tumultuous phase of his personal and professional life since the havoc of the late twenties which produced Lily Connolly and *Twenty Thousand Streets Under the Sky*.

II

Hamilton was sanguine about the new novel. He aimed at 200,000 words and promised Michael Sadleir that he would deliver it on the first day of 1949. The final work proved to be even longer, about 250,000 words, but it would take three novels and almost five more years to finish it.

Writing in the week after his forty-fourth birthday, Hamilton felt afflicted by the 'advancing years, which make one so blasé and bored about one's own life'.[16] He was seeing less of friends, especially Bill Linnit, who had married the previous year. He repeatedly told Bruce that his drinking was under control, but the control allowed for a higher limit. He sent Michael Sadleir a cheerful postcard itemizing the expenses of a holiday in Ireland:

Good but *damp* Emerald:

	Prices.
Plain drunk	8/6
Fighting "	12/3
Blind "	18/-
Dead "	22/-[17]

Far from accelerating to meet the optimistic deadline, progress on the novel slowed and then ceased altogether, causing Hamilton to become 'idle and depressed'.[18] Once more he blamed it on his surroundings, and at the end of the year he decided to attempt a bold change of scene. Though terrified by the prospect, he rented out his Albany flat, and bought a house on the Isle of Wight, which he described as a 'tiny place', for the substantial sum of £4,500.[19]

Gradually, the varying conflicts in Hamilton's life became irreconcilable. He felt a recurring need to flee from his domestic life, yet at the same time he began to find the discomforts caused by change intolerable. His arrangement with Loïs, though designed for his convenience, chafed on him increasingly as the division between his work and his social life, London and the country, became eroded.

The Isle of Wight was an almost instant disaster, because of 'climate, people, length of journey from London, and a million other things it would take too long to go into.'[20] He went through a 'dreadful period of trying to *force* myself to like it' and then gave up. The property was quickly resold, at a loss of £500, and Hamilton was back in Albany. As always, the organizational minutiae of life were beyond him. When Loïs had been away on war work, he had confessed to being unable even to tie up a parcel on his own. So the 'bore and hard work of moving in, and now all the ditto of getting out' had been a torment, though he admitted that 'the main burden fell on Loïs'.[21]

Suddenly Hamilton saw everything in his life going wrong. He had been unable to write 'and this finally gnaws into the soul and drives one to the bottle.'[22] Lalla had been behaving in a 'tempestuous and wild manner' which had culminated in violent epileptic fits. Based on the medical advice which he had received (and kept from his sister), Hamilton believed this was most likely to be a sign that her cancer was recurring.

Then there was the loss of the friendship of Bill Linnit who had 'been a terrific source of strength during the last six years'. After Linnit's marriage, Hamilton considered that he had not merely forsaken him but had ' "changed", abandoned his old friends and, I fear, become a Socialite! – some say a Social Climber!'[23] Having been the bachelor about town, he was now playing the role of the respectable husband and Hamilton felt betrayed. He considered the strain caused by the rift was as severe as that induced by the Isle of Wight fiasco.

Hamilton's torments at this genuine crisis in his life were an almost comic mixture of the trivial and the genuinely extreme. Repairs were in progress at Albany and the builders 'banging and hammering *from morning to night for months on end*' caused Hamilton profound misery. The summer was one of '*unmentionable* heat – damp, thundery, oppressive and *incessant*'.[24] A further result of the Isle of Wight transplantation was the loss of his long-time secretary. A major tour of *Gaslight* was being arranged and acting friends were pestering him with requests for parts in it: 'how can one work if one has to answer all these letters in one's own hand, and go and be polite on the telephone?'

The long-awaited appearance of the film of *Rope* was a terrible blow, made worse because Hamilton had allowed himself to proceed despite his misgivings about the cinema: 'I had thought that working with Hitchcock was going to be heaven, and put everything I knew into it. However, he utterly rejected my script, got someone else to write it, and finally produced a film which *I* think (and all intelligent friends agree) was sordid and practically meaningless *balls*.'[25] In later years, Hitchcock himself conceded that the film was a failure, but he blamed the very technical considerations that had attracted him in the first place, in particular, the use of single takes: 'When I look back, I realize that it was quite nonsensical because I was breaking with my own theories on the importance of cutting and montage for the visual narration of a story.'[26] Nevertheless, *Rope* remains one of the most remarkable technical experiments ever attempted in the commercial cinema. The film's most significant failure is not in its lack of editing – with extraordinary ingenuity, at certain crucial moments Hitchcock makes use of composition and camera movements as a form of montage without cutting – but the failure to find a satisfactory way of ending the work, which is as much of a problem in the original play. Three years later Hitchcock remedied the mistake, if mistake it was, in one of his masterpieces, *Strangers on a Train*, which, though based on a novel by Patricia Highsmith, is essentially a deeper exploration of the same themes. The theatrical bravura of Hamilton's play cannot disguise its shallowness, its use of an atrocious subject without any attempt to explore it. In *Strangers on a Train* the two strangers meet, one a hero, one, Bruno, a psychopath. Bruno imagines the idea of two men, such as themselves, agreeing to commit each other's murders. He then proceeds to kill the hero's hateful wife. The hero is appalled, but have not his unconscious wishes been acted out? This film really does pierce the barrier between our ideas of normality and evil.

It is at least arguable that Hamilton's objections to the film were not because Hitchcock betrayed his play but that he brought out its implications too painfully. François Truffaut has argued that Hitchcock was 'a singular man, not only by virtue of his physique, but also by virtue of his spirit, his morality, and his obsessions. Unlike Chaplin, Ford, Rossellini, or Hawks, he was a neurotic, and it could not have been easy for him to impose his neurosis upon the whole world.'[27] Hitchcock used the suspense narrative in the most commercialized of art forms to express his highly personal fears, impulses and fantasies. In adapting *Rope* he took the jejune cerebral exercise that was Hamilton's text and attempted to tease out what it was that had given the play its perverse effectiveness. Hamilton claimed that the result was sordid, but this very quality is one of the potent attractions of the play. Hitchcock introduced a series of unpleasant, ironic jokes about the murder that has been committed at the beginning of the film, but then the action of the original play was itself an extended sick joke, perpetrated by the two young murderers. Hamilton's repulsion is almost a refusal to recognize that its peculiar power comes from the fact that we are watching action choreographed for the amusement of two psychopaths. Hitchcock also got closer to what had been one of the almost unmentionably shocking aspects of the original Leopold and Loeb case, the homosexuality of the two murderers. The unspoken story behind Hamilton's play is that of forbidden sexuality and the forbidden act of violence, the complicity of lovers and the complicity of criminals.

It is scarcely surprising that Hitchcock found Hamilton's own treatment of his play unsatisfactory. Hamilton's public face was that of a charming but private man. If he was to explore dark impulses in his art, which may or may not have been fantasies of his own, then he wanted to be strictly in control. *Rope* is an unsatisfactory film. Losing the power to edit, Hitchcock seems also to lose the power to control the tone and the performances, which are notably uneven. Yet this also gives the film a creepy, exposed effectiveness. Hamilton saw notions from which he had dutifully distanced himself twenty years earlier blown up on to a vast screen and made darkly hilarious.

Truffaut said perceptively of Hitchcock's work that 'the love scenes were filmed like murder scenes, and the murder scenes like love scenes',[28] and this was never more obvious than in the brazenly shocking opening sequence of the film in which we see Brandon and Philip (as they are called in the film) strangling (the likewise renamed) David Kentley. It is also one of the most viscerally homoerotic scenes ever filmed, charged with passion and danger.

The film deeply shocked Hamilton and, by his own account, it produced a drastic response that would transform his life. For some time, it is not clear how long, Hamilton had been attracted to a woman he knew. After seeing *Rope* he got drunk and became depressed. He phoned her up and went round to see her. This was the only specific occasion in his life when he would insist explicitly to Bruce that, in Bruce's own words, 'unequivocal love-making' had taken place.[29]

20

Ursula
and the Death of Lalla

I

It seems impossible to establish exactly when Hamilton first met Lady Ursula Stewart. Bruce suspected, or at least said he suspected, that the relationship had begun in a desultory way as far back as the war. But then, Bruce's later feelings on the subject may have encouraged him to surmise that it was a routine affair which Hamilton had deludedly blown up into something larger. Hamilton's own account seems to contradict this. Between his complaint in a letter to Bruce about the noise in Albany and the intolerable heat of the summer and the departure of his secretary, he refers almost casually to the woman whom he would for some time identify only as the 'Other':

Then I suddenly got involved in a terrific Amour! You would imagine that this might have been a bright spot – and in a way it was and is – I have never been made so happy, or had anything so astonishingly reciprocated, in my life – but in actual practice it has brought about a terrific nervous strain, and friction between Loïs and myself.[1]

Hamilton decided the only solution to all his problems, and the intensive drinking that resulted, was an escape and he went to a nursing home for two days, after which he claimed to have cut out drink, started to eat properly and to be walking for two hours each day in Regent's Park. His first impulse was to attempt to find Ursula, or La as she was called – another 'l' sound – a place in his life which might avoid upsetting the balance. His optimistic plan was to find himself a room where he could sleep and work, and which would then allow him to visit both Loïs and La.

This plan proved impossible to fulfil because his feelings for La could not be neatly contained. According to Hamilton, who liked having his difficulties resolved by someone else, usually Loïs: 'The transitional stage was *awful* – the seriousness of the attraction becoming more and more apparent to Loïs, and the quarrels becoming deeper and deeper, longer and longer, hideouser and *hideouser*.'² Everyone was ill, Hamilton was drinking more heavily than ever. There was no choice but to make some sort of separation, although he claimed still to be 'extremely amicable' with Loïs and to be seeing a lot of her.

La and Hamilton rented a tiny house in Hove, 'you could almost put all of it into my sitting room at Albany', and Hamilton, now writing and hardly drinking at all, pronounced himself better than he had been in his life, or since his early days in Norfolk, at least. In this temporary haven, he attempted a portrait of his still-anonymous lover for Bruce:

I can only say that she is by no means a glamorous girl – mature (42) – thin (extremely) – and extremely nice and polite and shy to meet.* (*And practically a teetotaller, you will be glad to learn! Also been married twice, and is still married!) . . .

The point, really, though, is that I have been made sexually happy for the first time in my life, and do only hope that a merciful providence will make this amazing turn in my life one which will bring about *renewed productiveness* and complete emancipation from the bottle, which will now, I trust, be *my* slave.³

At the age of forty-five, Hamilton was finally experiencing a full relationship with a woman. There is some doubt about whether his marriage to Loïs was ever consummated; any sex that there was between them was patently unsatisfactory and soon dispensed with. His earlier encounters with prostitutes were unsatisfying and it may have been that Hamilton exaggerated the pleasure he derived from the brief affairs he had under the influence of Bill Linnit. Certainly he never made any qualification in his statement that he had achieved sexual happiness for the first time with La. There is even the possibility that Hamilton had never previously had full sexual intercourse with a woman. Now he had a dangerous glimpse of the possibility that his life could be different from the previous unhappiness and confusion, that a relationship with a woman could involve sex, friendship and intellectual companionship, all at once.

Ursula Chetwynd-Talbot was born in 1908. When Lalla wrote to Bruce about her, she was most struck by La's title. She was the eldest of three daughters of Viscount Ingestre, who was the heir to the twenty-first Earldom of Shrewsbury, Premier Earl in Peerages both of England and Ireland and Hereditary Great Seneschal or Lord High Steward of Ireland.[4] Her father died of pneumonia in 1914 and it was Ursula's young brother, John, who became the 21st Lord Shrewsbury. Ursula's mother was soon remarried, to an American diplomat, and Ursula spent much of her childhood out of Britain.

She has been described as 'shy to a degree of suffering'[5] and, like Hamilton, she was an observer. According to her younger sister, 'you could almost hear her listening to people's dialogue.'[6] In early years, though recognized as artistic, she was praised, if at all, in conventional terms, for her decorating and flower-arranging. Her first husband, Hector Stewart, died suddenly of a rare illness, and sudden deaths would awkwardly punctuate the fiction that she would later write. In 1942 she married his cousin, Lieutenant Commander Michael Stewart. Like so many hastily contracted in wartime, the marriage was not happy.

In her early forties, Ursula was elegant, even striking, in appearance, but not a beautiful woman. Hamilton acknowledged this and Bruce put it more strongly, dismissing her as 'thin and not beautiful; the nature of the sexual attraction she had for Hamilton was far from clear to me.'[7]

Hamilton's Marxist political beliefs did not preclude a certain fascination with intricacies of aristocratic nomenclature. When he finally revealed her name to Bruce, the explanation took two paragraphs:

She is the sister of an Earl (Shrewsbury) and this means that it is one of those titles you carry about with you whoever you marry. (Thus, she was Lady Ursula Stewart when I first met her.) The *names* this woman has had! She was born *Miss* Ursula *Talbot* (Talbot being the Shrewsbury family name), 'Miss' because the grandfather was still alive. Then she became *Lady* Ursula Talbot. Then (3) Lady Ursula Stewart. Then (4) Lady U. Stewart *again*! Then (5) Laura Talbot – the struggling writer. And then (6!), at Hove Street, Lady Ursula *Hamilton*! You may think this rather weird (I mean why not Mrs Patrick Hamilton?) but the complications were such that it was necessary to employ this device in order not to be exposed as *flagrantly* living in sin.

And now she is hovering between Laura Talbot, Lady U.*S.*, and Lady U.*H*.! Absolutely fantastic – you should see the variations in names when she gets a large post.[8]

La talked of changing her name to Laura Talbot, her pen-name, by deed poll, but Hamilton resolutely opposed this, asking rhetorically, 'Wouldn't it only call attention to yourself – make you seem exhibitionistic? *Do* people abandon titles?'[9] On other occasions he would display a concern with his illustrious military ancestor that is reminiscent of his father, alerting Bruce to 'the most astonishing' coincidence: 'Colonel Wildman (Thomas) was aide-de-camp, at the battle of Waterloo, to L.T.'s great (or great great) grandfather – Lord Anglesey. Lord A. had his leg blown off at this battle . . . Such coincidences make me say to L.T., when being silly and sentimental, that our *Fates are Linked*!'[10]

One of La's attractions was that she was a writer: 'She has had two novels taken by Macmillan,' he boasted to Bruce.[11] Yet in his letters to Bruce he was never to mention her fiction again, let alone give the impression of having read any of it. She started writing late and, according to Bruce, she first met Hamilton when he was asked to give an opinion on her first novel when it was about to be published, though this is unlikely.[12] Her first published novel, *Prairial*, bears traces of Hamilton's influence, most notably in a character who seems clearly to be based on him.

The Hamiltons, almost all writers at some time in their lives, can seem like a family of books, mingling and conversing. The beginning of *Prairial*, with Emily being dressed by her maid, Alice, may have reminded Hamilton of his mother's fiction, though La writes about the milieu with a more nonchalant and less enamoured authority. In its way, this is an impressive, and surprising novel, a luscious, feverish reworking of *Lady Chatterley's Lover*. Emily falls in love with and becomes pregnant by one of her husband's tenant farmers. Bruce and Hamilton's novels are full of sexual failure, humiliation and disappointment. There is nothing in any of their fiction like the beginning of the chapter following Emily's first act of infidelity. Perhaps it gives a sense of the release from sexual inhibition that Hamilton was granted for the first time: 'Emily stretched in the soft bed luxuriously, re-living the details of the night. Her limbs ached from the hard ground, with satiety, with sheer physical tiredness, and with satisfaction.'[3] The reader gradually discovers that Emily has been motivated, not by love, but by real madness. In a genuinely disturbing climactic scene, she attempts to kill her baby girl by tying her to a tree where she will be stung by nettles and wasps. At the end of the novel she has been committed to an asylum.

A choric voice in the novel is provided by a heavy-drinking painter called Edward, who has a father called Bernard. His conversations with Emily about his drinking are like a little anthology of Hamilton's thoughts on the subject. She accuses him of drinking himself to death: ' "Not to death, my dear Emily, to avoid death. Life without drinking is a sort of death, and I don't want death." '[4] She attempts well-meaning assistance as she, and so many others did for Hamilton, by encouraging him to eat:

'If you ate more – '
    'I should drink less. I know, it's one of your illusory theories.'[5]

And his drinking is constantly contrasted with her madness, and with its relation to his creativity:

'If I could paint like you, Edward, I shouldn't drink.'
    'Oh, yes, you would,' he said, 'from frustration, or despair, or from satisfaction when a thing's finished. Or because you hate the dealers, and the critics, and the milling hordes who have never held a paint-brush and think they know better.'[6]

One of his concluding, drunken dicta, ' "It's the torshured – hic – who torshure – hic" ',[7] is a paraphrase of a statement in the novel that Hamilton was then writing: 'It is a mysterious and hideous truism that the oppressed are often much more harsh with the oppressed than are the oppressors.'[8] Laura portrays Edward's drinking as an element of his dignity and integrity. Eight years later, the view of the subject in her fiction would be far harsher.

While Hamilton and La were living down in Hove, he briefly achieved a new, precarious balance. He walked a great deal around an area full of memories of his boyhood with Bruce. There was 'hardly a single square *yard* which does not bring to mind a thing done, a thing said, a thought

thought – either by you or me.'[19] On weekends, he would return to Albany to stay with Loïs. He reported on the arrangement with satisfaction: 'All goes well with me, and my strange, strange triangle is, I *believe*, working out better for all three than if it had never occurred. Touch *wood* . . . Anyway, I am amazingly well and even more amazingly non-alcoholic, and *working hard at my novel*.'[20]

The conviction about the mutual benefit was not shared by La. She had her own social circle, a group of upper-class women whom she used to see regularly. Hamilton's interest in her milieu was not accompanied by any wish to enter it, and indeed he strenuously discouraged La from meeting her old friends. They soon came to see Hamilton as a sinister figure who had virtually kidnapped La. In the following years she would see them only occasionally on fugitive visits.[21] Hamilton's friends, by contrast, were by no means discouraging. Some of them who had twenty years earlier advised Hamilton to have sex with Lily Connolly in order to break her spell over him, were now urging him to make a complete break with Loïs 'as being the "man-of-the-world" thing to do – but I *know* they are wrong.'[22] Hamilton was paralysed. After what he termed the 'Hove experiment', he found that he could 'neither go *forward* nor *back*': 'I know now that I simply *cannot* abandon Loïs. Whatever my *inclinations* (which are curiously mixed), my *conscience* will not allow it. Twenty years of marriage creates an unbreakable bond, and to throw her out of my life utterly would be too cruel – out of the question.'[23] He felt complicatedly bound by his conscience to La: 'I do not think I have the strength of character to give her up.'[24] The result was barely tolerable for any of the three, and financially draining for Hamilton. La moved back to her flat in Chelsea. Hamilton finally gave up the Albany set and, for the large sum of £3,500 (he lamented that it would have cost closer to £600 before the war), bought a converted stable on an old estate outside Whitchurch, a small village near Pangbourne in Berkshire. With a slightly pained irony he christened the new dwelling Albany Stables.

The good news was that his drinking was under control, with nothing but two or three whiskies in the evening, though he was smoking heavily. He pronounced himself philosophical. The two women were philosophical also, though in sharply contrasting ways. Loïs was unwilling to give Hamilton up and was content to continue in her supporting role. More than two years after Hamilton's affair had begun, she nervously re-established contact with Bruce, telling him contentedly that the Albany Stables were

small after Henley and Albany, but much much nicer, and much easier to run. We have a Polish peasant to help in the mornings from 9–12, and the rest I do. The sitting room was 3 horse boxes, my room 2, & the bathroom (mi*nute*) a hole for dumping manure! The rest consists of the old harness room (now the entrance hall) and the groom's 2 rooms. (One now the kitchen & the other Master Pat's room.) There is a large hay loft up above, which makes a gorgeous glory hole. It's a very clever reconstruction which you will soon be seeing for yourself.[25]

She told Bruce with proprietorial intimacy that 'P. is working well, and is a different creature when he's down here in the country. *What* a change from the black Albany days.'[26] She worked hard to put the house in order and to turn the jungle outside into a garden. If Hamilton had a refuge with her where he could come and work in peace, her chances of outlasting her rival must have seemed good.

La was not so phlegmatic. Hamilton complained in hurt tones that while Loïs was behaving immaculately, La '(whom I rather adore and who *couldn't* be a nicer character) hits me over the head with trays and dials 999 to have me removed by the police! . . . So what *is* one to do!'[27] Inertia continued to be his response. Then, one morning, while lying in bed, Hamilton was accorded a revelation:

I can only say that a sort of voice (my own) said to me:–

'*Difficulties* and *Disaster* ARE Life. That is why Life is such *Fun*.'

I suppose this is only another way of saying 'Face *up* to things' or 'Take things *easily*' or 'See the *funny* side of life.' All the same it has helped me *incredibly*. Over things like money and tray-hitting at any rate![28]

II

By 1951, Lalla's drinking was finally out of control. When Hamilton heard that Bruce had lent money to 'this wretched, miserable creature', he reacted with a near hysterical anger, exacerbated by Bruce's physical distance from what was happening: 'in lending her money, you are not really helping a distressed sister – you are just pouring *gin* down her throat.'[29] By March, their cousin Frank Bridger was telling Bruce that he could no longer provide help for her. Not only had Lalla been turning up drunk at his home but he had then been threatened with legal action by her husband, Bertie, for 'harbouring her'.[30] By May their 'wretched sister' was in hospital.[31]

Hamilton's fears of three years earlier about the recurrence of Lalla's cancer proved to be justified. It had spread to her pelvis and a specialist told Hamilton that she had six months to live at the outside. She was heavily drugged and told that she was suffering from 'rarefied bones' and that she might never walk again. On hearing this she told Hamilton that she was glad to know the truth as she had hated the air of mystery.[32] He never considered telling her she had cancer: 'I may *conceivably*, in the future, think it wise to let her know that she is dying, but (on everybody's advice) must never let her know it is from cancer. People (particularly women) apparently *hate* such an idea. (I don't quite know why – *I* wouldn't mind, would you?)'[33]

When Hamilton was a young adolescent, Lalla had talked to him of her sexual intrigues. She had found him employment in the theatre and facilitated the staging of *Rope*. He had read his earlier novels aloud to her and rewritten them in the light of her comments. Now, except for brief intervals, she communicated with nothing but a 'a sort of Falstaff "babbling" '. There was little to do but watch her die. In September Hamilton spent many hours holding her hand as she lay confined to her bed, now barely taking any food:

She still lies more or less in the dark, and she is, I must say, intensely piteous. But she is drugged during most of the day, and knocked out with morphia at night.

My conscious mind is, of course, rejoicing at seeing the end in sight – but down in the subconscious there is great distress – a misery which haunts one all day.[34]

The experience made him think of his last remaining close relative. Hamilton urged Bruce not to cancel his projected trip to England, 'if only for my sake. I can't tell you how I am missing your company and counsel just at this time. I can't think I've ever missed it more in my life – and that's saying a great deal.'[35] At the end of September 1951 she died, aged fifty-three. Hamilton wrote to Bruce after the funeral, at which he experienced mixed emotions:

I can't possibly write to you one of those foolish *cliché*-ridden letters about how peaceful and girlish she looked in death, and all that. No doubt the wretched Bertie will do that. . . .

I went to the funeral yesterday (it was at the Hampstead Parish Church in Church Row). It was quite dignified but, of course, like all funerals, unpleasant (particularly as it was an internment, not a cremation). There were about twenty-odd people present, and Bertie *just* succeeded in not making *too* much of an ass of himself or in taking *too* much of the limelight.

I'll tell you all about this when we meet. It is so difficult to describe Bertie's mixture between real and intense sorrow and his faint enjoyment of it all.

It is, of course, the happiest of events – on the surface at any rate. What goes on beneath the surface of one's mind is a different matter.[36]

21

The West Pier

I

In the summer of 1950 Hamilton received in the mail a press cutting from the *Evening News*. It was headlined, 'Inspiration':

Patrick Hamilton has sought the inspiration of his birthplace [*sic*] Brighton, to complete his new book which is due at his publishers in September. It is the first of a series, which will certainly develop into a trilogy, about life in England from 1911 to the present day. Tentative title is 'The West Pier'. – And a New Play. Hamilton was brought up in Brighton until he came to London where, in a series of grim Edwardian 'rooms', he wrote and struggled for a living, finding inspiration for such books as 'Craven House', 'Hangover Square' (a story of the public houses of Earls Court) and his play 'Gaslight' in which Robert Newton and Rosamund John are appearing at the Vaudeville.

He tells me he has promised Bill Linnit a finished play script by Christmas. Its subject? Blackmail.

The cutting was accompanied by an unusually frosty letter from Michael Sadleir:

We appear to learn a certain amount about you, your plans and progress from the gossip columns of the press, but get no direct information from you to your publishers as to what the latter may look for. That surely is a little unfriendly and into the bargain causes us some small inconvenience as we get occasional enquiries about Hamilton prospects, as do our travellers and hitherto we have nothing to say.[1]

In the midst of chaos, his peripatetic progress from Albany to the Isle of Wight, back to Albany, to Hove, and later to Chelsea and Whitfield, Hamilton was managing to write. He was placatory to his aggrieved friend and publisher, and by September he was able to report that he was 'absolutely *racing* ahead with *The West Pier*.'[2] He believed that if he 'stayed in bed all day and drank a great deal of whisky in the evenings', as he had when he finished *Hangover Square*, he could have it finished by the end of September. But he no longer believed his health could tolerate such a regime, so he proposed the end of October: 'I feel that the book is good up-to-standard Hamilton. Also (touching wood) I have a feeling that all this long hideous period of unproductivity has come to an end, and that I'm going to be a writer again.'[3]

A frequent word in reviews of *The West Pier* is 'sociological'.[4] And indeed Hamilton begins *The West Pier* almost in the style of a social scientist attempting to classify psychopaths like his hero, Ernest Ralph Gorse, or similar types, such as 'the poisoner Neil Creame, the bath-murderer George Smith, and many others of a similar way of thinking'.[5] In the sequel he lists even more names in an almost comical attempt to demonize Gorse by association managing, incidentally, to mis-spell the name of Thomas Neill Creame in yet another way:

He had a touch of Burke and Hare of Edinburgh (though he was never a heavy drinker); he had a touch of Dr Pritchard of Glasgow; a touch of the multitudinously poisoning Palmer; of the strangely acquitted Miss Madeleine Smith; of Neal Creame, the Lambeth harlot-poisoner; of George Smith, the bath-murderer; of Frederick Bywaters, Ronald True, Sydney Fox, Frederick Mahon, Neville Heath and George Haigh.[6]

The direct reference of the name, Ernest Ralph Gorse, is to the murderer Neville George Heath, a con-man who committed a series of murders involving savage mutilation of his female victims. (This is hinted at in *Mr Stimpson and Mr Gorse* – the second novel in the trilogy – when Gorse jokes about his own name: 'Not Furze. Or Broom. Or Bracken – or Heather, or anything like that'[7]). Hamilton repeatedly breaks off from the narrative to assure us of Gorse's evil and the final sentence of *Mr Stimpson and Mr Gorse* tells us that Gorse will finally be hanged.[8] It is difficult to understand how the connection with Neville Heath could ever have been taken seriously. Heath, sixteen years younger than Gorse, was crucially a part of the spiv era of the late forties, and would make no sense put back into the twenties and thirties milieu in which Gorse moves. In his celebrated essay, 'Decline of the English Murder', George Orwell makes a distinction between the traditional pre-war murder, the 'domestic poisoning dramas, product of a stable society' and the war-time variety exemplified by the 'meaningless story' of the Cleft Chin murder, 'with its atmosphere of dance-halls, movie palaces, cheap perfume, false names and stolen cars'. If anything, Hamilton was more interested in the traditional older version, but it must be remembered that Gorse commits no murders in the books. Arthur Calder-Marshall is almost alone among critics of the novel in pointing this out, that the Gorse Hamilton tells us about is entirely different from the Gorse that we see, a minor swindler of three women and one man whose frauds are never even reported to the police.[10]

The seed of Gorse is to be found a quarter of a century earlier in *The Siege of Pleasure*. Jenny, drunk for the first time, is tempted by the sleazy charms of Andy, for whom she is throwing over Tom, the decent young man who really loves her:

In fact, was he not superbly eligible? He was no common 'pick-up'. He was the owner of a car; he consorted with the retired military; and all his talk went to prove that he was 'in a good way'. If she played her cards right, there was no end of what she might get out of him. She had him round her little finger already.[11]

Andy is a villain of a small kind, serving only to expose weaknesses that would have been exposed anyway. In *The West Pier* Gorse is given Andy's attributes, though the military connection and the car are fraudulent, but in the same way he is an instrument, in Hamilton's hands, for probing his characters' flaws. In the description of Gorse's youth there are fine moments of Hamilton's peculiar brand of suburban horror, such as the remarkable scene in which he makes his terrified white mice participate in swimming races in the bath. Later in the book, and to an even greater extent in the sequels, Gorse becomes a cypher, like Swift's Gulliver, who exists in relation to the particular society in which we find him. More than this, all the narrator's talk of Gorse's depravity disguises his status as a perverse, oblique self-portrait. He attends Hamilton's prep school and then, like Hamilton, he leaves early when his family moves to

Chiswick where he attends Colet Court. At this point their paths diverge and it is as if Gorse is then Hamilton's dark double, leading a parody of his creator's life. Colet Court was the school that prepared boys for St Paul's public school and that is where Gorse goes. Hamilton did not, because he left after his unhappy dormitory experiences and ultimately followed Bruce to Westminster.

Almost systematically, Hamilton provides Gorse with the details of his own life. He wears a Westminster School tie to which he is not entitled. At the crucial moment of defrauding Esther Downes in *The West Pier*, he shows her a ring with a fake family crest, the precise ring that Hamilton himself wore. There are more examples in *Mr Stimpson and Mr Gorse*. Like Hamilton, he has a 'curious passion for the theatre', can act well in private but on stage is 'something worse than hopeless';[12] he eavesdrops in pubs in order to learn about his victims; he 'was a great walker and did most of his thinking while he walked';[13] he is an expert on prostitutes in Soho in 1928, though he is not sexually attracted to them.[14]

Almost covertly, Hamilton is exploring the notion that the skills with which Gorse preys on his victims' weaknesses and vindictively manipulates them are comparable with his own as an artist. This is explicitly raised at the moment before Gorse displays the Hamilton family crest to Esther:

All this wealth of inventive detail was convincing Esther more and more. Nobody, she thought, could possibly *invent* detail like this.

And, in fact, Gorse, had he not been what he was, might have been a highly successful novelist.[15]

In a rare lyrical moment, Hamilton observes the hapless Ryan, Gorse's ancillary victim, tinkering with his motorcycle: 'Men are at their best when quietly absorbed in the workings of a machine. There is something charming, disinterested, and childlike about it.'[16] This is significantly different from the thoroughly interested way in which Gorse busies himself. By being expert on the banal minutiae of daily life, as a consequence of their particular callings, both Gorse and Patrick are cut off from it. They can never lose themselves in the simple activities of life as Ryan can. The gift, as we have seen in this already-quoted passage, is also a curse: 'Too much thought is bad for the soul, for art, and for crime. It is also a sign of middle age, and Gorse was one who had to pay for the precocity of his youth in the most distasteful coin of premature middle age.'[17]

The West Pier is a flawed novel. One critic wondered: 'Does [Hamilton] perhaps nudge and interfere too often? I think he does.'[18] Two kinds of nudging take place. There is the author as sadistic puppeteer who colludes with Gorse in manipulating and thwarting the other characters. The world of the book is a bleakly retributive one in which not only are circumstances arranged so that Gorse's plot never comes to light, but the characters are not even permitted to escape from the novel into oblivion. In cruel final touches, the rest of the lives of Bell, Gertrude and Esther are all summarized with ghastly reductiveness. The less acceptable form of nudging is in the authorial tone, which is insistent to the point of being garrulous or, on occasion, tiresomely intrusive. Hamilton ceaselessly analyses his characters as if they were chess pieces in a problem, and the reader sometimes feels nagged at, or addressed as if at a public meeting.

Nevertheless, it is a formidable achievement, even disregarding the circumstances in which it was written, and Michael Sadleir's immediate reaction was one of delight:

I admire your book beyond measure. It is a triumph of deceptive simplicity, of mosaic-like construction, of laugh-aloud fun flickering over an abyss of infamy. What a HORROR Gorse is! And will there be no retribution until 3 or 4 more books from now? I can hardly bear it.

The ingenuity with which, out of perfectly ordinary – indeed trivial – material you have devised the web of villainy, prevented the victims stumbling on the truth – and all with a cast of 5 people and within the space of a square mile – is masterly. And of course the funny bits . . . ![19]

The publishing process took its course, though Hamilton felt more nervous than ever before, confessing that 'after all this time (during which people have been saying that I'm a drunk and so forth) I'm so desperately anxious to make a come-back, and start absolutely on the right foot.'[20] More tentatively, almost shamefacedly, Hamilton also allowed himself to express the first stirrings of a new literary ambition: 'I feel that I have really got on to something with Gorse – that it might turn out to be my wretched little *Comédie Humaine*.'[21]

What Hamilton did not know was that deep misgivings were being expressed about the book. Michael Sadleir had sent a proof copy of the novel to J. B. Priestley, in the hope of eliciting a favourable comment for the dustjacket. He quickly received a reply:

Dear Michael,

I have now read THE WEST PIER and am rather worried about it. The trouble is, that it does not seem to me really as good as HANG-OVER [*sic*] SQUARE or THE SLAVES OF SOLITUDE. It contains, of course, a good deal of admirable writing, very characteristic of Patrick, and no doubt will serve very well as an introductory volume to later and, I imagine, stronger stories about this unsavoury character. But with the best will in the world – and nobody enjoys this writer's odd mannerisms and close observation more than I do – I do find this particular story very slight and in danger of seeming to be little more than an anecdote padded out. I hate to say this and I shall be very much obliged if you will keep this opinion from him, but I must be honest about my feelings, and I do not feel that this is a book that asks for the big drum.[22]

Sadleir replied on the day after he received Priestley's discouraging letter and confessed to a startling change of opinion:

Dear Jack,

Having just re-read THE WEST PIER in proof I must confess that I entirely agree with your letter. I thought better of it in typescript, but that was undoubtedly mainly affectionate enthusiasm.

You ask me to keep your opinion from Pat. Now this is going to be very difficult – if not impossible. He is tremendously eager to have your opinion and now that the proof is in, is bound to ask me whenever I see him. As a matter of fact I see him tomorrow, but I can put him off on this one occasion, provided I have some ammunition against the next encounter.

Would it meet your scruples if I supplied him with an abbreviated version on the lines of the enclosed? This of course I should do by letter, giving no sign that it was anything but a complete communication. Please emend in any way you wish, and send back as soon as maybe.

Thank you in any case for reading the book so quickly. Naturally, my recantation as stated at the beginning of this note is highly confidential vis-a-vis anyone. I am in a rather delicate position.[23]

The term 'delicate' could be considered prissily inadequate for Sadleir's relation with Hamilton both as publisher and old friend. His revision of

Priestley's criticisms can have done little to soften what must have been a terrible blow:

I have now read THE WEST PIER. It contains of course a good deal of admirable writing very characteristic of Patrick, and no doubt may serve very well as an introductory volume to later and stronger stories about this unsavoury character. Nobody enjoys this writer's odd mannerisms and close observation more than I do, but with the best will in the world I find this particular story very slight. I do not feel that this is a book that asks for the big drum.[24]

Hamilton did not have much regard to critics and he had never been part of any literary group or clique providing him with support. He was much admired for this,[25] often by writers who chose not to follow his example. Instead, Hamilton had relied more on a group of male friends, all older than himself. Men like Michael Sadleir, J. B. Priestley and Bruce Hamilton were not fools, far from it, but they all had a conception of the novel that was, ultimately, different from Hamilton's disturbing, idiosyncratic comic gift. Sadleir was a nineteenth-century pasticheur, Priestley a stolid comic realist descended – in more ways than one – from Henry Fielding, and Bruce wrote thrillers of the most traditional kind. None of them could have been expected to respond to the sheer peculiarity of Hamilton's project, about which the author himself was far from clear.

When Bruce read *The West Pier* in the late summer of 1951, he feigned greater enthusiasm than he felt and then wrote a long letter making a series of criticisms. He was stung by Hamilton's having borrowed an episode from *Pro* and he made a whole series of objections to Hamilton's treatment of their schooldays, as if his brother had unfairly, as well as inaccurately, plundered their joint source of raw material. He may also have suspected that the overt idea for Gorse came from his thriller of fifteen years earlier, *Middle Class Murder*, which has as its protagonist a scarcely classifiable psychopath. In fact, one of the weaknesses of *The West Pier* is that it contains too much that is similar to the following passage by Bruce:

Then you get the true middle-class murderer, a figure of awful menace and awful fascination. Most frequently the subject has always had a screw loose somewhere – a streak of congenital depravity. Less common is the type, normally of pacific and unassuming disposition, who sets however a definite limit to what he is prepared to endure, and once that limit is passed will hazard everything, disgrace, and even death, to relieve himself of the burden. To this type it seems Tim Kennedy must be allocated.[26]

He complained that Hamilton had not really got under Gorse's skin, when the *donné* of the character, indeed the whole series, is that he is inscrutable. More cruelly, he said the same of Esther Downes. The result was that Hamilton concluded his very long point-by-point defence against Bruce's criticisms by admitting to 'cold feet' and rather pathetically asking: 'will you, my dearest Ecurb, when you next write, encourage me up to the hilt – pointing out any other merit you can think of in the book? You know well enough that your encouragement now as in the days of "Modernism(!)", means more to me than anyone else's on earth.'[27]

II

As soon as Hamilton had finished *The West Pier* he began work on a new stage play called *The Man Upstairs*. 'I am pathetically hoping to recoup my fortunes with this play,' he confessed. Although he thought he had begun with the 'best 1st Act ever', the second 'alas, is at present *dreadfully flat.*'[28] By the end of the year it was finished, with Hamilton confiding promisingly that 'its main theme is blackmail – only *physical*, not mental blackmail – the subtly made, but unmistakeable threat of serious physical violence if a certain amount of money is not forthcoming.'[29]

Hamilton's two great theatrical successes were founded on two outstanding ideas. In contrast, *The Man Upstairs* relies on a run-of-the-mill idea, involving fraudulent blackmail. Worse still, in order to achieve the disappointingly mundane resolution, Hamilton relies on an absurdly unconvincing technical device, a radio which, for no good reason, has been rigged up between the hero's flat and the flat above, and which has been left on by mistake.

Rope and *Duke in Darkness* both contain unconvincing long speeches, but at least they were related to the play. When Hamilton in a prefatory note directs that the ' "war" speech in *Act Three* should not be omitted, for it is picked up at the end of the Act, and plants the "moral" of the play', it seems more like an expression of hope than accomplishment and the nervous quotation marks seem all too justified.

When a fake twin, a disguised version of a character comes on stage (a device later used in Anthony Shaffer's highly successful play, *Sleuth*), we seem a long way from the young playwright whose play could cause a Broadway audience to scream in anguish. In a stage direction, Hamilton tells the reader how effective this is:

Detecting and observing this facial resemblance of one imaginary 'Non-identical' twin to another should be extremely fascinating to an audience now practically in the know; and an actor should be able to find many ways of exploiting this fascination – making, by his different facial expressions, in the different lights in which he stands, an extraordinary similarity and remarkable dissimilarity.[30]

It could be argued that the fascination ought to be enacted rather than dictated. Yet the play does have its eerie moments and one of the greatest theatrical talents of the age, Orson Welles, was interested enough in it to seek to acquire the film rights (though not sufficiently solvent to pay for them).[31] Perhaps an enthusiastic management might have made something of it, after much rewriting. But O'Bryen, Linnit and Dunfee were not enthusiastic and the delay before production was as great as it had been with *The Governess*.

Hamilton had now regained the writing habit. While complaining about the delay in producing *The Man Upstairs*, he was able to write enthusiastically about a radio play which Val Gielgud had been attempting to chivvy out of him for years:

The theatre is an absolutely *chaotic* state – merit or appallingness having absolutely nothing to do with financial success.

My own play is *supposed* to appear during the New Year – but whether it will or not Heaven knows.

The radio play is also scheduled for some time in New Year. It is probably going to be called *Telephone Pest* and the subject is interesting. Have you read about this minor (but very nasty and growing) social menace? I mean people (men) who telephone women who live alone, and then, after an innocent and intriguing opening, begin to pour forth streams of unutterable obscenity. They do this, sometimes, for a matter of weeks, adopting different disguises, voices and personalities. I know about half a dozen women who have suffered from this (including Lalla when she was at Orange Street and L.T. recently at Cygnet House) and I have heard about dozens more.

The men, who usually phone from public boxes (and no doubt masturbate themselves therein), are frequently caught by most ingenious and rapid police work and the whole thing is very fascinating.

But, you will be wondering, how on earth have I got round the problem of broadcasting obscenity? I think I have done this most adroitly, Val Gielgud having praised me for 'enormous ingenuity'.

I've also managed to make the play – apart from three minutes only – *entirely* in telephone conversations – which makes for good listening. And I think the play is interesting at any rate – though whether it is exciting I can't say. It runs for about 45 minutes.[32]

But there is nothing more to *Caller Anonymous*, as it was finally called, than that. A barely characterized woman receives the calls and the man is soon arrested, and is then crudely denounced by the woman in a manner dimly reminiscent of the end of *Gaslight*. Hamilton's 'enormous ingenuity' consists merely of fading out after the 'innocent and intriguing opening'. The police apprehension of the wrongdoer is undeniably rapid, though whether ingenious or not is impossible to say since we are not shown how they do it. It presumably depends on the unspectacular enough science of tracing calls. The play is by some way the least interesting of Hamilton's performed or published works.

III

At the end of 1951, Hamilton wrote to Bruce in anticipation of his forthcoming visit: 'I shall also look into the matter of a pied-a-terre in London. (This means really, of course, that Loïs will – because she is so much better at that sort of thing.)'[33] At the end of February 1952, when Bruce, whose wife, Aileen, was remaining in Barbados, was on the verge of sailing, Hamilton wrote him a long letter as a guide to the byzantine affairs that would be awaiting him on his return. The first problem was where Bruce could stay. Hamilton's divorce from Loïs was now proceeding at high speed and he wasn't sure whether he, as the divorcé, might be forbidden to stay at Albany Stables. Laura was staying in a cottage near Salisbury that Hamilton had rented: 'This is very near her mother's house,' Hamilton assured Bruce, 'and so I can leave her there alone as long as I like.'[34]

Hamilton's anxiety about any sort of arrangements, no matter how trivial, were now such that he decided that he would meet Bruce not at Paddington Station, with all the problems with luggage that entailed, but next door at the Great Western Hotel, where Hamilton had booked a room for Bruce for three nights. There was a final warning:

Be prepared for a shock when you see my face again after all this time! Although, I think, I'm amazingly young in general health and outlook, I haven't worn at all well in my face – which is terribly seamed and lined and makes me look a lot older than the 48 years I'll be in a few weeks' time.[35]

Their first meeting was ominously unsuccessful. Once more, Bruce was struck by a change in his brother:

He was as usual immaculately dressed; and, slim as ever, he did not look much older. But his hair, now always uncovered, was in a state of almost bedlamite disorder, his eyes were a little wild, and, before he saw me, I thought to myself, 'He's had two or three already.'[36]

Hamilton insisted on going to Bruce's room to sample the duty-free whisky that Bruce had brought with him. He became very drunk and the evening ended with a terrible argument.[37] To Bruce, Hamilton seemed to be behaving like their father at his worst, and on this visit he came to believe that Hamilton resented him. In Bruce's opinion, the possible explanations for this resentment included his disapproval of Hamilton's politics and his drinking, his feeling that Hamilton's creative gifts were in decline, his marriage, his return to Barbados. Another possible reason he doesn't mention is the effect that years apart must have, even on the closest of friends or relatives. There was also, whatever the conflicting views about Hamilton's powers, the continuing disparity between their achievements.

Hamilton's domestic complications were also an obstacle. Bruce was almost as close to Loïs as Hamilton was, and resented La much as

Hamilton had resented Aileen. Their first meeting was polite and amicable, but the two never became close and on the very next day Hamilton and Bruce drove up to Albany Stables to stay with Loïs.

Bruce's return coincided with the possibility of an upturn in his fortunes. His last book, a thriller called *Let Him Have Judgement*, published five years earlier, received some favourable reviews, both in Britain and the United States.[38] This story of the revenge on behalf of a wrongly hanged man against a judge who is living a double life is even more poorly plotted than is usual in his work. It begins with the condemned man writing a letter. The story depends on the curious chance that the recipient of the letter from the condemned man (who is in the United States) finds himself in the next bed (in the dormitory where he is opening it) to the one person in the world with information that can be used against the judge who is to blame for the miscarriage of justice.[39] But it has a certain effectiveness and it was by far Bruce's most commercially successful book. It was widely translated and sold particularly well in the United States. Then it aroused the interest of the actor, Raymond Massey, who adapted it for the stage under the book's American title, *Hanging Judge*, with the participation of the distinguished film director, Michael Powell, for whom Massey had starred in *A Matter of Life and Death* in 1948. When Hamilton heard about it he was sceptical, recalling his own experience with the still-born adaptation of *The Midnight Bell* for Robert Milton in 1932. Nor did he think *Let Him Have Judgement* was suitable for theatrical adaptation. 'So you are wise not to build on it,' he concluded, 'though it is absurd to predict about anything in the theatre.'[40]

Hanging Judge was produced, with half the finance provided by the Chrysler company of America. For once, Hamilton did not even attempt to display enthusiasm or interest in his brother's work, soured by the continuing failure of *The Man Upstairs* to attract interest.[41] At the end of his life, Michael Powell looked back on the play as one of his happiest memories:

It was a big production. There was a hung-jury scene, which naturally called for twelve good men and true, and although some of them were understudies and some of them were doubles, that meant a big company to take on tour. The main setting of the London Club, based upon the Garrick, called for a half-a-dozen good speaking parts, and then there was the interior of the judge's weekend cottage, and a vignette of the judge himself sentencing a murderer.[42]

The cast was top class as well, led by Godfrey Tearle (who had played the villain in Hitchcock's *The Thirty-Nine Steps*) as the judge. The out-of-town tour went well and at the end of 1952 the play was thought good enough to open at the New Theatre (now the Albery) in the West End. The result, Powell recalled, was disappointing after all the excitement: 'Well, it did go for a month or two, but not long enough for it to be a big success and for Ray to be able to sell the film rights, or transfer the play to New York. Still, nothing to be ashamed of.'[43]

Twenty years later, when Bruce was writing the memoir of his brother, he must have thought ruefully of his own West End experience when he cited Hamilton's prudence in writing plays with one set and a small cast, thus minimizing costs and increasing the 'ability of a run to survive a few weeks of moderate business.'[44] As Powell recalled, *Hanging Judge* needed to fill a 'big, first-class house'[45] to be profitable and it was never quite able to sustain this.

The other source of hope for Bruce was the publication of his novel, *So Sad, So Fresh*, 'which I believe to have been the best work of which I was capable'.[46] Again, Bruce was hurt by Hamilton's lack of interest and a year later Hamilton was crossly exclaiming that he hadn't read it and couldn't until he got some '*reasonable* peace of mind', though he attributed his omission to the seriousness with which he took Bruce's work. When he finally read it he was severely critical, faulting the book for being autobiographical without transforming the material. He denied that the general reader 'could possibly take much delight, or even much interest, in' characters and situations that were there only because they had happened when the Hamilton family were living in lodgings in the twenties.[47]

Hamilton saw it as a misguided change of direction, and he could have added that the change had led Bruce back to the beginning of Hamilton's career. What is almost tragic about *So Sad, So Fresh*, Bruce's dullest book, is that it is little more than a lame, humourless reworking of Hamilton's sparkling debut, *Monday Morning*, though the tone is climactically darkened when the hero kills his romantic rival and serves a prison sentence. The heroine, whom the by-now-middle-aged hero marries at the end, is even called Marya, the brothers' name for Maruja Mackehenie, who had inspired the beloved in the original book.

La had also published a book this year, her second novel, *The Gentlewomen*. Laura Talbot was a better novelist than Bruce, and this story of a woman struggling to preserve her archaic snobberies when she is hired to superintend the children in an aristocratic family, is skilful and intelligent. It just isn't very interesting. There are good things in it, such as a scene in which a children's lesson on 'The Lady of Shalott' is devoted entirely to the question of whether to call the poet Lord Alfred Tennyson or Alfred, Lord Tennyson:

'But why not Lord Alfred Tennyson?'
'Is his brother a marquess?'
'Was, you mean; Lord Tennyson is no longer alive, Ruth.'[48]

But the arcane details of snobbish manoeuvrings can become tiresome, even when being mocked. According to Bruce, whose reports on La must always be treated sceptically, Hamilton disliked this novel which, 'while showing sensitive perceptions, was excessively preoccupied with such trivialities as the propriety of having armorial bearings on carriages or cars.'[49]

22

Mr Stimpson and Mr Gorse

Hamilton wrote *Mr Stimpson and Mr Gorse* under conditions fully as oppressive as those under which he had written its predecessor. At the time of Bruce's return to England in 1952, Hamilton was spending much of his time at Albany Stables, which was where he worked, and describing himself as 'behaving enormously, almost dangerously, well – and working like mad.' He was writing ten pages a day. Even when Bruce came to visit, Hamilton insisted on going to bed straight after supper.[1]

A move with La to a cottage in Stapleford proved disastrous. The water supply failed completely, provoking 'an almost complete break-down in L.T.'s health'.[2] This was accompanied by a demand from the Inland Revenue for £3,000 in unpaid taxes. Furthermore, La was divorcing her second husband and Hamilton considered it a matter of principle that he pay all the court costs. 'How I've kept my head above alcohol and managed to go on working, is a *miracle*.'[3]

Though the output had slowed, the novel was getting written, and he even had a title, *A General in the Family*;[4] he continued to be optimistic, even gleeful. His description of Gorse in the following letter shows how divided Hamilton was between considering him to be a satirical device and a portrait of evil:

The book, I think, may be the fun I hoped it to be. The atrocious banalities between Mrs Plumleigh-Bruce (Anglo-Italian) and a Mr Stimpson (Estate Agent) are right up my street, and are more and more making Gorse an absolutely delightful character in swindling them. He retains, however, I hope, his awful, murderous menace – and one is keenly looking forward to his ultimate visit to the gallows.[5]

With an effort extraordinary for a man in his circumstances, Hamilton finished the book, now called *Signature to Crime*, in the summer. He confessed with nervous satisfaction that 'Writing a book is fairly all right, but reading it is rather frightening.'[6] Just under three weeks later, on a Sunday, Michael Sadleir wrote to Hamilton describing his reaction to the novel. It must be quoted entire because it may be this letter more than anything else, more than the drink, the domestic chaos, the allegedly failing powers, that destroyed Patrick Hamilton's literary career:

My Dear Hen

You asked for a handwritten note as soon as I had finished your book, and here one is. But I fear you will dislike reading it as much as I dislike writing it. Candidly I am gravely embarrassed what to say about *Signature to Crime* which, despite great technical virtuosity, gives an impression of petulance and of personal prejudices so peevishly over-stated as to render the characters mere cock-shies.

This promises badly for the book's reception by critics and public. It will be thought disagreeable and unsympathetic, because there is not a tolerably likeable person in it. It will strike such reviewers as do not relish your particular and highly individual brand of nonsense (and the notices of *The West Pier* showed that certain recalcitrants do exist) as laboured and facetious. Thirdly, sustained mockery and relentless scarification, dealt out by a novelist to characters whom he has purposely presented as grotesque marionettes, bring weariness to a reader and make him long for relief.

Of course the book has excellent qualities, and the author's 'signature' is unmistakeable. It is constructed and contrived with great skill, and a complex chronology – occasional slips apart – is handled with mastery. It is crammed with evidence of your astonishing capacity for retaining and reproducing the absurd conversations and deplorable mentality of absurd people. For this reason I enjoyed the ludicrous arguments between the Major and Stimpson, and Mrs P[lumleigh-]. B[ruce]'s diary – though perhaps there is a shade too much of this.

But the limericks and stories, the cross-words, cigarette-tappings and so on struck me as a bit far-fetched and exaggerated. About the Major's poem I have uneasy doubts. It might be thought to make mock of Armistice Day, and consequently resented.

Well, this is enough for now. Maybe more than enough. I only wish it could read differently. I must now get other opinions; and meantime will note down the few ambiguities and apparent contradictions which struck me. They are not important.

Yours, M.S.[7]

It was not even signed Quarles, as was his jovial custom. This was a chilly, brutal letter from a friend of nearly thirty years, and it can be seen as the final disastrous result of Hamilton's having his publisher as his best friend. Such a letter to a long-established and successful author from his publisher would have been inconceivable in a purely professional relationship. Rather, it bears the traces of a shocked and disappointed friend.

Michael Sadleir was now in his mid-sixties and unable to recognize a masterpiece of comedy which struck so forcibly at his own social prejudices. He could appreciate Hamilton's merciless scrutiny when it was applied to the acting profession, to the deracinated working classes, to the petit bourgeoisie. But when Hamilton treated the pieties of the middle classes with scorn and contempt, this was too much.

About two years later Edmund Wilson, then the most influential and respected literary critic in America, wrote an equally devastating letter to a novelist who was less well-known and a good deal poorer than Hamilton:

Now, about your novel: I like it less than anything else of yours I have read. The short story that it grew out of was interesting, but I don't think the subject can stand this very extended treatment. Nasty subjects can make fine books; but I don't feel you have got away with this. It isn't merely that the characters and the situation are repulsive in themselves, but that, presented on this scale, they seem quite unreal.[8]

Though it was accompanied by a fervently positive message about the novel from Wilson's wife, Elena, this letter was potentially more damaging for Vladimir Nabokov than Sadleir's was for Hamilton. Nabokov was by now in his mid-fifties, painfully establishing himself as a writer in his second language and he had written what he was convinced was his masterpiece, *Lolita*. Because of its theme, the novel was considered unpublishable and now it had been dismissed by a man who was not just one of his closest friends but also the critic who had played a major part in making the reputations of contemporaries like Ernest Hemingway and F. Scott Fitzgerald. But where his own writing was concerned, Nabokov was imperturbable. If he was deeply hurt, and he must have been, he showed it only in the three-month delay before his response, which began: 'Belatedly but with perfectly preserved warmth I now want to thank you for your letters – Elena's was especially charming.'9 And that was all. He never mentioned the subject again to Wilson and his own view of what he had written remained unchanged. It is a myth that masterpieces are uniformly greeted with hostility on their first appearance, but it would be more true to say that ageing critics lose their ability to spot something new. Old critics are displeased by new styles of writing much in the way that they resent new colours of buses or shapes of milk bottle. Life gets steadily worse and the subject matter of novels becomes more unpleasant. Edmund Wilson, one of the first defenders of *Ulysses*, now professed repulsion at the similarly shocking content of *Lolita*. Michael Sadleir, who had happily published Hamilton's dismal Stalinist tract, *Impromptu in Moribundia*, in 1939, now objected that elements in his book might provoke 'resentment' at the idea that a poem commemorating the First World War could be a subject for comedy. T. S. Eliot recognized the problem in his later years, and made it a policy, when he worked as a publisher, to show manuscripts to younger colleagues before arriving at a definite judgement.10 *Lolita* was published almost clandestinely and became an international bestseller, while also coming to be considered one of the major novels of the century. At an age when Hamilton had ceased publishing altogether, Nabokov embarked on what was virtually a new career, with a succession of important books.

Mr Stimpson and Mr Gorse is no *Lolita* but it is a remarkable advance on its predecessor, as well as being an entirely different sort of novel. *The West Pier* is an austere book with a certain vein of horrible humour, but *Mr Stimpson and Mr Gorse* is one of Hamilton's major comic achievements. The weaker parts of the book are those that are most reminiscent of *The West Pier*, where Hamilton discourses in jocular, pseudo-sociological fashion on the class of colonel's wives, from which Mrs Plumleigh-Bruce comes, or too-insistently assert Gorse's evil.

What is new in the book is Hamilton's use of Gorse as an instrument in what seems like the first chapter in a savage anatomy of English life. The blackly hilarious portraits of Mrs Plumleigh-Bruce, Mr Stimpson and Major Parry are fired by the narrator's scorn, even hatred. Admittedly, Hamilton is an embarrassment for those who believe that authors should have a parental affection for their creations, as if the satirical rage of a Hogarth or a Rowlandson were illegitimate artistic impulses. Nor does this preclude a horrified pleasure in the material, for Hamilton was a connoisseur of boredom, stupidity, complacency, bogus sentimentality. He returned to old ground in the novel. Major Parry's composition of his 'November the Eleventh poem in honour of the glorious dead'[11] is a crueller and funnier version of a similar scene in *The Midnight Bell* where Mr Sounder has composed a sonnet.[12] He had portrayed the effect of escalating drunkenness, notably in *The Siege of Pleasure*, but never with the comic skill with which Gorse scientifically plies Mr Stimpson with drink before leading him astray in Soho.

The portrayal of Mrs Plumleigh-Bruce is something entirely new. The kitsch decoration of her house, the grotesque 'Oirish' with which she addresses her maid, and, above all, the cadences of her diary, brilliantly rendered, show that Hamilton, far from being in decline, was at the height of his comic powers. Our last sight of her, exiled to the sea-front, is horrifying, leaving her like the victim of a metamorphic fable: 'And Mrs Plumleigh-Bruce's rich, regal, mouthy, throaty, fruity, haughty and objectionable voice became a recognized noise in the wind and desolation of the hopeless and helpless sea-front.'[13] It is no wonder that John Betjeman, with his fascinated horror for bad taste and the minutiae of bourgeois life, cited this as one of the modern novels he particularly admired. Michael Sadleir was lamenting the book's 'sustained mockery and relentless scarification' barely four years before John Osborne and Kingsley Amis would turn those qualities into a new literary movement. In general the reviews were unsympathetic, censuring Hamilton for the hatred he displayed towards his characters.[14]

One of the more distinguished critics to review the book, Walter Allen, wrote in sorrow as a fan of Hamilton, whom he memorably described as 'the poker-faced connoisseur of the seedily third-rate; he clumps through the spiritual slums of urban man like a plain-clothes police sergeant'. Allen argued that Hamilton ought to have written a different sort of novel, with complex, rounded characters, whom readers could respect, if not like:

But in this book Mr Hamilton has very cunningly dodged the novelist's real issue by going back to the pre-history of the novel, going back, in fact, to that seventeenth-century literary exercise, the Character. Just as writers like Earle and Fuller wrote the Character of a Hypocrite, of a Miser, of a Fair and Happy Milkmaid and so on, in his new novel, Mr. Hamilton gives us Characters of a Snobbish and Frigid Colonel's Widow, a Lecherous Business Man and a criminal Psychopath. They are, as it were, accretions of generalisations about broad categories – real or otherwise – of human beings, given an illusion of life by Mr. Hamilton's air of knowingness about their haunts and habits; so much so that they sometimes appear almost as the secretions of their circumstances. Challenge the generalisations and the conviction departs.[15]

It may be that critics of Hamilton's generation were too quick to dictate what a novelist's 'real issue' might be. Allen's interesting argument raises, while intending to dismiss, the question of whether a novel must be just one thing, dealing with narration in a certain realistic tradition which Allen himself followed in his own, now largely forgotten, novels. Why not, for example, the examination of types that John Earle and Thomas Fuller attempted in the early-to-mid-seventeenth century?

A biographer should refrain from offering advice like a retrospective agony aunt on what ought to have been done, or from predicting what might have happened, like an astrologer. Nevertheless the reception of *Mr Stimpson and Mr Gorse* must be seen as a decisive failure in Hamilton's life. In the midst of domestic disaster he had struggled to complete a novel with which he was pleased. More than that, he felt himself to be tremulously on the brink of an important sequence of works, perhaps something like the long work that J. B. Priestley had called for in his introduction to *Twenty Thousand Streets Unders the Sky* twenty years earlier. If at that moment he had had an enthusiastic publisher, or even a publisher sufficiently conscious of his author's and his company's interests to think that the scheme was worth encouraging, or even, failing that, a friend who believed that Hamilton needed emotional support when he was at his most vulnerable, then his career and his life might have taken a different course.

Certainly Hamilton was in no condition to adopt Nabokov's silky insouciance. Ten days later he was writing to Sadleir about the text for the duskjacket of the novel in a tone of almost ghastly humility: 'Very many thanks for the blurb to *Signature to Crime*. I do not think this could possibly be better. Among other things it most adroitly deals with the defects of the book, many of which will, I fear, remain, even in the revised version.'[16] Hamilton accepted Sadleir's criticisms without any resistance. He had almost no choice, since the only other person he could turn to was Bruce, whom he already suspected of being unsympathetic to *The West Pier*. Hamilton may also have feared that Bruce would not be in a generous mood after having received Hamilton's severe criticisms of *So Sad, So Fresh*. Hamilton's problem with the Gorse sequence was much the same as he saw the dilemma in his private life. When Bruce wrote to his brother describing this as his 'in some ways least satisfactory period', Hamilton responded as he did when his more worldly friends suggested he abandon Loïs. He had made a commitment and could not go back on it. He admitted that he had not even dared to send a copy of the book to Bruce:

I was afraid of adverse criticism from you – and I felt it would be much better to discuss it on your return.

It is the one book of mine that Michael Sadleir hasn't liked, and, on the *whole*, cannot be called a success.

I myself am not really satisfied with it – but I *do* think that it has *countless* 'patches of great brilliance' (to quote your expression about my third period.) In fact I'm certain these patches are as good as anything I've ever done.

Now to the main point of my mentioning this.

If you *haven't* read it *please don't*. It'd be so much the better to wait till I can talk to you.

But if you *have* – then tell me,

BUT

don't say anything discouraging about it!

Allude to it only *briefly* and, *even if you have to lie through your teeth*, agree with me that it has these 'patches of great brilliance'.

I don't think I'd have ever embarked upon a series (almost a serial) about one character, if I had known what it entailed. When one writes an inferior isolated book one can, after a year or so, just write it off as inferior. But with one of a series, one's confidence is shaken, and one's work and enthusiasm about the whole thing is seriously endangered.

In point of fact there are only going to be *two* more books – making four in all – and I have high hopes of pulling the whole thing out of the fire yet![17]

The only unconvincing sentence in this letter is the final one because in every other detail it reads like the testimony of a man no longer able to undertake the arrogant leap into empty space that any writing of serious fiction must entail.

23

Divorce and
Unknown Assailant

I

From the beginning of 1953 onwards, Hamilton allowed domestic events to take their course. In June, his divorce from Loïs became absolute and a year later, he married Lá. His decision to marry was impetuous, but not romantically so:

I came to the decision with enormous suddenness – a Marxist Dialectical Leap – the change from Quantity into Quality – the *Quantity* of misery, unfairness and damage the previous situation had been causing to *all three* of us *suddenly* making a real qualitative change in my attitude.[1]

Albany Stables was sold and Loïs found a flat back in Henley. Hamilton bought a small house for himself and La in Hyde Park Gate Mews, just a hundred yards from the park. Nothing much had changed. If Hamilton had been weaker, he would have stuck with Loïs. If he had been more determined, he would have left her entirely for Laura. Instead he would spend the rest of his life vaguely drifting between them, whether out of habit or a misplaced sense of obligation. He had principally used the delay before marrying La to turn their relationship into a more turbulent version of the relationship that he was unable to leave behind. The two wives – who hated each other – were both understandably dissatisfied with an arrangement that cast them in the respective roles of frying pan and fire, and it did nothing but harm to Hamilton. His expectations of his domestic life began to be prudently limited. When in London he walked regularly in Kensington Gardens, attempted to drink less ('what is for me practically *nothing*') and kept his mind busy with chess and an attempt, which he was to take up recurrently in his life without significant results, to learn Latin. He guardedly reported to Bruce, as he generally did in his periods of reform, that he was a different person:

Above all I am mentally so much calmer, and this is a tremendous help in my private life with La. If only *one* party can keep calm, the really hideous hitting rows do not take place. Short words there must always be from time to time, of course – but that applies to any people living together.[2]

He cannot have been greatly cheered by the publication of La's third novel, *Barcelona Road*, a patent and unhappy attempt to fuse the worlds of Laura Talbot and Patrick Hamilton in a distorted version of their own relationship. The heroine is Lady Lilah, a name which seems to derive from the sound of someone attempting to say Lalla, La, Laura and Loïs simultaneously. She has married beneath her, and come to live in suburban Hove with her new husband, the once-successful journalist, George Shincombe (just as Patrick and La had lived together briefly in Hove Road): 'Poor George was such a "trier", such a struggler – so sincere and hard-working, and his luck had gone out lately, and there was no doubt about it that he loved her, and George, thought to be so "brilliantly clever" during his "fashionable" period, was certainly not a fool.'[3] There is a certain interest in seeing the Hamiltonian worlds of the pub and seedy provincial life portrayed not with horrified obsession but bored social disdain. Lilah is half revolted and half fascinated – 'it is his awfulness which fascinates me'[4] – by the caddish local dentist, Rodney: 'At least, Lilah thought, Rodney had not made the "gaffe" of wearing a white tie: that pitfall which lay in wait for the unwary, that stamper of provincialism.'[5] Laura Talbot does not endorse Lilah's snobbery and the book ends neatly with George escaping and Lilah trapped in suburban Hove. But the book depends to an almost pornographic extent on the degrading excitement of an upper-class woman giving herself to a middle-class professional man, much as a novel set in the Deep South of America might be about the daughter of a plantation owner giving herself to one of her father's slaves.

It was a difficult year. *The Man Upstairs* was finally produced but failed inconsequentially in the provinces. Hamilton felt so let down by Linnit and Dunfee (as the company was now called) that he broke with it, thus depriving himself of another friendship on which he had relied, albeit less in recent years.[6]

Everything served to cast him down, including the coronation of Queen Elizabeth II. This in itself was objectionable to Hamilton, but he was also becoming agoraphobic and the terrifying crowds prevented him from getting to Lords: 'And one is *depressed* as well as terrified. Nothing is worse for the soul, or can make one feel more *lonely*, than the knowledge that one is going against the masses (mostly Labour-voting, needless to say).'[7] But there was generally an element of conscious self-parody even in his bleakest expressions of gloom, and he concluded this diatribe with a poem (Eugene Goosens was a celebrated musician and conductor of the time):

> *On Being Kept Awake by a Cuckoo at Whitchurch at 5 a.m.*
> Oh, blithe newcomer (often heard,
> No doubt, by Eugene Goosens).
> Oh, Cuckoo – shall I call thee bird
> Or just a bloody nuisance?[8]

At other times he descended into drink and self-pity, comparing himself to the captain of the Glamorgan cricket team who had reputedly lost the toss twenty-four times out of twenty-eight attempts.[9] In January 1954 an attempt to return to golf and good health at the Hurley course, outside Henley, 'ended up in misery and drink'. Hamilton was baffled by his failure: 'Why is it that at the moment I can do *nothing* right? I don't think it's all my fault.'[10] And, once again, the Inland Revenue was after him:

This isn't nice as my expenses (before I *eat*, smoke, drink or take a bus) amount to £48 a week! You'll hardly believe this, but this is how it goes:

£120 a month to Income Tax	= £30
£10 a week to Loïs	= £10
£6 a week for H.P.G. Mews	= £6
£2 a week for 'help'	= £2
	£48!

And I'm not *earning* £48 a week, my dearest Ecurb! So where it all ends I don't know.[11]

Over the previous thirty years of his life, Hamilton had gradually constructed an existence which moved between a series of fixed points on which he could rely. A comfortable income, a secure domestic environment where he could work, family members with whom alone he could be emotionally intimate, a number of business cronies whom he could see whenever he wanted, and the work which justified his existence.

During these terrible years in the mid-fifties, the worst of his life, they all faded away. Much of Hamilton's activity was directed towards trying to pretend that all was as it had been. He sent Michael Sadleir a long poem about an innovation he had encountered while at the London Library.[12] The six pages of couplets, intricate and skilful, must have taken a great deal of time to compose, but Sadleir was now sixty-five, he had just become Chairman of Constable, and he was no longer disposed to play facetious undergraduate games in the way he had been when in his forties and fifties. Three weeks passed and Hamilton had to write a rather lame follow-up: 'Did you get my 144-line poem about the goings-on at the London Library? It didn't exactly require an answer, but I somehow thought I would hear from you.'[13] Sadleir's reply soberly avoided competing with Hamilton's attempt at youthful high spirits: 'I am very sorry to have seemed unappreciative of the L.L. poem, but I have really been too busy to devise a response worthy of its theme, and my once powerful poetical talent has alas deserted me.'[14]

Hamilton spent a 'wifeless' weekend with Bill Linnit in a 'desperate attempt to revive our painfully declining friendship'.[15] It was a doubly disillusioning experience. He was confirmed in his dislike of Bill Linnit, whom he described as 'now dreadfully woolly-minded in every way, and only seems to seek the acquaintance of the (phoney) "upper-class" people whom his wife is so agonisingly and obviously anxious to cultivate.'[16] (The use of both quotation marks and parentheses demonstrates the depth of Hamilton's scorn.) Not only that, Hamilton decided that he no longer cared much for golf either, because the game no longer taught him anything. As Hamilton, the compulsive autodidact, put it, 'isn't the whole point about *any* activity (recreational or otherwise) that you are incessantly *learning* something?'[17]

Hamilton had hoped that his marriage would paradoxically improve relations with Loïs and that he could 'go and stay with her a lot' at her new flat in Henley. 'Could it be that the Glamorgan Captain . . . has won a toss at last?' he wondered.[18] His first extended visit, just a couple of months later, was a disaster: 'We made each other *miserable* and finally agreed that we can't any more spend *long* periods together.'[19] The result, as with most of his setbacks now, was an alcoholic binge.

There were occasional enthusiasms. He described chess as his salvation,[20] though for him the game was rarely a social activity. He was more interested in chess problems or playing through old master games. A more improbable souce of interest was the idea of adapting for the stage Stetson Kennedy's celebrated exposé, *I Rode With the Ku Klux Klan*.[21] A radical born in Florida, Kennedy had infiltrated the racist organization and uncovered a wealth of incriminating material which proved to be 'the single most important factor in preventing a postwar revival of the Ku Klux Klan in the North.'[22] To Hamilton, Kennedy represented an ideal, a radical man of action, that was utterly beyond him. Bill Linnit was encouraging but, Hamilton's initial excitement notwithstanding, it is difficult to conceive of a project less appropriate for the author of *Rope* and *Gaslight* than this journalistic, political drama set in the steamy Deep South of the United States. A month later the play was 'in abeyance for the moment'[23] and that was largely where it stayed.

Hamilton was now fifty but talking like a man of extreme old age. He quoted a familiar saying: 'As we grow older the years grow shorter but the days grow longer. . . . Don't you find the days, on the whole, painfully long? I sometimes wake up in the morning and wonder how on earth I'm going to manage to get through the 16 hours or so before I'm in bed and asleep again.'[24] This was not an attitude but a symptom of illness and after another alcoholic binge he was tempted to undergo the 'Dent Cure', from which Michael Stewart, La's second husband, had already benefited. Hamilton cancelled the treatment, because, he said, Dr Dent was 'now old and very past it'.[25] But he was deeply impressed by Dr Dent's book, *Anxiety and Its Treatment – With Special Reference to Alcoholism* – the title alone could hardly have failed to secure Hamilton's interest. He was particularly struck by Dent's contention that alcoholism is

a *disease* like any other. I think most people would concede this – but only superficially. An alcoholic is still subconsciously looked on as a *sinner* – one who jolly well ought to pull himself together. He is not pitied like, say, a chronic sufferer from bronchitis or what-have-you.

I suppose this is largely because he makes such a bloody nuisance of himself, or becomes such a *bore*, or, in the later stages of his disease, loses his character and resorts to all sorts of dishonesty (either intellectual or technically criminal).

All the same, it *is* a disease like any other, and (what non-alcoholics so seldom realise) an extremely agonising one – worse, in a way, than other diseases, because the agony is moral as well as physical. You don't blame yourself for losing your job and bringing your family to ruin if it's due to chronic arthritis – but you *do* if it's due to chronic alcoholism.

I'm not saying that character cannot be of any assistance in dealing with this disease. There is a bit in Dent's book which is engraved in my mind. He says: – 'Whenever anyone runs away from any discomfort he becomes more acutely conscious of that discomfort. Let a man shield his eyes from the light and they will rapidly require ever more shielding. There is no limit to this. The eyes may demand complete darkness and the fear of light becomes so intense that all kinds of fantastic precautions will be taken against any possible light entering the eyes . . .'

He is thinking of alcoholism in particular, but applies what he is saying to countless other ailments caused by addictions – constipation (aperient-taking), indigestion (alkali-swallowing), sleeplessness (barbiturate drugs) and so on and so forth. The point is that the taking of remedies (except on occasions) increases the ailment. Poor Mummie, in her goodness of heart, by plugging me with aperients in childhood nearly made me a victim of constipation for life.[26]

II

For Hamilton, writing *Unknown Assailant*, the third Gorse book, was like preparing a lamb for the slaughter. He was shackled to the remnants of his friendship with Michael Sadleir and the idea of moving to another publisher seems never to have occurred to him. Disconsolate, discouraged and just wanting to get what was now reduced to a trilogy over with, he expanded a short story into a very short novel. He couldn't even bear to go through the physical process of writing. Instead he hired a typist to whom he attempted to dictate a rough first draft. His scheme was to correct this and then have it properly typed. The plan went awry almost from the first since, due to alleged failings of the typist, the result of what he dictated was 'practically *gibberish*'.[27] Hamilton's testimony here must be treated with some caution. Logistical arrangements had always provoked almost intolerable anxiety in him, and now, facing the end of his published writing career, he could hardly have chosen a less propitious time to attempt an entirely new method of composition. The unfortunate typist was disposed of and then Hamilton attempted to type the first draft but was defeated by his own exhaustion and exasperation. Then La stepped in and took Hamilton's dictation, which she did 'beautifully – but it was a great strain for both of us.'[28]

Unknown Assailant is quite unlike anything else Hamilton ever published. When Henry James turned to dictating his novels, late in life, his already voluminous sentences became meandering linguistic rivers with clauses leading off them like tributaries. The effect of this method of composition on Hamilton was quite different. His prose became spare, with short, staccato sentences. In contrast to the characteristic, highly finished style of his earlier work, *Unknown Assailant* frequently reads like a sketch for a novel. Though a minor achievement, it is a haunting, valedictory work.

Hamilton disposes of Gorse in this book not by killing him, as he had threatened in the past, but by launching him into a community that is, in various ways, immune to him. In *The West Pier* Esther Downes derives much of her sense of selfhood from her life savings. In *Mr Stimpson and Mr Gorse*, Mrs Plumleigh-Bruce places a similar value on her reputation within her tiny community. By depriving the women of their goods, Gorse steals their souls.

Ivy Barton, 'a decidedly foolish but very good and loveable girl',[29] is very different. By failing to put up any resistance of Gorse, she shows herself as, in an important way, untouchable:

Ivy was curiously disinterested in money, even in her own savings, which she had put by reluctantly and simply because her mother had told her that it was the correct and necessary thing to do. They bored her, and she could think of nothing nicer than taking them out of the Post Office and using them in the more glamorous way to which Gorse said they would be put.[30]

Gorse further damages Esther Downes by violating her relationship with her family, but his manoeuvrings can have no effect of this kind on Ivy:

'The truth was that Mr Barton, who did not care for his daughter in the smallest way, had absolutely no interest in her savings, apart from mildly resenting the fact that she had any. The only thing which would have aroused his interest would have been her losing them through her own folly.'[31]

In her dogged honesty, Ivy forces Gorse to turn his fraud into a straightforward transaction. He must reveal himself as a thief. He drives her into the country, ties her up and steals her money. This is the only moment of open violence in the trilogy but even here Hamilton exaggerates the 'bestiality' of what is going to happen, before telling us that Gorse 'certainly did not want a dead body on his hands',[32] which makes him a curious rival to sadistic murderers like Neville Heath and George Smith. Just before the attack, Hamilton tells us that Gorse 'liked to tie women up in order to get the impression that they were at his mercy, and he also liked to be tied up by women and to feel that he was at theirs'.[33] Hamilton's statement that 'It is foolish to call this a perversion' has been taken as a confession to the reader – and, more directly, it must be assumed, to La, to whom this was being dictated – that this is Hamilton choosing a moment to exculpate his own preferred sexual practices. But this is to miss the point made by the rest of the sentence: 'it is merely a rather emphasized form of the sadistic or masochistic element underlying every physical relationship between man and woman, or, if it comes to that, man and man, or woman and woman.'[34] It is not perverted because that is what sex is really like.

By exposing so nakedly the brutality of the male-female relationship, Gorse permits Ivy to transcend it. Almost unobtrusively, he departs from the book, taking the black retributive world we expect in Hamilton's writing with him. Not especially distressed, Ivy shakes off her bonds. While walking along the country road, she meets a telegram boy, Stan Bullitt, who is the first thoroughly good, active character Hamilton ever created. Stan asks where she got her bruised wrist:

'Oh – it's such a long story!' said Ivy. 'It's such a long *story*!'

'Well,' said Stan Bullitt, still gently holding her hand. 'Every story has to come to an end at some time – doesn't it? And sometimes it has a happy ending – doesn't it?'

'Yes!' said Ivy, as he went on examining her wrist.

'The point is to *make* the happy ending – isn't it? And the only way to do that is to *do* something about it – as far as I know . . .'[35]

In *The West Pier* Hamilton had guaranteed the misery of his characters by grimly recounting what would happen in the rest of their lives. He grants Stan his success by putting him beyond the cruel workings of the world, telling us that he was killed 'in the very early days of the Second World War':

The news of his death made Ivy bitterly unhappy, and yet perhaps, seen objectively, it was not an entirely unhappy thing.

Whom the gods love, it is said, die young. And Stan was peculiarly fitted to do this – to die in all the glory of his boisterousness, cleverness and superb physical health. Stan, if he had lived, would probably never have been able to adjust himself to the harsh exigencies of maturity, and, later, of middle or old age. And, if only doing what he did for Ivy, if only for enabling her, with his overwhelming personality, to escape permanently from her father, he had not lived in vain.[36]

That this (leaving to one side the marriages cobbled together at the end of Hamilton's first three novels) is the happiest fate accorded to any of Hamilton's characters, is the clearest demonstration of his bleak, stoical pessimism. In the case of *Unknown Assailant* all pessissism was justified. He must have known that Michael Sadleir would not like it and his fears were justified. In May 1955 he wrote to Bruce, almost in despair:

The book, which is called *Unknown Assailant*, is, I think, neither better nor worse than *The W.P.* and *Mr S. and Mr G.* Michael S. has told me that he dislikes it a good deal (but at any rate he is publishing it, and I think he will do this quickly).

My relationship with this man has become more strained than ever, and I don't think this is because my work has (as you and I agree) deteriorated in the Gorse books. There's something more to it than this – something I can't put my finger on.

I can't *tell* you how depressing it is to have a publisher who does not even *feign* the *smallest* enthusiasm about one's work.

I know the Gorse books are inferior, but they're not as bad as all *that*.

I've thought about this matter a lot, and I have an idea that the inferiority is to some extent due to the nature of the *theme*, which, for some reason, cannot be treated in a fine and delicate way – the sort of crochet-work I've tried ever since

The Midnight B. A rather *loose* manner of writing is somehow *demanded*. However, I may just be making an excuse for writing loosely.

Having an unenthusiastic and damping publisher is rather like being a carpenter compelled to use a hopelessly blunt saw. You begin to lose interest in your work, and consequently you do it badly.

On top of all this M.S. had become, in his correspondence at any rate, insufferably *rude*. (You always thought he had this quality.)[37]

For the first time Michael could not even bring himself to write the blurb for the book's dustjacket and wrote a chilly letter to Hamilton asking him to do it himself, as 'there may well be some point you would like stressed about the new story.'[38]

The reviews for the book were mixed. John Raymond, the leading British authority on the works of Georges Simenon, had patronized *The West Pier* on its first appearance.[39] Now he described the trilogy as masterly and the new novel just as good. The effect was rather spoiled by the novel's being referred to as *The Unknown Assailant*, reviewed fourth in a batch of five novels and bracketed with the fifth – Richard Gordon's *Doctor at Large* – as 'two excellent entertainments'.[40] Isabel Quigly, in the *Spectator*, was ecstatic, but, sadly, she was recalling the great achievement of *The West Pier* which had seemed likely

to give almost a new meaning to fictional realism. Without comment, without moralising, he managed to suggest a disease that, while far-fetched, was also contemporary and pointed; a valid ugliness, a purpose in the dreary record of squalor. *Unknown Assailant* falls off from this high standard of horror. . . . the imaginative accuracy of his early treatment of Gorse has flattened into mere documentary, and Gorse has become – for the present, at least – a figure out of a sociologist's casebook.[41]

Four months later Hamilton wrote to Martha Smith about a new book he had started and to assure her that he was now back on the straight and narrow path after his literary wrong turning: 'Oh I can't tell you how happy I am – still happy – to be free from Gorse!'[42]

24

Breakdown

Hamilton and La's house in Hyde Park Gate Mews was convenient and possessed certain attractions. Hamilton was generally amused by signs of his near neighbour, Winston Churchill: 'Although in London, this place is *gloriously* quiet and restful. I write this looking out on Sir Winston's house and garden. (The elderly low comedian, by the way, is now in residence again, and cops lurk about . . .)'[1] But the house was 'inconvenient to run' and was gradually exerting a depressive effect on the couple, partly because since his late twenties Hamilton had found London difficult to bear for extended periods. The major rail strike in the summer of 1955 only made things worse. In practice, Hamilton never had much sympathy for industrial action by the proletariat, in England at least. This he found a 'singularly depressing and, *I* think, rather muddled, strike.' He was confirmed in a feeling he had had for some time that the proletariat was 'as moribund a class as the "aristocracy".' All it apparently wanted was a television set, and worse still, he had heard that in some areas people had 'put up television aerials without *having* a television set! Just to pretend to the neighbours that they've got one!'[2] And he could fairly claim that his lack of sympathy with the proletariat began at home. At the end of the letter in which he complained about it he also lamented his own discomforts, at the hand of his home help: 'I've had a tricky time since the 11th. Mrs Ham had a heart attack and has left us. And we simply could not *find* any other "help" of any sort.'[3]

Though he was in London, Hamilton felt himself starved of one of the principal qualities by which the capital justified itself for him: intellectual companionship. Estranged from Bill Linnit and Michael Sadleir, he abruptly announced that he was 'off' Claud Cockburn and no longer saw him. The lone substitute was another lapsed friend of Cockburn's, the minor literary figure, John Davenport, who is now seen of significance, if at all, as a friend of Dylan Thomas.[4] Almost half-heartedly Hamilton attempted to turn him into another paternal figure: 'J. D. – though at *periods* a heavy drinker and occasionally violent in drink – is, like yourself [Bruce], very much my intellectual superior – (though, I suspect, he can't write for toffee). It is glorious to have someone you can *learn* from.'[5]

In September 1955 Bruce, now the principal of a new technical institute in Barbados, returned for a year-long visit (the last he would make until his retirement) and Hamilton, presumably recalling their last disastrous reunion, made a prudent suggestion: 'By the way, I think it would be a good idea if, on our first meeting on your return, we do not meet at *night*, but for a glass of beer or two in the *morning*. This just to *start off* on the right foot.'[6]

Bruce felt even more hopeful when he heard that Hamilton, at La's insistence, had finally agreed to take the Dent cure. At first it seemed as if the cure, albeit harsh and intensely resented by Hamilton, was working. Although Bruce watched over his brother, and attempted to enforce the medication that was a part of its final stages, his attempt to rescue Hamilton disintegrated, with considerable bad feeling between the two brothers. Bruce claimed that he did not greatly blame himself for this,[7] and he had no reason to, but the fact that he made the protest may indicate his sense that he was entirely the wrong person to be Hamilton's nursemaid. Apart, they were closer than they had ever been, and in these last years Hamilton channelled most of his literary powers into his long, sometimes almost book-length letters to Bruce. But their meetings were uniformly disastrous. Unfairly or not, Hamilton now considered his brother a prig and perhaps even a bore. Bruce no longer had much regard for Hamilton's writing and he despised what he had, in Bruce's view, reduced himself to. On one painful occasion, Bruce returned from a concert at the Albert Hall which he had attended in spite of Hamilton's objections: 'I can only describe the expression on his face, as he asked me if I had enjoyed myself, as a puffy sneer. It would have been hateful if it had not been so pitiable.'[8] The cure ended with Hamilton drinking more heavily than ever, and each relapse left him at a lower level.

Bruce's response to the failure of this visit to England was to begin a (never-to-be-published) novel, ominously titled *A Case for Cain*. It is a barely disguised memoir of his relationship with Patrick, with many direct references and quotations. He describes the whole of his life as 'practically dedicated to something hardly short of the worship of his brother. At the novel's crisis, Bruce does introduce a grim note of fiction, leaving his wife (an obvious portrait of Aileen) and, as the title suggests, murdering his brother, beating him to death with a golf club.

Patrick had decided earlier in the year that he should attempt a move back to Norfolk, with La, though he worried to Bruce that 'the part of the world you and I knew is now overrun with GI's (raping girls right and left) and aeroplanes.'[9] Then, improbably, there was what seemed to be a miracle, as he explained to Martha Smith:

It would be impossible to tell you by letter about all the intricacies of the really beastly time I've had in the last three months or so. It's enough to say that I've miraculously survived – survived even the ill-advised 'cure' (about which I'll tell you when we meet!) – and that I'm now, honestly, feeling better than I've ever felt in my entire life.[10]

For a nominal rent of ten shillings a week, Hamilton and La had been offered Highfield House, in Blakeney, Norfolk, while its owner was away. (He agreed to their tenancy both because he was a distant friend of La's family and because he had acted in a production of *Rope* when he was a schoolboy.) The large house facing south suited Hamilton perfectly, with 'an absolutely unspoiled view of miles of the most rural part of Norfolk – a garden big enough to turn into a miniature Golf Course (which I've done) – some goldfish, believe it or not, in a sort of stone pond – what more could you want?'[11] Hamilton was not drinking, though ominously proposing to return to occasional consumption now that he had cured himself. He was working on a new book, and even thinking once more of the Ku Klux Klan play. He at least contemplated a radio adaptation of *Hangover Square* and while discussing it he reported to Val Gielgud that he was 'more or less odiously well. But I don't put this down to the exertion of moral strength. Simply getting away into the country.'[12] None of these projects ever advanced substantially. Three months later Hamilton gave up the *Hangover Square* adaptation because he considered the novel impossible to adapt to another medium: 'On reading the book again I have found that its whole interest, and indeed its whole tension, resides in the atmosphere it gives of a ghastly sort of underworld of drunks and hangers-on in Earl's Court, just before the war.'[13]

Bruce saw the worst of Hamilton during this period. Stalin had died in March 1953 and Hamilton was dismayed not just by the death itself but also by the denunciations which followed, though these did little to shake his basic political convictions, which were a matter more of faith than reason. He also witnessed some bickering between Hamilton and La.

The truly damaging blow – which Bruce did not witness – was a piece of cruel bad luck: his expulsion from the 'paradise' of Highfield House. The owner sold it, arranging with Hamilton and La that they could move into another house just a quarter of a mile away. But while the first house was sold, the second deal fell through: 'Consequently one is without any proper warning, completely homeless – and what happens now God knows.'[14] La went to stay with her brother and Hamilton returned to Loïs who was herself living with a friend at Sandgate in Kent but 'by the grace of God, there is just at present a vacant room there.'[15]

This was one blow too many. There remained a curiously obstinate rationality about Hamilton's depressions, and, for that matter, his attitude towards his drinking. Perhaps damagingly, he always believed that his problems were straightforward affairs that could be solved by a change of circumstances, a new regime, exercise, fitness, a hit play, an esteemed novel. He now experienced the most severe depression of his life, together with an absolute inability to think of anything practical that could be done to deal with it. He was insecure about his writing, and he was no longer wealthy – kept from penury, he claimed, with a degree of exaggeration, entirely by the continuing worldwide proceeds from *Rope* and *Gaslight*.[16] After a disastrous few days down in Hove, during which Hamilton learned that Bill Linnit had died, Bruce had returned to Barbados. Hamilton's remaining friends, from whom he was anyway now detached, knew nothing. Michael Sadleir's suspicions were only aroused when, in September, he received a letter from the London Library. He had been Hamilton's sponsor for membership, and the Secretary was inquiring why Hamilton was not replying to inquiries either about overdue books or his annual membership fee.[17] Michael wrote to Hamilton and Martha wrote to Loïs to find out what was going on. Loïs replied by return of post, speaking first of her own unfortunate circumstances:

I'd *love* to see you both again: I've been very much cut off from the old friends since my divorce. Now, of course, I'm kept busy in this small (and rather threadbare) flat, doing the old job of 'housekeeping' without a servant of any sort. Hamilton is still here with me, anyway until November; then – I don't know.

Yes, his condition is a sad one indeed. His body is so well, but his mind so fretful, and uninspired for anything; and because of this he is, for the time being, doomed to idleness, which, in its turn, makes for more gloom and introspection. The doctors say it is menopausal melancholia: *I* think it is, and I also think it will pass, whether it is a matter of months or even years. He needs a home, Martha, with a background of his long-established roots: and this is our aim and hope, but how it's going to be achieved we cannot for the life of us see at the moment. I can only do what I can when I can, and keep my fingers crossed.[18]

Even Loïs was underestimating the drastic nature of Hamilton's depression, not surprisingly because it was something new, even for his scarred psyche. Hamilton was unable to express what he was feeling at the time, but when the crisis was behind him he wrote the longest letter of his life, fifty pages to Bruce, beginning on 3 December 1956 and completing it on 30 January 1957.

Of course, nobody who has not been through this illness can possibly understand it fully. Nor can anybody who has been through it possibly explain it fully. To talk of 'depression' or '*hideous* depression' or '*unspeakable* depression' – all sound so *tame*! People can only think of the most ghastly depression they themselves have ever been through, and imagine that this sort of thing is going on all the time in the case of a sufferer from this illness. But to think this is not really to touch even the *fringe* of the real horror, which, although indescribable, I must nevertheless, attempt, feebly, to describe to you.

Imagine, then, that you read in the papers about a small boy who had been made by his parents to 'stand in the corner' of a locked and empty room *all day and all night for a year* – the only relief he gets being in the five hours of sleep which he takes on his feet (still conscious, in the moments of his waking from this coma, of the torture which awaits him next day). You have, of course, to imagine that this is physically possible.

Now imagine that you yourself are this small boy. Go, if you like, into the corner of a deserted room *now*! And stand up in it for only twenty minutes. (Or *two* minutes! Try it *now*!)

And, having endured the twenty minutes, think of the *next* twenty minutes, and the twenty minutes after *that*, and then the *hour* after that, and then all the *hours* after *hours* after *that*, before you get your next coma! And then the *days* after that, and the *months*, and the *years*!

Think of the counting of every *minute*, the watching of every *hour*, while waiting for the brief coma, which is *so* brief and useless!

Is not this a fair description of hell? – one might say *eternal* hell!

But this, really, is not all. If you or I were put in such a corner we *might* work out *some* scheme for coping with it – let's say writing a novel in one's mind and, as a daily task, memorising what one has written.

But such pleasures are denied one! – for one simply can't take the *faintest* interest in *anything* to *do* with the mind! (This is really another way of saying that the horrors of solitary confinement are nothing compared to it.)

Here I must concede that one was at least saved from *worry*! A million pounds (income tax free) given one – death of one's dearest (you, Loïs, La) – a new world war – *complete* destitution – all bores, bores, *bores*!!!

I have used this *feeble* simile of standing in a corner permanently because in such a situation the horror *really* would derive from the fact that one would be *deprived of anything to respond to*, all day and night. Well, is not this the same as being unable to respond to anything? Do you follow me at all?[19]

Though he had frequently suffered from depression, he seems never before to have been drawn to thoughts of suicide. Now he contemplated it incessantly. He revealed to his brother that this preoccupation had begun during their days in Hove before Bruce returned to Barbados, a visit when Bruce had been baffled by Hamilton's withdrawn, passive misery, even though he appeared scarcely to be drinking. There had been no fear of death or extinction, and no religious feelings of any kind. Instead he was preoccupied by the details, the practicalities, of suicide. How should it be done and would it hurt? He was tempted by open windows and high places, or throwing himself in front of a train, or deliberately being run over by a car but he was afraid to do it and, understandably, given his vivid memories of the aftermath of his accident, afraid of the pain if he survived. The possibility of an overdose reminded him of the effect the death of their mother had had on them: 'And if one did it at "Halstead" with Loïs, there was the horror involved for her – I mean discovering me in the morning, and having to wait *hours* before *announcing* it, in case she should have me saved by doctors. (You will remember that poor Lalla went through this sort of horror.)'[20]

In September 1956 Hamilton had a long-standing appointment with Dr Dent to discuss some aspect of his alcohol 'cure'. As soon as he saw Hamilton's condition, he dropped all talk of this and said: 'Well – this looks like a case for ECT.' Hamilton didn't know what this was until it was explained that it was electro-convulsive therapy, a form of treatment that Hamilton had already been offered to treat his alcoholism and had turned down. Dr Dent immediately made an appointment with a Dr J. A. Hobson, 'one of the leading pioneers and exponents of this treatment', Consulting Physician in the Department of Psychological Medicine at the Middlesex Hospital. Dr Hobson dealt with such cases at the Woodside Hospital in Muswell Hill, north London. On the night before the appointment, about a week later, Hamilton was staying alone in a hotel near the hospital and suffered a panic attack in which he nearly threw himself out of the window of his room. Dr Dent had him admitted to a clinic while Hamilton drank himself into a coma with whisky, from which he was woken by Dr Dent who had to plead with him to keep his appointment. He drank whisky in the car on the way to the hospital, in the waiting room and entered Dr Hobson's room taking his bottle with him. Hamilton, with his keen interest in crime, was predisposed to be impressed by Dr Hobson, 'a tall, good-looking man of forty-five', who, just three years earlier, had given evidence for the defence on the mental state of the sex murderer, John Reginald Christie. (In fact it was to Dr Hobson that Christie had made his first detailed description of the murders.[21]) But when, with a confidence, which he had heard from doctors so often before, Dr Hobson announced that he would cure him, Hamilton only felt worse. Dr Hobson obtained a room for Hamilton on the spot, 'turning into another room an elderly clergyman who was in for dipsomania (but still drinking and quite happy!).'[22]

Hamilton was first treated with 'Deep Sleep Treatment', a series of injections to subdue him, but this did nothing to allay his anxieties and after three days he fled to Loïs in a worse condition than when he had arrived. He was coaxed back and feebly attempted to be a co-operative patient. 'At one time I made a wretched attempt to sand-paper and varnish the frame of a stool – but gave up after about a quarter of an hour. Nor was I interested in Billiards, ping-pong, lectures or reading!'[23]

Nowadays E C T is frequently portrayed as a brutal, archaic treatment that was only ever used as a form of coercion by repressive medical institutions, often to stamp out awkwardly nonconformist individuals. Certainly it is an extreme form of treatment, deliberately inducing a fit by passing an electric current through the brain. It had originally been developed, in the late 1930s, because it was thought, wrongly, that epilepsy and schizophrenia could not occur together. Hence, the argument went, if fits were induced the schizophrenia would be cured. This didn't work but it was observed that 'the most striking changes occurred not in schizophrenia but in severe depressive disorders, in which it brought about a substantial reduction in chronicity and morbidity.'[24] Even now, little is known about why the procedure works but it is still used when it is essential to bring about improvement quickly. According to a standard text book:

The strongest indications are therefore an immediate high risk of suicide, depressive stupor, or danger to physical health because the patient is not drinking enough to maintain adequate renal function. Less strong indications are persistent severe depressive disorder despite an adequate trial of antidepressant drugs; and a depressive disorder causing extreme distress requiring rapid relief.[25]

The treatment was duly administered and Hamilton responded to it in typical fashion:

I was a month there, and it was like having seven minor (and not so minor as all that) operations in a row. For an hour after each of these you suffer from an almost complete and really terrifying loss of memory – not knowing who, where, or what you are, what you do, where you live, if you have any friends, if you are married and so on and so forth. You pester the nurses with endless panicky questions, and can't really understand their answers. After this one just has a not very bad headache.[26]

The temporary amnesia that is a common effect of the induced fits caused Hamilton some alarm:

It is supposed to affect the memory for two or three months afterwards, but if it has done this to me it is very slight indeed (though it has blotted out little bits of the later depressed periods), and, anyway, I'd rather have been turned into a cretin for the rest of my life than go on enduring what I was enduring.[27]

He was as depressed as ever after the first treatment but he had promised to submit to a course of six. When the sixth was over he felt he was the same but Dr Hobson assured him that he was cured, 'And the patient is always the last to know. . . . Always the *last*. . . .'[28] Dr Hobson jovially suggested one more treatment, 'so that you're done to a turn', and Hamilton agreed. On the afternoon after the seventh, La called and Hamilton told her of Dr Hobson's absurd notion that he was better: 'And it was here that *she* surprised me, saying, in a tone almost of confidence, "Yes – I think you *are* better." '[29]

She left with Hamilton a book about the nineteenth century Staunton murder trial. It was well chosen, not just because of Hamilton's interest in murders but because the case of Louis Staunton, tried with several members of his family for the murder of his wife and child, is like a brutal, working-class version of *Gaslight*[30]:

And then, after she had left, and (I think) at about six o'clock in the evening, I was mooning about my room when it occurred to me that I might *conceivably*, only *conceivably*, have a look at the book after supper that night.

And then, some time before supper time, I can vividly remember lying on my bed and being struck by what I considered an idiotic, rambling thought.

It would be funny, wouldn't it (I thought) if history repeated itself, and La's coming to see me, and leaving that book, resembled *Bruce*'s coming to see me, at No 99 years ago, and my suddenly telling him I was better! Needless to say I dismissed the thought as utterly fantastic, and went on glooming.

Nevertheless, this is exactly what *happened*![31]

Nothing spectacular occurred. He began to read the book: 'And then (still before breakfast, I think) I had a sort of inspiration. Why not (I thought) get some *more* little things to cling to?'[32] Hamilton decided to go to Foyles bookshop in central London and buy a *Teach Yourself French* book. He knew exactly where it was, on the same shelf as the *Teach Yourself Shorthand* which he had bought a year previously to brush up on what he had learnt by correspondence course back in the early twenties.

He also bought a work of popular, exhortatory philosophy, *Belief and Action* by Lord Samuel, a 'sad, sweet, morose, lost-looking' man with whom he 'used to have morose, cosy chats at the end of Omar Dinners'. He went to a café over the road, was 'enraptured by the book, by the fact that I was able to be enraptured by it'. The improvement continued and Hamilton decided that he really was cured. 'It is not what they call "nothing short of a miracle",' he wrote to Michael Sadleir and Martha Smith, 'it is a miracle.'[33]

Hamilton's autodidactic zest had returned: 'As you can imagine, I am in a sort of pit-ponyish dream of delight at the sudden transition to normality – at being able to *respond* to things again, to take interest in them, to laugh, above all to *read*!'[34] His new enthusiasm manifested itself in various ways. He had vague, never-to-be realized plans for a novel: 'I have even something half in mind already – this with a Sandgatish background. I am right in the midst of a fascinatingly ghastly middle-class society here – and in which the women's countless dogs all wear overcoats, and people, when they haven't seen you for some time, say "Long time no See" etc. etc.'[35]

More characteristic of this period of his life was a plan for a reference work that could be compiled in fragments. He had become interested in synonyms and he asked Michael and Martha for advice as to how he could obtain *Webster's Dictionary of Synonyms*, which was published in the United States. By return of post they informed him that they had bought the book and would give it to him as a present. Hamilton replied:

I do not think you would ever be able quite to know how absurdly happy your letter made me! Merely to have learned that you had traced the book, and that I might *possibly* get hold of it – this would have been happiness enough. Then, to have learned that you had actually acquired a *copy* and that it was waiting for me – at this my happiness would have been simply overflowing! But to learn that all this happened and that it had been offered to me as a present by my two oldest chums – really this was going *too* far![36]

The breach in the friendship had been healed. He arranged to meet them for dinner in London – with Loïs – before returning to Norfolk.

At this propitious time Hamilton received another pleasant surprise, in John Betjeman's 'City and Suburban' column in *The Spectator* in the final issue of 1956. It was headlined, 'Moustache or Clean Shaven?':

Even literary gents, and I suppose I must call myself one, have their literary heroes. To me these are those who never go to parties nor are seen on television nor are heard on the wireless, but are just names on printed pages. They never even publish portraits and biographies of themselves on their dustwrapers. I have sought out and found a few. I knew Anthony Hope. I have met Ralph Hodgson, and 'Bartimeus' is a friend of mine, but I have never heard anything about the personality or appearance or age of one of the best English novelists, Patrick Hamilton, whose *Hangover Square, Slaves of Solitude* and *Mr Stimpson and Mr Gorse* seem to me in the top class of English novels. What is he like? Has he a moustache or is he clean shaven? Where is he now? Is he happy? I am inspired to wish him a prosperous New Year.[37]

25

Recovery

I

The electro-convulsive therapy worked on Hamilton. After the autumn of 1956 he never again experienced the inert despair that had tempted him to commit suicide. One could go further and claim that the treatment also cured him of being a writer of fiction. There is a natural tendency in literary biography to attribute a decisive value to the work. Everything else – other responsibilities, commitments, friends, lovers, family, with all their importunate demands – are only of significance in the degree to which they help or hinder the production of works of art. This is rarely how it seems at the time. It was not the job of Dr Hobson to untap Hamilton's literary inspiration, but rather to prevent him from killing himself. After his recovery, Hamilton often talked of having ideas for books but he never did anything more than doodle ineffectively at them, in the spirit in which he would begin to compile reference books or teach himself Latin or mathematics. This most professional and determined of writers never again produced a work that could conceivably have been offered for publication. He had once been uncannily skilful at remodelling the material of his life into works of fiction. Now he turned inwards, satisfying his 'wonderful new urge just to scribble'' with long letters to Bruce and rough, scattered attempts at memoirs which might make some sense of where he was. He also, against all the odds, achieved a precarious, partial contentment.

It would hardly be possible to claim that the final years of Hamilton's life were happy. Things had gone wrong too early and too profoundly for that. He had begun his career by impudently sketching out a possible career:

Anthony had it all lucidly ordered in his mind. He imagined Life, more or less consciously, as a sort of play in three logical Acts and a Prologue. He had just done with the Prologue. The three Acts were (1) fiery youth leaping splendidly to the zenith, (2) replete, mellow middle age, and (3) sedate decay. With a wonderful curtain in Death, bang in the centre of the stage.[2]

The first act was triumphantly achieved, but opinions differed on what had gone wrong with act two, soured, perhaps, by early success. J. B. Priestley suggested that

in ordinary terms he left his youth behind for many years of middle-age. But while knowing all this – and indeed a lot more than this – I cannot help seeing him from first to last as a gifted youth, living in some boarding-house and breaking out of his solitude every night to sit in a pub, keeping very sharp eyes and ears hard to work. . . . Again, though he tried living in many different places (always in England), he never appears to have really settled down anywhere, never become a member of a community, but was always, so to speak, the restless and sceptical outsider, still the gifted but lonely youth.[3]

When Hamilton returned to Norfolk, he felt that a miracle had occurred but the circumstances of his life were unchanged. They were inherently unstable and were likely in their different ways to worsen. As before, his drinking fluctuated, but the periods of abstention were rarer and the binges were more severe in their effects on a system less able to tolerate them. His reliance on Loïs and La had tried them both to a point where neither could be a stable support for him. His capacity and will to work had declined and his contacts with the theatrical, publishing and broadcasting worlds were now a wasting asset. Even if he had been seriously inclined to write something new, there were fewer and fewer friends likely to contact him with the suggestion of a new play, or even the revision of an old novel.

This was the context in which he had experienced despair. His attitude after the treatment was more mellow and accepting, with even a perhaps necessary degree of numbness. He reported to Bruce an almost alarming list of things to which he had taken a new dislike: cricket, discussion of which composed so much of his relationship with Bruce; chess, which had occupied so much of his time; golf, which provided so much of his exercise; film and the theatre, which provided virtually all his money. The latter two he said were not in the same category anyway, 'for I had almost completely lost my taste for them while in the best of health.'[4] Some of his enthusiasms returned, and he regularly played correspondence chess with Dr Hobson, who was a far more accomplished player. But even those activities which Hamilton resumed were on a more intermittent, disengaged level. Yet it may be that it was this very inertia that enabled Hamilton to achieve the 'sedate decay' he had imagined for himself in his first novel. What he had not anticipated is that it would begin when he was in his early fifties, an age at which his father had joined the army in the First World War and sought service near the front line.

By his own report, Hamilton's politics remained remarkably unshaken. He admitted, with a cheerful iconoclasm, that, whereas he had previously abstained from voting in general elections, he now intended to vote Conservative. He insisted that this showed no abandonment of his Marxist convictions but was a rational accommodation of changed circumstances. The curious result was that his Marxist analysis had brought him to a position indistinguishable from that of his father. His reasons were, that now that the dream of Marxist Socialism was '*meaningless*, I feel entirely justified in selfishly pursuing my own *material* and *cultural* interests. These, naturally, will be those of my own nation, and my own nation is, I think, likely to be best served by the Tory party.'[5] Hamilton's 'almost pathological hatred of the Labour Party', as he himself described it, was already well established but now he felt an equal contempt for the British working class, 'which has proved itself *despicably* incapable of what might have been its historic task, and, instead of the Red Flag, has hoisted a stout and defiant Television Mast against the evils of capitalist exploitation.' The Tory Party was equally to be supported because of its supposed opposition to America: 'I don't know which I hate most – Labour ascendancy within or American domination without.'[6]

The Suez Crisis had also angered Hamilton, though in a different way to most writers of the time:

I am with that section of the Tory party which believes in taking the firmest possible hand (or stand) with Egypt!

I believe (as Marxists must) in the sacred rights of *majorities*, and, now that there is absolutely *no* thought anywhere of international revolution and consequent world-union, I do not see why pip-squeak corrupt little nationalist messes should be permitted to be in a position absolutely to *ham-string* (and this is really happening over the Suez business) *vast organisations and populations* such as those of Great Britain or France. (This, surely, is the attitude Russian took when she had no nonsense with 'poor little Finland'.)[7]

Hamilton's Marxism was both deeply held and as entirely idiosyncratic as his father's fascism. He may well have been the only Marxist, perhaps the only person, in the world to defend the British invasion of Suez by claiming that it was as praiseworthy as the Soviet invasion of Finland.

II

When Bruce told Hamilton that he was making another visit to England, partly to cover the Test series between England and the West Indies for a Barbados newspaper, he reacted nervously: 'On the last occasion, as far as I can remember, apart from your two visits to Norfolk you were having to cope either with my alcoholism or my depression! I don't know which was worse for you – I rather imagine the latter.'[8]

The Bruce who arrived in England was now routinely and harshly critical of his brother. When, in a letter to Bruce, Hamilton repeated as his own a statement about a Keats biography that Bruce had made to him, Bruce saw this as a sign of his failing mind. Even by Bruce's own admission, the statement had been made during the brief crisis in Hove when Hamilton was at his most acutely suicidal and might have been forgiven some vagueness as to where a straightforward aperçu had derived from.[9] Because of Bruce's professional commitments, their meetings were few and desultory, and in Bruce's eyes the beneficial effects of Hamilton's treatment had now worn off. He found him woolly-minded and repetitive.[10] Just before Bruce's return, the two spent an unsatisfactory week together in a rainy Oxford in which each was bored by the other. Much of the time was spent in pubs with Hamilton drinking whisky, Bruce, constrained by money and disapproval, drinking beer. The week ended in what Bruce described as a 'calamity – to me it seemed no less'. This was simply a visit to a variety show in which Bruce saw Hamilton, 'tighter than usual', repeatedly telling a woman in the bar that he had had several plays of his own performed in this theatre:

It was, to me, unspeakably dreadful. Not because he had got drunk and was making a bit of a fool of himself – though indeed, being usually an unobtrusive drinker in public, he seldom did this. It was the *sort* of fool he was making of himself. What filled me with an inexpressible sense of loss was the realisation that I might have been sitting with my father. 'I've had several plays of my own on here.' 'I'm an author myself, so I don't want any trash.' What was the difference? Thus, after nearly forty years, a full cycle had been completed. This was where we came in.[11]

Detached readers are likely to find themselves excluded from, or even puzzled by, the emotions aroused by this event, just in the way that intense family feuds are incomprehensible to outsiders. Bruce was fighting a long-standing psychic battle of his own here, involving complicated rivalries and rejections, love and hate, towards both his father and brother. The evening, during which Bruce admits that he scarcely spoke, while making his horror at his brother's behaviour obvious, ended with Hamilton drunkenly attempting to initiate a real fight with Bruce, who sullenly refused to respond.

Later, when Bruce had left England he wrote a conciliatory letter and received a warm response, but Hamilton would not agree with his brother that the differences could simply be ignored as trivial:

I think, though, that this relationship *must* involve (in a Marxist way) its opposite – and so the occasional disturbance is caused. Indeed these disturbances are, as I see it, *inherent in the situation* – beginning from the days when, while I was *worshipping* you as a 'Magnet' prizewinner, I was at the same time *blackmailing* you about your private life.[12]

For Hamilton their relationship was a struggle for supremacy that had begun in childhood and had never been resolved. And now that the other Hamiltons were dead, Bruce had become the focus of all Hamilton's torn, complicated feelings for his father, mother and sister, and for himself. Hamilton never found any answer to the enigma of why he drank, but his search for an answer was almost entirely in the years of very early youth, in the world he now shared only with Bruce. Hamilton's fragile recovery had substantially been achieved by the act of saying that he had recovered. Under the sceptical, disapproving scrutiny of Bruce, his new equilibrium was almost impossible to maintain, and more difficult as Bruce's displeasure became increasingly obvious.

26

Sedate Decay

I

At the end of 1957 and the beginning of 1958, Hamilton suffered a 'succession of catastrophes', which 'came under the headings – emotional and material'.[1] Within six weeks, several old friends died. Two – the 'farce-writer and old drinking friend', Vernon Sylvane and Anthony Ireland, who had starred in the first production of *Rope* – were described by Hamilton as '*nostalgically* very important to me'.[2] But they did not represent the authentically bad news, though Hamilton showed some of his new resilience by summing it up with a grim reference to the recent Munich air disaster in which half of the Manchester United football team had been killed:

Then, of course, the *real* blow, Michael Sadleir. You can imagine how much this upset me – but perhaps not fully imagine – for I myself could not have imagined how much it would (and still does) distress me. It somehow gave me a delayed reaction to Bill Linnit's death (which, as you know, I never *properly* reacted to because of my depression when it happened). As well as being my dear friends, they were both so closely bound up with my *writing* life – as well as my concrete, business, *everyday* life. This is hard to express but I think you'll understand. The two pillars have now collapsed – the two vitally important eggs have been destroyed with the basket.

And then, just to complete the business, Audrey Heath. I hadn't seen her for years, and so it should, really have meant nothing. But it did, for it was she who started me (and you) upon my/our writing life.

One feels like a surviving player for Manchester United![3]

If there had been even the slightest possibility of Hamilton publishing again, it had now gone with the death of Michael Sadleir on 13 December 1957. He had turned his professional associates into a surrogate family, and had depended on them for encouragement and praise. Sometimes Michael Sadleir and Martha Smith had been – in Hamilton's mind – his readership as well as his publishers. Now Martha, who had no authority within Constable anyway, had retired and he knew almost nobody in the organizations who had once constituted almost his entire personal and professional world. When, later in the year, Bruce inquired about where he should attempt to place a play he had written, Hamilton replied helplessly that he no longer knew who was actually working at Heath's agency, or whether Linnit and Dunfee still existed.[4]

The losses were painful, but they only confirmed the existence of a gulf that Hamilton had already accepted and he was able to report to Bruce that his health was excellent, 'All things considered – but then a lot of things have to be considered!'[5] And there was at least one news item from which he was able to take hope, the launch of the Sputnik satellite which showed the Soviety Union humiliating the United States in the space race.

The greatest disturbance came from what was to be Hamilton's principal source of stability in his final years, his accommodation. The caretaker who came with Long Acre, his rented house near Blakeney, had suddenly moved away and Hamilton, even with La and a hired help, was dismayed by the challenge: 'All that happened was that, after a *hideous* period at Long Acre, my spirits grew lower and lower (though there was never the slighest sign of the old depression) while my spirit-consumption grew higher and higher – reaching a bottle-a-day level on my trips to Henley and London. So I thought I'd better go into the Cooler for a bit.'[6] Hamilton returned to the attentions of Dr Hobson at the Woodside Hospital for a five-day treatment of injections of insulin in the morning and super-Vitamin B in the evening. It was here that Hamilton began his first attempt at an autobiographical work, tentatively titled, *Memoirs of a Heavy Drinking Man*. It was explicitly modelled on George Gissing's scarcely fictionalized account of his own literary exile,

The Private Papers of Henry Ryecroft, written in 1903, the final year of his life when he was just forty-six. There are passages in this strange, retrospective work that must have spoken directly to Hamilton:

As I walked to-day in the golden sunlight – this warm, still day on the far verge of autumn – there suddenly came to me a thought which checked my step, and for the moment half bewildered me. I said to myself: My life is over. Surely I ought to have been aware of that simple fact; certainly it has made part of my meditation, has often coloured my mood; but the thing had never definitely shaped itself, ready in words for the tongue. My life is over, I uttered the sentence once or twice, that my ear might test its truth. Truth undeniable, however strange; undeniable as the figure of my age last birthday.

My age? At this time of life, many a man is bracing himself for new efforts, is calculating on a decade or two of pursuit and attainment. I, too, may perhaps live for some years; but for me there is no more activity, no ambition. I have had my chance – and I see what I made of it.[7]

Hamilton saw Gissing's book as a 'personal document whose main theme was poverty'. His own version would be similar,

a personal history, whose main theme is an illness. The illness, in its mildest form, may be called heavy drinking: in its acutest form it may be called imperatively necessary drinking. In this acute form drink is as much wanted by the victim as sustenance is wanted by a starving man, or even, perhaps, as insulin is wanted by a diabetic.[8]

Hamilton's text begins with an inconsequential discussion of 'noisy' and 'quiet' literature and then meanders into a discussion of drink in literature, which he considers on the whole a neglected subject: 'There has always been a lot of heavy drinking in novels, of course, but nowadays – apart from certain American novels, whose authors, attempting to be tough, reveal nearly always an inward, slushy, and, alas, typically American sentimentality – heavy drinking is left to the "humorists".'[9] Then Hamilton finally reaches the incident which inspired this meditation, and the impulse to emulate Gissing. As he was lying in his private room, two medical students arrived and began to question him assuming, wrongly he said, that Hamilton was an alcoholic:

Was it hereditary? Did I think it was something inherent in the constitution, or was it the result of nervous strain – of some underlying frustration, or major diaster in my life? Could it be traced to unhappiness in childhood or boyhood? And many other rather naïve questions of the same sort.[10]

These questions – as recalled, embellished, or even invented by Hamilton – are more significant than any solution he could have found. To answer the questions one by one: yes, his father was also an alcoholic, and according to Bruce their drinking followed a simple pattern (though for Bruce this showed a common moral failing). Yes, his attraction to the ideas of Dr Dent was his insistence that drinking was an illness and was linked to a constitutional anxiety. Yes, Hamilton was emotionally and sexually frustrated for almost his entire life. He seems to have suffered from an inability to achieve sexual consummation and this encouraged his drinking. When he finally did enjoy sexual fulfilment, this caused more problems in his life than it resolved. Yes, his life and career had been blighted by the single disaster of his car accident, damaging him both professionally and personally. It put him out of action for almost two years when he was on the brink of establishing himself as a writer, and it scarred his face, accentuating all the feelings he had had about his own unattractiveness. And finally, yes, he could see how the roots of the drinking could be seen both in the insecurities of earliest childhood and the agony of his adolescence, when he first turned to drink as a source of comforting oblivion. Indeed Hamilton uses these questions as a transition to an account of the anxieties of his early childhood.[11] Each question is like a spoke on the wheel that leads to the alcoholic compulsion at its hub.

II

While Hamilton was attempting this difficult exploration of an obsession, La was publishing a novel, *The Elopement*, on the same theme, which shows that her husband was not the only victim of his alcoholism. Like Hamilton's jottings, it is an exploration of why people drink. But where Hamilton begins with questions, Laura Talbot begins with a glib maxim, an epigraph derived from Dr Dent's *Anxiety and Its Treatment*: 'Children after puberty should be told there has been addiction in the parent or grandparent, just as they should know of any other hereditary weaknesses. They must be warned that they may be more liable to fall victims to drink than their fellows.'

The Elopement tells the story of a provincial rector who, it is almost needless to say in Laura Talbot's work, has married beneath him.[12] The plot is nothing more than a demonstration of the truth of the epigraph. The rector's ancestors have been drinkers and he sees the genetic curse emerge in his daughter, Nell, who takes gradually to alcohol, sabotages her own chance of marrying well and elopes with her sister's fiancé. The two forms of delinquency, alcoholic and sexual, are linked in a positively Victorian fashion, with one tiny step leading inexorably to another. The novel is caught up in the confusion of which Hamilton had complained to Bruce.[13] If alcoholism is a constitutional condition that is inherited, then it is no more a matter for moral censure than other inherited conditions, such as haemophilia. But as Hamilton had observed, it is judged differently, and the novel contradicts itself by indicting Nell for her supposed weakness, just as Bruce believed that Hamilton was recapitulating Bernard's weakness yet condemned him for it.

It is, perhaps, unfair to regret that *The Elopement* was not equal to the complex drama of its inspiration, the Hamilton family, which had been for Lalla, Bruce and Patrick both a refuge and the source of inherited torment compelling them to re-make the mistakes of the previous generation. In fact the book is a reductive fable, the most routine of Laura Talbot's novels, but the scenes in which the Rector talks about the impossibility of helping an alcoholic seem truly heartfelt:

'The self-deception of the one who watches is almost as great as that of the one who drinks. I try to deceive myself into thinking I've cured Mrs Kelly through kindness, but every time I think so she gets drunk again. I give money I can't afford to Clarice's father and he takes it with promises – he takes it to the public house. I try to think I help them, but I don't, I only deceive myself into thinking I do. I can't because I don't know *how*. I don't *know how*, Myrtle! But why should I? Doctors don't know – they don't even try to find out! All I can do is study the character – I try to help the character and I fail, because it's something beyond character, but what? *What?*'[14]

In fact, the novel's epigraph provided an escape from the responsibilities of her subject, the need to explore character or motivation. If alcoholism is a simple illness, then all that is needed is a simple cure and the Rector prays that medical science will soon provide one:

'For all we know, there may be someone amongst us now – some young man somewhere perhaps, searching, struggling, experimenting; facing opposition, frustration, ridicule even, but with enough genius and courage and luck – he'll need the luck – to persevere until he hits upon the truth and finds the cause, and perhaps, through the cause, the cure.'[5]

In the same year, Bruce's last, and by some way least interesting, published novel appeared. As if Hamilton's own failure to write had affected his older brother, *Too Much of Water* is the first of Bruce's books that owes nothing in theme, style or setting to the work of Hamilton. It is a light-hearted whodunnit set on an ocean liner bound for the West Indies, and is nervously dedicated 'To Aileen who found it fun'. Uninventive and unengaging, it is perhaps most notable for the facile optimism of its final page, unique in any work of the Hamilton family since Bernard's fiction. The conclusion is provided by Mr Bennett, a west country farmer: ' "We been through some serious experiences, sad and serious. I en mean at all we should forget them, nor the poor people we lost from our company. But here we are, and here's the world we're still living in, praise be; and the onliest thing is to make the best of it." '[16] Bruce found it difficult to follow this advice over the next few years. He went through periods of intense depression and this inevitably coloured his last perceptions of his brother.

III

When Hamilton returned to Norfolk he reported, as was his custom, that he was in better condition than he had ever been in his life before, 'looking 10 and feeling 30 years younger'.[17] Most promisingly of all, La had managed to obtain a flat eastwards from Blakeney along the Norfolk coast in Sheringham. He later described it as

a sort of suburban house with a garden . . . divided into four flats. You can see the sea from it (about 500 yards away) – and the golf course can be cut into (dodging the Club House) by walking for about three minutes. I'm very attached to it and don't ever want to leave it. But I expect that sooner or later I'll have to, or want to.[18]

The mechanistic approach of Dr Hobson had made a considerable impression on Hamilton and he claimed that what he owed him was 'absolutely fantastic'.[19] He insisted that he had now 'got the better of this illness permanently.' He felt a new security 'caused by the abandonment of any idea of complete teetotalism or "cure".' He was now keeping himself to a small amount of beer and a gin and tonic in the morning and no more than three large whiskies in the evening 'and I haven't the slightest desire to break it – in fact usually I can't take full advantage of it.'[20] His strategy for maintaining this, by his standards, negligible intake was to have a small whisky which he would continually replenish with water.

Hamilton would now occasionally visit London. In November 1958 he was invited by Dr Hobson to attend what was a 'potentially *very* drunken' occasion, the annual dinner of the Society for the Study of Addiction to Alcohol. It might have been thought that Hamilton was a patient the Society might have wished to keep out of sight but he reported that it was 'gloriously successful'.[21] Bruce nervously sent Hamilton *Too Much of Water*, urging him: 'Don't bring your heaviest critical artillery to bear on something more or less written as I went along.' But Hamilton, perhaps feeling free of any kind of literary rivalry, wrote back warmly: 'The whole book gave me a feeling that you have it in you to write a book exceeding all your others. I don't mean that you *still* have it in you, I mean that you *now* have it in you!'[22] He claimed that he was himself working slowly at new fiction, but his principal effort was devoted to a new draft of his memoir, whose commencement he dated 2 February 1959.

The new version dispensed with the ruminative opening of before and began in more stirring style fitting an epic of alcoholism:

One who has had a very serious illness has travelled far: he has been, involuntarily and without glory, an explorer of the first magnitude.

He has entered wild, terrible and grotesque regions and climates, and here he has daily endured pains – great and small, of the body and the mind – quite ununderstandable by the average man.

He is allowed to make no preparations for his adventures into which he is, as it were, shanghaied. And soon after the first part of the journey – after the first mild or painful symptoms, that is to say – he is incessantly living in the fear of death, which may overtake him during the outward expedition, at the appointed destination, or even on his return.

He is compelled to submit to extremes of heat through fever and extremes of cold through shock. He is on duty all the day, and he keeps long night vigils.[23]

The metaphor is sustained through visits to the exotic natives who inhabit hospitals, those 'palaces of pain',[24] and he compares the heroism of the sufferer from illness with the population of London who behaved with such fortitude during the Blitz. While disclaiming experience of the most extreme forms of alcoholism, Hamilton writes more frankly about what he actually did than he had ever dared before. Bruce underestimated the consistency of his brother's insight into his own condition, even when it was at its worst:

But the writer, in spite of his manifold encounters with the malady, is unable to claim, probably, to be amongst the really great, good and brave explorers. He has travelled far, and has had many wild and frightening adventures; but he has never fully visited those famous localities which demand superhuman endurance if the traveller is to survive at all, or to survive with his mind and body intact. He has passed, at a very near distance, the many terrible isles of Delirium Tremens, but he has never solidly landed at any of them. He has been permitted to gaze into the black, seething waters of ultimate alcoholism, but he has never been wholly sucked down into them. And he has come away, from all his adventures seemingly unscathed and in good health.

All the same he should be able to claim the rank of an explorer of sorts, if only because he has so often been made extremely ill by his drinking – ill either for extended or only brief periods.

In the brief periods the manifestations have followed a more or less conventional and obvious pattern. There have been errors or breakdowns in gait, balance or sight – staggering, reeling, falling down flat, seeing two objects instead of one, and so forth. The writer had often been assisted or actually carried to bed by friendly porters in clubs or hotels; and, in the absence of these helpers, has gradually and with intense concentration climbed, using his hands and knees and elbows instead of his legs, the stairs upon stairs leading to the heights of his bedroom.

In the extended periods the behaviour has been less obvious to the ordinary onlooker, but much more painful to an intimate friend: for it has involved drinking almost unintermittently from morning to night, as well as in the middle of the night, and deception has been used.

The writer has fraudulently contrived to put whisky into the cup of tea which has been brought to him in bed in the morning, and gin into his bedside glass of water – finding Gordon's gin preferable to Booth's when doing this, because the colour of Gordon's gin resembles water more closely, and is therefore more likely to confuse the judgement of anyone entering the bedroom.

He has never been gratuitously aggressive or offensive when drinking. This is simply because he does not belong to that rather unusual class of drinker, whose members, quite often, drink comparatively very little. But he has frequently been remarkably silly and, above all, repetitive.

Nor has he ever disclosed a secret when drinking. Very few drinkers, however drunk, do this: that they do this regularly is a fiction of the worst kind of fiction-writer.

And, oddly enough, in spite of all his errors in gait, balance and sight, he has never spent a night behind prison bars.

This he believes to be decidedly unusual. For most of his own friends, who on the whole have drunk much less heavily than himself, have at some time or another had to submit to this small humiliation – small because usually the punishment is most humanely, or even humorously, administered.[25]

Obviously Hamilton could still write, but he was now like an unwell, satisfied, very old man taking leave of life. There were bits of his old life left. He would occasionally take the train into London, and if he was travelling from Henley and arrived at Paddington then he would walk the more than two miles through Bayswater, Hyde Park and Piccadilly to the London Library, where he would borrow popular fiction that he recalled from his childhood. He would pay largely nostalgic visits to the Saville Club where he got some 'intellectual stimulation'[26] but he now found London 'impossibler and impossibler' and spent most of his time in Sheringham, where he claimed to be happier than he had ever been in his life.[27] His Marxism was as secure as ever and he was impressed by Nikita Khruschev: 'I particularly like the way in which he is incessantly rebuking those who go too far in their denigration of Stalin.'[28] Apart from this, his opinions became increasingly blimpish. The Germans were racially bad, the Americans were deplorable, the Italians were 'pretty low', Teddy Boys had too much money. He was particularly worried about the attraction of 'Youth' to coffee bars since he considered that coffee was 'a very dangerous drink – for young and old – often worse than alcohol'.[29] Hamilton, the chronicler of seedy subculture, was left hopelessly adrift by its newer manifestations.

His latest hopeless literary project was an anthology of rhyming slang, but he had no urgent need for money. When he learned from Bruce – who was now sixty years old – that he had sold his house in Barbados for £4,000, he jocularly threatened to borrow a fiver from him and then revealed that he was earning £4,500 a year, largely from performances of *Rope* and *Gaslight* by the despised Americans. This was a comfortable sum, though he complained that income tax made him feel 'practically ruined'.[30]

A letter from Martha Smith emphasized that there was now no one left to chivvy Hamilton into any sort of activity. Few people in his life had ever taken him – 'poor Hennie', as she still called him[31] – less seriously, or been more affectionate. She briskly assumed that he was now on the 'straight and narrow and are not getting any of your old troubles.'[32] She contemplated his domestic arrangements with detached amusement: 'I gather you still go periodically to Henley and hope that Loïs is keeping well. What a strange life you lead with your "women"!'[33] But she was sixty-five now and writing bravely of retired life. (Orange Street, the Constable office, was 'rather a bore – a lot of chat with half a dozen chaps, taking up a lot of time and achieving nothing.'[34]) She did not even make a pretence of expecting that they would meet again.

If Marxism was Hamilton's macrocosmic philosophy, his microcosmic philosophy was now Oblomovism. This was derived from Ivan Goncharov's 1859 novel about a man who refuses to get out of bed, though Hamilton knew it only from Lalla's description.[35] His own version was partly a personal code of worldly renunciation and partly an excuse, but Bruce's view of this as ominous self-deception[36] must be set against the cheerfulness with which Hamilton promulgated his philosophy of stasis: 'I am very well, but very lazy – almost a complete Oblomov. . . . I am reading a lot – and enjoying it enormously.'[37]

He continued to spend time with Loïs, including his fifty-sixth birthday, but when at Sheringham his habits were rigid, 'infuriating, but easy to understand', in his own words:

The 'musts' are: –

(1) I must have a glass (of beer) in front of me for one hour before lunch every morning.

(2) I must have a glass of whisky in front of me for two hours before supper every night.

(3) I must go to sleep every afternoon.

(4) I must go to bed after supper, which is usually at around nine.

You will notice, I no longer have any real *zest* for alcohol just as I've no longer the same zest for sex.[38]

When Bruce visited England in the spring, he found that Hamilton's actual consumption at Sheringham was higher than the above schedule would suggest. He would drink three or four glasses of Guinness in the morning. After a short walk he would start drinking gin, then eat a small lunch without much appetite. He would sleep in the afternoon, the brothers would have tea at four o'clock. Then when Bruce went for a walk, Hamilton would change into his pyjamas and dressing gown and start drinking whisky. He would, with minimal assistance from Bruce, finish the bottle, then they would eat a light supper and Hamilton would go to bed at about nine. He smoked steadily through the day. Bruce saw him do no work. Hamilton's activities consisted mainly in writing letters, re-reading light literature: Sherlock Holmes, P. G. Wodehouse, cheap Westerns.[39] It may be that Hamilton's routine was disrupted by the presence of Bruce, and that his intake increased slightly due to the pressures of the relationship, but there is little doubt that, though there were occasional periods of restraint, his alcohol intake was now increasing dangerously.

Hamilton was still relying on Loïs as a source of refuge and even nursing. Indeed, according to Bruce, he at times considered leaving La for Loïs, forming the characteristically impossible scheme of continuing to live in the Sheringham flat, to which he was attached, but with Loïs instead of La. This stratagem, nebulous to begin with, evanesced entirely when Hamilton arrived at Henley in the middle of a near fatal drinking binge, where he was aided by Loïs and a young friend, Timothy Boulton, who recalls a maudlin, obviously drunk Hamilton suddenly entering the house with the announcement that he was dying. These irruptions had already become familiar to Boulton and the spectacle seemed as much ludicrous as tragic.[40] For Loïs it was different. She decided she could no longer put up with a situation she had already, it might be thought, tolerated for far too long. Henley could not longer be a bolt-hole for him. Bruce helped her to pack up such of Hamilton's possessions as she still retained.

At the end of 1961 it was not obvious which of the Hamilton brothers was in the worse state. In the first half of the year, Bruce had suffered a mild heart attack. Hamilton responded to the news by recommending 'a *shot* at my way of life – i.e. doing bugger all.'[41] Though Bruce recovered, he was then almost disabled by a depression that by his own account was to afflict him for several years. This may well have been brought on, or at least exacerbated, by the shattering news that Cresset, who had published his previous five novels, had rejected his new book, *Destroying Angel*, a biographical study of Shelley. Hamilton responded with sympathy: 'Although I haven't read it, I *know* that it is a good book. You are incapable of writing a bad book. *I* have managed to do this more than once.'[42] Though Bruce can no longer have held serious hopes of achieving success as a novelist, this was a cruel blow for a newly retired man. He was to publish just one more book, the memoir of Hamilton eleven years later.

Meanwhile, La's novel, *The Last of the Tenants*, was published. It is a strange, melodramatic tale of a woman living alone in a Norfolk village, tormented by rumours that she has killed a baby. When she is judged to be indirectly responsible for the death of another baby, she drowns herself during a flood. Though it is never stated, it is clear that La responded to the East Anglian setting by writing a modern version of Crabbe's *Peter Grimes*, but with a woman as the protagonist. Skilfully told from three different viewpoints, it is the most convincing of her novels and though there are one or two tiny personal references (the leading character is recommended to read *The Private Papers of Henry Ryecroft* – 'it will come to you as a balm'[43]), it is a book that seems successfully to have transcended the influence of her husband. Its promise was never fulfilled, for this was the last novel she published.

27

The End

While there can be no doubt that Hamilton's world was constricting and his health deteriorating, he was not always as passive as he appears through Bruce's eyes. As a letter written in the summer of 1961 shows, he still took an occasional lively interest in the news, particularly when it concerned an old friend, now gone to the bad as a Labour MP:

I am in a *furious* temper this morning – because of the confirmation of the news that German soldiers are to train in Wales.

I note that only seven Labour members objected to this, and that K[enneth]. Robinson was not amongst these members. Both you and I put our money on the worst sort of horse when we backed this little worm.[1]

Nor was he entirely reclusive. Despite his distrust of the species, he not only encountered a Teddy Boy but invited him and 'his pansy friend' back for a drink at his house. They were 'extremely nice and polite', though Hamilton complained that they had arrived at 7.30 in the evening, finished off an entire bottle of whisky and a half bottle of brandy belonging to La, and only left at 1.30 a.m.

What the Teddy Boy thought of Hamilton remains a mystery, but others who met him for the first time during this period were charmed by him. In September, Hamilton complained of the effect of eight children, La's nephews and nieces, who were staying at the boarding house next door: 'And The Patter of Little Feet is extremely exhausting.'[2] But Hamilton's gruffness masked an essential good humour. He is remembered as a 'very kind, albeit bedridden, gentleman' by one of these children, Charles, Lord Ingestre, who would later become the Earl of

Shrewsbury.[3] And, though he had resolved never to play chess again, Hamilton cheerfully attempted to teach Charles to play chess, while fearing that, at eight and three-quarters, he was already too old to become a master. When the party finally left, 'I gave the eldest boy my folding Chess Set and it seemed to please him a lot.'[4]

Three years earlier a young novelist, Angus Hall, had written to Hamilton asking when the fourth Gorse book would be appearing.[5] This was an unpromising start, but on a rainy day in the autumn of 1961 he telephoned Hamilton while on a visit to Norwich. 'Do you drink?' Hamilton asked. 'Avidly,' replied Hall. 'Come round at six, then,' Hamilton said and hung up. Being a particular admirer of *Mr Stimpson and Mr Gorse*, Hall was surprised to find its author living in a house that would have suited Mrs Plumleigh-Bruce. The man he found there was gentle and welcoming. The two of them drank heavily and talked of cricket. Then Hamilton showed him his means of financial support:

He lifted the lid of a large, sombre chest and pointed to the dozens of unopened press cuttings envelopes that lay inside it. 'Behold, my income,' he said apologetically. 'I never read them, but they're all reviews of *Rope* and *Gaslight*. There isn't a week goes by without someone somewhere in the world staging my plays. They've given me a modest income for many years now, and I need never work again. Writing a money-making play is very simple, really. Just give the actors something good to say. I used to be one myself, once, and I know that's all they're interested in – good, long, self-indulgent speeches.'[6]

After this woozy travesty of his achievements in the theatre, they ate dinner with La, with Hamilton reluctantly consuming a little lightly boiled fish. When the young author asked how 'such an honourable and obviously mild person' as Hamilton could have created a monster like Gorse, Hamilton adopted his sociological demeanour:

'People often wonder that about me,' he murmured, 'but what I was trying to present was a "black" social history of my times. There were so many "white" portraits of the twenties and thirties that I wanted to show the other side of the picture. After all, those were the decades in which Hitler rose to power. No one that I read was writing anything about him and the evil he represented.'[7]

Hamilton portrayed himself to Hall as someone with no interest in what had happened since the war. He would not travel abroad – 'horrible place, abroad', he commented – or fly, or read anything new. For exercise, he played occasional rounds of golf on his own and was now drinking very heavily indeed. His whisky was stored in crates in the kitchen. He told Hall of his new novel, of which he had written the four chapters that were all he would ever complete. *The Happy Hunting Ground*, as it was called, was about a young farm hand who entices his girlfriend away with the promise of London, but in fact the novel would have ended with her joining him in a suicide pact:

Hamilton again smiled reflectively as he told me of this. 'It's a good title,' he said. 'London's a place where you're forever hunting for happiness – and even if you find it it's soon taken away from you. I can't explain why this idea of achievement and revocation appeals to me so much. There's no bile that I know of poisoning my system. But I feel that death is not far away from me. Once I've gone they can take my body and give it to the dustmen for all I care.'[8]

As Hall left, Hamilton shook his hand and offered some gnomic advice: 'Remember one thing, always keep away from barmy people.'

Yet Hamilton's condition was more serious than it appeared to his awed young visitor. At the beginning of the year, during his final visit to Woodside, Hamilton had been warned that if he did not stop drinking he would be dead within a year. Two months later, in April, he sent a cheerful telegram to Bruce announcing that he was 'STILL IN GLORI- OUS HEALTH AND WRITING BOOK'[9] but there is no evidence that he made the slightest attempt to stop drinking. He was now suffering from cirrhosis of the liver, a condition caused by his drinking which made his liver increasingly unable to fulfil the function it had performed so heroically for so long. His only concession to the doctor's advice and to La's desperate entreaties was to dilute his whisky with large quantities of water. This would not have been sufficient to keep him alive and Bruce later wondered whether he was attempting a slow suicide, but concluded that he 'had always the ability to put distressing things out of his mind' and was probably just refusing to consider the inevitable consequences of his actions.[10] In all likelihood, Hamilton's illness was now too far advanced and the testimony of Angus Hall suggests that he was fully aware of his imminent end. Deliberate suicide would have been uncharacteristic. It is more likely that he lacked both the will and the inclination to make the drastic changes that would have prolonged an uncomfortable and burdensome existence. He had acknowledged that he lacked the courage that had led his mother to take her own life. He could at least wait unheeding, as Lalla had outside Ellen's door, and let events take their course.

It could be seen as something of a triumph that, by the late autumn, Hamilton was in any condition to receive an admirer with the charm and dignity he displayed. But in 1962 the effects of his liver disease became evident. He began to feel nauseous, his skin took on a yellow hue. His sleeps became longer and he was sometimes almost comatose. Another typical symptom of liver failure was the weakness of his limbs; he could barely walk and suffered two serious falls. His world now shrank from Martincross to his bedroom.

By July he could not even write to Bruce and was forced to dictate to La that he was 'still recovering from the remains of bronchitis and a bruised rib.'[11] He claimed, though, that the truth was that he was 'suffering from Oblomovism'. He had recently begun to read Goncharov's novel, but so true was he to its protagonist's spirit that he grew bored and couldn't finish it. He was seeing almost no one but John Davenport wrote to him sympathetically:

I am drinking like a quarter of a fish, so we shall make up one between us, a small one. A sprat, say.

Very much looking forward to seeing you. It's been an absurdly long time since we explored King's Lynn and discovered it wasn't there.[12]

Davenport managed a valedictory visit. The very last person Hamilton asked to see was La's nephew, Charles, for whom he had developed a great affection and it was arranged that he should visit for two nights. Thirty years later, the Earl of Shrewsbury recalled his visit:

He had as I recall a certain bottle problem, as many artistic people have. . . . He was charming, and spoke to me at length about his love of cricket. He gave me a cricket ball – which I still have – which he swore had been used in a test match. He also told me that he longed to write stories of the Wild West! This may have been a figment of his wide imagination, but it seemed to be an interest of his.[13]

Hamilton talked of the boy after he had left: 'One of the last things he said before he became incoherent was "I love Charles. I love that boy. I wonder why he is so attractive . . . Charles *is* terribly attractive. Beautiful – I imagine Lord Alfred Douglas must have looked rather like that, but he, I suppose, was rather a little beast." [14]

By August Hamilton could barely walk at all and La was privately acknowledging in her letters to Bruce that the end was inevitable. He was almost entirely bedridden, but he was still drinking whisky, sometimes in tea. His stomach became bloated, as it filled with fluid that was yet another by-product of a failing liver. Yet amidst the collapse there were moments of piercing clarity. The last letter to Bruce, dictated once more to La, was brief, barely thirty words. Bruce had asked him if he could recall two nonsense verses that had been composed in sleep, one by each of the two brothers, back in the late twenties. Hamilton replied:

> I have suddenly remembered our dream verses. Yours was:
> 'Something akin to warrant if life were emeritus.'
> Mine was:
> 'Life into life with avid egress flows,
> Warm by degrees and curiously ennose.' [15]

This semi-conscious association was an appropriate end for their intense, bitter, loving relationship. 'You know, Bruce and I had a wonderful relationship,' Hamilton said to La near the end. 'We were more than brothers.' [16] Hamilton's own couplet could be taken as referring to his own state, though 'avid' is not quite the right word for a process so passively allowed to occur. By August he was suffering from a variety of ailments – he even had to endure the extraction of a tooth – and was only occasionally lucid. In the first week of September, Hamilton's kidneys began to fail, a typical symptom of advanced liver disease. He was close to death and by the middle of the month a nurse was staying on the premises to provide the full-time care he now needed. La allowed Loïs to visit and stay for a few days, a comfort to Hamilton who was now insensible to the friction between them. Hamilton now only got out of bed to go to the bathroom, but Loïs found him surprisingly cheerful; 'He was even up to singing and laughing.' [17] He faced death without any remorse or fear. During Loïs's visit he constantly quoted a stanza from Swinburne's 'The Garden of Proserpine':

From too much hope of living,
From hope and fear set free,
We thank with brief thanksgiving
Whatever Gods may be
That no life lives for ever;
That dead men rise up never;
That even the weariest river
Winds somewhere safe to sea.

On Friday 21 September Hamilton became severely ill and on the following day he was even worse. His general practitioner, Dr Geldard pronounced his chest and heart 'not at all good'.[18] Hamilton was now in pain as the effect of the repeated injections and pills diminished. It seems most likely that in the final days, as Hamilton's liver began to fail, he became encephalitic, which would explain his alternate sleepiness and intense alarm. On the Sunday morning he slept fitfully. In the afternoon La sat with him lighting cigarette after cigarette and holding them in his mouth. Hamilton was 'very confused and wild, still asking for Nembutal'. Dr Geldard came and told Hamilton: 'You need *sleep*, my dear fellow, you're tired out, you must sleep, I'm going to make you sleep.' 'You won't, you know,' Hamilton replied, and laughed. 'We'll see,' Dr Geldard said and gave him an injection. 'Now you'll sleep. Your wife is with you and you'll sleep.' 'You're a good doctor and a good man,' Hamilton said and fell asleep, holding La's hand.[19] Later that Sunday evening, on 23 September 1962, he died without regaining consciousness.

Hamilton had been born into a family of minor novelists. Another was present at his death bed. Over the years of their marriage, Hamilton had gradually excused himself from reading La's novels.[20] He might have been grimly amused, though, by the style in which she reported the death which he had himself anticipated so heedlessly:

I got into a dressing gown, listened to P.'s breathing, then went into the kitchen, snatched a biscuit and cheese, washed up the tea, too tensed up to sit and do nothing, then went to listen to P. again – there was silence. I have never been in a house where there has been a death before – it seemed to be filling the whole house, engulfing it – the silence of snow. I couldn't go in.

I stood in the passage in the dark not knowing what to do. I went again and again to the doorway, listened, and the silence became more and more overwhelming. I stood in the passage again and then in the drawing room doorway till Matron came. I said, 'The silence, this silence', and then I could see that she had heard it.

I was afraid he might have called me, but both Matron and Dr Geldard said this was impossible, his heart failed in his sleep, he was unconscious. How merciful, they say that had he lived any longer the complications would have been terrible.

I saw him the next day. He looked very peaceful, his beautiful mouth firmly shut, all the blemishes and the bloatedness of his illness gone. I thought it beautiful and terrifying . . .[21]

As Hamilton himself knew, in bad literature the corpse always looks peaceful, the ravages of the final illness have always disappeared.[22] Patrick Hamilton would have been crueller and funnier about his own corpse. He would still have noticed the blemishes.

28

Aftermath

Elegizing Yeats, Auden wrote that the defunct poet 'became his admirers'. There was one admirer at Hamilton's funeral. Angus Hall travelled from London. Michael Sadleir's son, Richard, represented Constable. The two wives were present. According to Bruce, 'the antagonism between the two grieving women was exhibited in so plain a way as to be almost unseemly'[1] but since he was in Barbados, this may just be conjecture. The only other mourners were two local friends of La's. There were no friends of Hamilton's and no relatives present.

Hamilton had left no instructions for his funeral. La asked that the penultimate stanza of Shelley's 'Stanzas Written in Dejection near Naples' be read:

> Yet now despair itself is mild,
>   Even as the winds and waters are;
> I could lie down like a tired child,
>   And weep away the life of care
>   Which I have borne and yet must bear,
> Till death like sleep might steal on me,
>   And I might feel in the warm air
> My cheek grow cold, and hear the sea
> Breathe o'er my dying brain its last monotony.[2]

The choice of poem was appropriate, if only because it was on a visit to Naples, thirty years earlier, that Hamilton had concluded that 'the *world* is very much *over-rated*'.[3] His body was cremated and the ashes scattered on the nearby Blakeney Flats.

According to Bruce, Hamilton wrote him a letter towards the end of his life about his will: 'You are *mentioned*, but as far as I can make out you don't get any bees and honey [i.e., money] unless you survive both Loïs and La.'[4] When the will was published after Hamilton's death, Bruce was not mentioned at all. Two-thirds of the estate was left to La, one third to Loïs, both absolutely. This meant that each of them could in turn bequeath their share to whomever they wished. Bruce was deeply hurt and told La that, in his view, the will 'did not give effect to what it was clear Hamilton had understood and expressed in his letter'.[5] La agreed and announced her intention to leave her share in Hamilton's royalties to Bruce: 'Why on earth should my "heirs" have it? Anyway, I haven't any "heirs".'[6]

La remained on relatively friendly terms with Bruce and Aileen. In 1964 she married once more, to a Dr Bill James, whom she had known for many years. The following year they moved to Jersey where he owned an estate and then, in 1966, they were both killed when the light aircraft, in which they were being flown on a day trip to Alderney, crashed into the sea.

Bruce proved not to be a beneficiary of La's will. Instead Hamilton's royalties were left to her own heirs, her nephew and niece, Charles and Charlotte. Bruce considered that he had been profoundly betrayed. In the original version of his memoir of Hamilton he concluded bitterly:

Thus, contrary to Hamilton's wishes and at the expense of the devoted Loïs, who had very little income beyond her one-third share of the royalties, most of the posthumous proceeds of Hamilton's work have gone to enrich the not altogether impoverished Talbot family, the senior members of which, in spite of having all the evidence fairly before them, have insisted firmly on their pound of flesh.[7]

Yet, deplorable though La's behaviour may have been, Bruce knew well that previously expressed intentions are irrelevant. Just a few pages before his denunciation of the Talbot family, Bruce wrote: 'It is my intention to have [La's letters], along with [Hamilton's] own and any such other significant material as I am able to salvage, put after my death into the hands of the British Museum Reading Room or such other responsible institution as I find willing to accept them.' In the event, the letters remained in the possession of his widow.

From the vantage point of the present day, the only question seems to have been whether two-thirds of Hamilton's estate would have ended up with Aileen's family or with La's family. The evidence clearly suggests which he would have preferred. He never liked Aileen. On the other hand, in his final weeks he developed an Aschenbach-like fondness for the young Lord Ingestre. He would, in all likelihood, not have been displeased that La's portion of his estate should now be in the possession of the Earl of Shrewsbury and Talbot.

It was a bitter blow for Bruce and Aileen just when they were returning home to England after Bruce's retirement. He had carved out a distinguished career for himself in educational administration. He had been appointed Chairman of the Public Service Commission and on his retirement in 1964, he was made a CMG (a Companion of the Order of St Michael and St George), for his services to Barbados. But he was not wealthy. When he moved back to Brighton with Aileen, the couple bought a small terraced house, perhaps a quarter of the size of the First Avenue house he had grown up in. He had made some slightly demeaning attempts to secure what he saw as his right to his brother's royalties. They proved futile.

The remainder of his life and Loïs's were lived in the shadow of Hamilton. Loïs lived in Henley until her death in 1975. She was active in the local Women's Institute and was always in demand at Henley functions for her piano playing. The attention she had devoted to Hamilton when he was alive was now transferred to his literary reputation, at a low ebb for some years after his death.

There was a revival in 1972 when Bruce's memoir, *The Light Went Out*, was published by Constable. Also re-issued were *Hangover Square* and *The Slaves of Solitude*, with new introductions by J. B. Priestley. In the following year, Bruce became ill and was found to be suffering from lung cancer. In March 1974 he died. The Hamilton family – Bernard, Ellen, Lalla, Bruce, Patrick – were gone. They left no descendants, only books.

Notes

My quotations from Bruce Hamilton's memoirs require some explanation. There are two versions of the first draft, *Patrick – A Tragedy*: a rough typescript (*Tragedy I*) and a fair copy based on it (*Tragedy II*), bound in four sections, the third of which seems to be missing. Since these are virtually identical I have quoted from the second, clearer version, except for the part of the book that is missing in the fair copy. Where a quotation is the same in all versions, I quote from the more accessible, published text of the memoir, *The Light Went Out*. Otherwise I quote from an earlier version but where there is an equivalent passage in the published version, I give a further reference, in square brackets.

The two typescripts of *Patrick – A Tragedy* are both in the Bruce Hamilton collection (now in the possession of Nigel Jones), as are the two versions of Hamilton's fragmentary memoir, *Memoirs of a Heavy Drinking Man*, and all the letters from Hamilton to Bruce. The sources of other manuscript material are cited in the Notes as follows:

BH	The collection of Bruce Hamilton
BBC	BBC Written Archives Centre
TEMPLE	The Constable archives, now in the possession of Temple University, Philadelphia, Pennsylvania, USA
CONSTABLE	The archives still held by Constable
FABER	The archives of Faber and Faber
SF	The collection of the author (consisting of further papers owned by Bruce Hamilton, bequeathed by his widow to Victoria Hill, who gave them to the author)

The other abbreviations used in the notes are:

PH	Patrick Hamilton
Bruce	Bruce Hamilton
Lalla	Lalla (Helen/Diana) Hamilton
Mem I	The first version of *Memoirs of a Heavy Drinking Man*

Mem II	The second version of *Memoirs of a Heavy Drinking Man*
Tragedy I	The first version of *Patrick – A Tragedy* (see above)
Tragedy II	*The second version of Patrick – A Tragedy*
TLWO	*The Light Went Out: A Biography of Patrick Hamilton*
20,000	*Twenty Thousand Streets Under the Sky*
Gorse	*The Gorse Trilogy*

Works of the Hamilton Family

For convenience, I have cited works by members of the Hamilton family by title only, in certain cases by short titles (see the list of abbreviations above). The works, confined here to published books, are listed under their respective authors in order of original publication. Where possible I have used the more generally available editions. Unless otherwise indicated the titles are of novels and the place of publication is London.

PATRICK HAMILTON

Monday Morning, Constable, 1925.
Craven House (first published 1926), revised edition (f.p. 1943), Cardinal, 1991.
Twopence Coloured, Constable, 1928.
Rope (a play), Constable, 1929.
Twenty Thousand Streets Under the Sky: A London Trilogy (f.p. 1935), containing *The Midnight Bell* (f.p. 1929), *The Siege of Pleasure* (f.p. 1932) and *The Plains of Cement* (f.p. 1934), Hogarth Press, 1987.
Gaslight: A Victorian Thriller in Three Acts (a play), Constable, 1939.
Impromptu in Moribundia, Constable, 1939.
Money with Menaces & *To the Public Danger* (radio plays), Constable, 1939.
Hangover Square (f.p. 1941), Penguin Books: Harmondsworth, 1974.
This is Impossible (stage and radio play), Samuel French, 1942.
The Duke in Darkness (a play), Constable, 1943.
The Slaves of Solitude (f.p. 1947), Cardinal, 1991.
The West Pier (f.p. 1951), *Mr Stimpson and Mr Gorse* (f.p. 1953) and *Unknown Assailant* (f.p. 1955), jointly published as *The Gorse Trilogy*, Penguin Books: Harmondsworth, 1992.
The Man Upstairs (a play), Constable, 1954.

BERNARD HAMILTON (PH'S FATHER)

The Light? Hurst & Blackett, 1898.
Wanted – A Man! Apply John Bull & Co.: (Late of Dame Europa's School). A War Story for Big Boys told by Bernard Hamilton (a political pamphlet), Simpkin, Marshall & Co., 1900.

A Kiss for a Kingdom, Or A Venture in Vanity, Hurst & Blackett, 1899.
Coronation, Ward Lock & Co., 1902.
The Giant, Hutchinson, 1926.
His Queen, Hutchinson, 1927.
The Master of Mirth. A Romance of Rabelais, Hutchinson, 1928.
One World – at a Time (Bernard Hamilton's 'Psychic History'), Hurst & Blackett, 1928.

ELLEN HAMILTON (PH'S MOTHER), PUBLISHED UNDER THE PSEUDONYM 'OLIVIA ROY'

The Awakening of Mrs Carstairs, George A. Morton, Edinburgh, 1904.
The Husband Hunter, T. Werner Laurie, 1907.

BRUCE HAMILTON (PH'S BROTHER)

To be Hanged: A Story of Murder, Faber and Faber, 1930.
Hue and Cry, Collins, 1931.
The Spring Term, Methuen, 1933.
Middle Class Murder, Methuen, 1936.
The Brighton Murder Trial: Rex v. Rhodes, Boriswood, 1937.
Traitor's Way, Cresset Press, 1938.
Pro: An English Tragedy, Cresset Press, 1946.
Let Him Have Judgement, Cresset Press, 1948.
So Sad, So Fresh, Cresset Press, 1952.
Barbados & the Confederation Question 1871–1885, Ph.D. Thesis, Crown Agents for Overseas Governments and Administrations, 1956.
Too Much of Water, Cresset Press, 1958.
The Light Went Out: A Biography of Patrick Hamilton, Constable, 1972.

URSULA HAMILTON (PH'S SECOND WIFE), PUBLISHED UNDER THE PSEUDONYM 'LAURA TALBOT'

Prairial, Macmillan, 1950.
The Gentlewomen (f.p. 1952), Virago, 1985.
Barcelona Road, Macmillan, 1953.
The Elopement, Peter Davies, 1958.
The Last of the Tenants, Peter Davies, 1961.

Epigraphs

The sources of the epigraphs are: Edward Mendelson (ed.), *The English Auden*, Faber and Faber (1977), 238; Vladimir Nabokov, *Lectures on Literature*, Weidenfeld and Nicolson (1980), 381–2; Julian Barnes, *Flaubert's Parrot*, Jonathan Cape (1984), 38; Nicholson Baker, *U and I*, Granta (1991), 9–10; Francis Wyndham, *The Times Literary Supplement*, 13 December 1991; Bruce Hamilton, unpublished journal, 1946, SF; PH to Bruce, 16 September 1951; PH, *The Slaves of Solitude*, 229.

Introduction

1 W. H. Auden, *Collected Poems*, Faber and Faber (1976), 147.
2 Cyril Connolly, *The Condemned Playground*, Hogarth Press (1985), 101.
3 Letter from PH to Bruce, n.d. [early 1928].
4 'Marriage can succeed for an artist only where there is enough money to save him from taking on uncongenial work and a wife who is intelligent and unselfish enough to understand and respect the working of the unfriendly cycle of the creative imagination. She will know at what point domestic happiness begins to cloy, where love, tidiness, rent, rates, clothes, entertaining, and rings at the doorbell should stop, and will recognize that there is no more sombre enemy of good art than the pram in the hall.' Cyril Connolly, *Enemies of Promise*, André Deutsch (revised edition, 1973), 127.
5 John Betjeman, *The Spectator*, 28 December 1956.
6 Valentine Cunningham, *British Writers of the Thirties*, Oxford University Press (1988).
7 Hugh David, *The Fitzrovians: A Portrait of Bohemian Society 1900–55*, Michael Joseph (1988), 144, 158–9, 245.
8 Julian Maclaren-Ross, *Memoirs of the Forties*, Penguin: Harmondsworth (1984), 9. Anthony Powell, letter to the author, 18 August 1991.
9 John Gross, *The Rise and Fall of the Man of Letters*, Weidenfeld and Nicolson (1969), 245.
10 PH to Bruce, 29 January 1954.
11 Alexander Cockburn to the author, 30 December 1991.

1 Family

1 *Gorse*, 238.
2 *Tragedy II*, 2. Of 'Ride Through', the supposed family motto, Bruce

reported: 'This we learned originated in spirited advice offered to Charles I on a desperate Civil War occasion by the Duke of the time, a quarrelsome loyalist who makes a rather poor figure in history. He was beaten by Cromwell at Preston in the Second Civil War, and lost his head not long after his master.' Ibid., 3.

3   PH to Bruce, 16 September 1951.
4   PH to Bruce, 16 September 1951.
5   *One World*, 20.
6   Ibid., 22.
7   *Mem I*.
8   *One World*, 22–3.
9   Ibid., 23.
10 PH to Bruce, n.d. [1928?].
11 PH to Bruce, 16 September 1951.
12 *TLWO*, 2.
13 *One World*, 24–5.
14 Ibid., 47.
15 Robert Hewison, *Footlights! A Hundred Years of Cambridge Comedy*, Methuen (1983), 190.
16 *One World*, 52.
17 Ibid., 53.
18 Ibid., 53–4.
19 *TLWO*, 2.
20 *Middle Class Murder*, 2.
21 *Tragedy II*, 146. The quotation is from Genesis 49:4.
22 *One World*, 55.
23 Ibid., 46.
24 Patrick Hamilton's mother, Ellen, was known as Nellie. His sister's nickname was Lalla. His first wife was called Loïs. His second was called Ursula, wrote under the pen-name, Laura Talbot, and was known as La.
25 *TLWO*, 3.
26 Bruce's notes for his memoirs of Patrick. SF.
27 PH to Michael Sadleir, 17 February 1951. TEMPLE.
28 *The Light?*, 95.
29 PH to Bruce, n.d. [1928?]
30 *A Kiss for a Kingdom*, 63.
31 *Wanted – A Man!*, 4.
32 Ibid., 20, 21 and, e.g., 10.
33 Ibid., 28.
34 Ibid., 30.
35 *Coronation*, 61.
36 Ibid., xi.
37 Ibid., 21.

38 Ibid., 157.
39 Ibid., 330–1.
40 *The Awakening of Mrs Carstairs*, 10.
41 Ibid., 30–1.
42 Ibid., 291.
43 Ibid., 295.
44 *TLWO*, 4–5.
45 *The Husband Hunter*, 6.
46 Ibid., 339.
47 This brochure is in the British Museum copy of *The Husband Hunter*.

2 Childhood

1   *To Be Hanged*, 215.
2   *Hangover Square*, 268.
3   *The Brighton Murder Trial*, 19.
4   *Pro*, 71.
5   *Gorse*, 268.
6   *Mem II*.
7   *Mem II*.
8   Ibid.
9   *Mem II*.
10 Ibid.
11 Ibid.
12 Ibid.
13 Ibid.
14 PH to Bruce, 16 September 1951.
15 Ibid.
16 *Mem II*.
17 *Mem I*.
18 Lalla's memoir, written in 1915. SF. *Tragedy II*, 16.
19 It is most likely that PH originally conceived *Gaslight* as being divided into two words – *Gas Light*. But neither he nor the published versions of the play's texts were ever consistent. Since the single-worded spelling was adopted unequivocally for the two film versions, that is the one I have adopted.
20 *Mem I*.
21 *TLWO*, 4.
22 *Tragedy II*, 13.
23 For example, Florence Keynes, mother of Maynard and Geoffrey, who was born in the same year as Ellen Hamilton, 'was deeply concerned about the health of her children, stuffing them with tonics and taking

great precautions against draughts[. . .]'. Robert Skidelsky, *John Maynard Keynes, Hopes Betrayed 1883–1920*, Macmillan (rev. edn, 1992), 57.

24 *Tragedy II*, 30.
25 Ibid.
26 Ibid., 45.
27 Ibid., 46.
28 *Gorse*, 15.
29 PH to Bruce, 16 September 1951.
30 *Tragedy II*, 63; *TLWO*, 10.
31 PH to Bruce, 30 January 1957.
32 Ibid.
33 *Craven House*, 39.
34 Ibid., 43.
35 PH to Bruce, 28 June 1954.

3 Leaving School

1 *Gorse*, 41, though Bruce remembered it actually marching 'right on to the playing area, disregarding the players, and began performing military evolutions to barked-out words of command.' *Tragedy II*, 73. Bruce made use of the incident in his novel, *Pro*.
2 PH to Bruce, 16 September 1951.
3 *Tragedy II*, 60.
4 *Mem I*.
5 *One World*, 143.
6 Dated 4 February 1917, in Siegfried Sassoon, *The War Poems*, Faber and Faber (1983), 68.
7 *Tragedy II*, 85.
8 PH to Ellen Hamilton, n.d. BH.
9 *Tragedy II*, 91.
10 Ibid., 92.
11 *The Slaves of Solitude*, 239.
12 *Hangover Square*, 75.
13 School Report. BH.
14 Interview in *Boston Evening Transcript*, 21 June 1930.
15 *Poetry of To-day: The Poetry Review New Verse Supplement*, July–August 1919.

4 Adolescence

1   *Tragedy II*, 187–8.
2   *TLWO*, 30.
3   *Tragedy II*, 138.
4   Interview in the *Boston Evening Transcript*, 21 June 1930.
5   PH to Bruce, n.d. [1931?].
6   *Tragedy II*, 146.
7   *Mem I.*
8   Ibid.
9   *Tragedy II*, 157. [*TLWO*, 33.]
10 Ibid., 149.
11 Ibid., 183
12 *Tragedy II*, 107 [*TLWO*, 38]. Bruce reconstructed this letter from memory and, as he himself observed, the reference to Vincent Crummles might suggest the letter dates from a later period when Hamilton was working in the theatre. The phrase, 'the author and barrister' occurs only in the later *TLWO* text and was a term, echoing Bernard's own usage, employed mockingly by the two brothers. Bruce may have been unconsciously recalling a letter drafted by Bernard many years earlier on Hamilton's behalf: 'Dear Sir, I wish to become a Boy Scout. My father the author and barrister, wishes me to do this. Will you kindly tell me how to set about it in the Chiswick area.' The young Hamilton innocently suggested a correction: 'Wouldn't it be better to say "*an* author and barrister"?' 'They'll know me, my boy, they'll know me,' Bernard replied. (*Tragedy II*, 84.)
13 PH to Bruce, 20 November 1928.
14 *TLWO*, 39.
15 PH to Bruce, 5 August 1959.
16 PH to Bruce, 28 July 1961.
17 *Tragedy II*, 191. This was the experience of other women who encountered Hamilton. Rosamund John, who acted in a touring production of *Gaslight* in 1949, remembers him only as 'very quiet and shy'. (Conversation with the author, November 1991.)
18 PH to Bruce, 10 October 1933.
19 PH to Bruce, n.d. [early 1934].
20 Charles Mackehenie to PH, 22 July 1946. BH.
21 Charles Mackehenie to Bruce, 2 March 1963. SF.

5 Apprenticeship

1   *Tragedy II*, 204.
2   As a 'shady blue-chinned seaman', a policeman and a 'scarlet-coated and bearskinned private soldier on sentry duty', *Tragedy II*, 213.
3   PH, account of his early life written for Constable. TEMPLE.
4   Ibid.
5   *Tragedy II*, 208.
6   Ibid., 214.
7   *Craven House*, 126–8.
8   See A. J. P. Taylor, *English History 1914–1945*, Oxford University Press (1965), 38.
9   Letter apparently lost, but quoted in PH to Bernard Hamilton, 28 August 1924. BH.
10 *Tragedy II*, 223.
11 Ibid., 225–6.
12 PH to Bruce, March 1940, quoted in *Tragedy I*, 180.
13 PH to Bernard Hamilton, 28 August 1924. BH.
14 *Mem I*.
15 *Tragedy II*, 229.
16 Arthur Conan Doyle, *Memories and Adventures*, Hodder and Stoughton (1924), 256.
17 PH to Bruce, 6 May 1955.
18 PH to Bruce, 5 August 1959.
19 Wilkes Barre, Pennsylvania is the home town of Lieutenant Dayton Pike in *The Slaves of Solitude*.
20 *Tragedy II*, 237.
21 Interview in the *Boston Evening Transcript*, 21 June 1930.
22 *Monday Morning*, 110.
23 Ibid., 60.
24 Ibid., 95.
25 Ibid., 123.
26 Ibid., 105.
27 Ibid., 214.
28 Both quoted in the first edition of *Craven House*, Constable (1926).
29 *Monday Morning*, 16.

6 *Craven House*

1   PH to Bruce, n.d. [16 February 1927].
2   Michael Sadlier to PH, 13 May 1942. TEMPLE.

3   *Craven House*, Cardinal (1991) 6. Unless specified otherwise, all quotations from *Craven House* are from this, revised, version of the novel.

4   Ibid., 22.

5   Ibid., 33–4.

6   *Times Literary Supplement*, 4 November 1926; *Christian World* review, cited in first edition of *The Midnight Bell*; *Manchester Guardian* review, cited in first edition of *The Siege of Pleasure*.

7   PH to Bruce, n.d. [summer 1927].

8   *Craven House*, 193.

9   PH to Michael Sadleir, n.d. [1926]. *Temple*.

10 PH to Bruce, 23 March 1948.

11 *TLWO*, 44.

12 *The Giant*, 18.

13 Ibid., 121.

14 Ibid., 151.

15 Ibid., 308.

16 PH recalls this in PH to Bruce, n.d. [16 February 1927].

7 The Young Novelist

1   *Tragedy II*, 257–8.

2   PH to Bruce, 10 March 1927.

3   Ibid.

4   Ibid.

5   PH to Bruce, 20 January 1927.

6   Ibid.

7   PH to Bruce, 10 March 1927.

8   PH to Bruce, 21 March (?) 1927.

9   PH to Bruce, 14 March 1927.

10 PH to Bruce, 6 April 1927.

11 PH to Bruce, 14 March 1927.

12 PH to Bruce, 10 March 1927.

13 PH to Bruce, 5 May 1927.

14 *Tragedy II*, 514.

15 PH to Bruce, 6 April 1927.

16 Arthur Calder-Marshall's widow, Ara, in conversation with the author.

17 See Michael Baker, *Our Three Selves: A Life of Radclyffe Hall*, Hamish Hamilton (1985), 234.

18 PH to Bruce, 6 April 1927.

19 Ibid.

20 *The Listener*, 13 July 1972.

21 PH to Bruce, n.d. [May 1927].

22 *20,000*, 153.

8 *Twopence Coloured*

1   PH to Bruce, May 1927.
2   PH to Bruce 27 May 1927.
3   PH to Bruce, summer 1927.
4   PH to Michael Sadleir, 13 September 1927, TEMPLE; PH to Ellen Hamilton, 15 September 1927. BH.
5   PH to Bruce, 29 September 1927, 26 October 1927.
6   PH to Michael Sadleir, 23 November 1927. TEMPLE.
7   PH to Michael Sadleir, 5 December 1927. TEMPLE.
8   PH to Bruce, n.d. [early 1928].
9   Michael Sadleir to PH, 4 February 1940. TEMPLE.
10   Cited in the first edition of *The Midnight Bell*.
11   PH to Michael Sadleir, 8 [February, PH mistakenly wrote January] 1940. TEMPLE.
12   *Twopence Coloured*, 48.
13   Ibid., 51.
14   Ibid., 227.
15   Dr Johnson 'for a considerable time used to frequent the *Green Room*, and seemed to take delight in dissipating his gloom, by mixing in the sprightly chit-chat of the motley circle then to be found there. Mr David Hume related to me from Mr Garrick, that Johnson at last denied himself this amusement, from considerations of rigid virtue; saying, "I'll come no more behind the scenes, David; for the silk stockings and white bosoms of your actresses excite my amorous propensities." ' James Boswell, *Life of Johnson*, Oxford University Press (revised edition, 1980), 143.
16   *Twopence Coloured*, 115.
17   Brian Aherne to PH, 29 August 1929. BH.
18   *Twopence Coloured*, 331.
19   Ibid., 333.
20   Ibid., 334–5.
21   Ibid., 336.
22   Ibid., 368.
23   *His Queen*, 19.
24   Ibid., 259.
25   *The Master of Mirth*, 53.
26   Ibid., 149.
27   Ibid., 150.
28   Ellen Hamilton to Bruce, 26 September 1928. SF.
29   *One World*, 185–6.
30   Ibid., 184–6.

9 Courtesans and *The Midnight Bell*

1 PH to Bruce, 24 August 1927.
2 PH to Bruce, August 1927.
3 *20,000*, 216.
4 PH to Bruce, August 1927.
5 *Tragedy II*, 129.
6 BH. The notes are undated.
7 Michael Sadleir to PH, 6 February 1930. TEMPLE.
8 *Craven House*, first edition, 160.
9 PH to Bruce, 3 February 1927. Bruce's description of his sexual initiation is in the unpublished novel, *A Case for Cain*, 82. SF.
10 PH to Charles Mackehenie, enclosed with PH to Bruce, 31 March 1927. BH.
11 PH to Bruce, May 1927.
12 Ibid.
13 *Gorse*, 418.
14 Ibid., 437.
15 PH to Bruce, 11 July 1927.
16 Ibid.
17 Ibid.
18 *20,000*, 55.
19 Lily Connolly to PH, n.d. [11 February 1928]. BH.
20 *TLWO*, 52–3.
21 PH to Bruce, n.d. [early 1928].
22 PH to Bruce, 10 June 1928.
23 Leslie Halliwell, *Halliwell's Filmgoer's Companion*, Paladin (eighth edition, 1985).
24 PH to Bruce, 10 June 1928.
25 PH to Bruce, 17 June 1928.
26 PH to Bruce, n.d. [December 1928].
27 PH to Bruce, n.d. [December 1928].
28 *TLWO*, 53–54.
29 PH to Bruce, 24 December 1942.
30 Michael Sadleir to PH, 4 February 1940. TEMPLE.
31 Michael Holroyd, introduction to *20,000*, 5.
32 Lily Connolly to PH, n.d. [April/May 1928]. BH.
33 *20,000*, 103.
34 Ibid., 177.
35 Ibid., 147.
36 Ibid., 165.
37 *TLWO*, 53. Bruce put this more tentatively in the typescript: 'He never went to bed with her at the time – though long after the fever had

run its course I think he once did; not very successfully.' *Tragedy II*, 266.

38 *20,000*, 39.

39 Ibid., 40.

40 Cited in the first edition of *The Siege of Pleasure*.

10 *Rope*

1 PH to Bruce, 25 April 1929.

2 *To Be Hanged*, 278–9.

3 Telegram from PH to Bruce, 22 May 1929.

4 Constable document. TEMPLE.

5 *Rope*, ix.

6 *TLWO*, 55.

7 Colin Wilson and Pat Pitman, *Encyclopaedia of Murder*, Arthur Barker Ltd (1961).

8 PH to Michael Sadleir, n.d. [1929]. TEMPLE.

9 Friedrich Nietzsche, *Thus Spoke Zarathustra*, translated by R. J. Hollingdale, Penguin: Harmondsworth (1969 edition), 43.

10 Cited in *The Midnight Bell*, Constable (1929).

11 In *English Drama 1900–1930: The Beginnings of the Modern Period*, Cambridge (1973), 204, 211, Allardyce Nicoll acknowledges that, before *Rope*,

the search for clever novelties and the desire to exhibit out-of-the-way stunts swamped the stage with pieces which had nothing save thrills and unexpected tricks to recommend them. . . .

Yet when [Hamilton] essayed to demonstrate what a thriller might be, all he could do was to invent a contrived macabre situation in which two undergraduates strangle one of their companions for no ostensible reason save to plume up their wills by committing 'passionless-motiveless-faultless-and-clueless murder', while, not content with this basic situation, the playwright further proceeded in a grisly manner to show how they place the body in a chest and then deliberately invite the dead youth's father and aunt, together with three of their friends, to come round for a party in what might be regarded as a parlour-mortuary.

We have moved far here from the old melodrama, and yet unquestionably these thrillers, even although in style they are often more polished and polite than the earlier popular plays, even although now they were being written by clever young highbrows, belonged to the same tradition. The only trouble was that, while both the melodramas and the thrillers abounded in plots that were absurd and episodes of a ridiculous kind, the emotions introduced into the former were sincere, the emotions introduced into the latter were essentially false.

To this accusation of contrivance, Hamilton could have responded that he had based his story on a real murder, had he not already denied it in his preface to the play text.

12 BBC Radio talk by Arthur Calder-Marshall, 5 September 1951. BBC.
13 *Rope*, viii.
14 Ibid., viii.
15 Ibid., ix.
16 Ibid.
17 Ibid., 14.
18 PH to Bruce, 23–7 April 1939.
19 PH to Bruce, 10 June 1955.
20 Author's interview with Kenneth Robinson, 11 February 1992.
21 Brian Aherne to PH, 29 August 1929. BH.
22 *20,000*, 392.
23 PH to Bruce, n.d. [late May 1929].
24 PH to Michael Sadleir, 22 June 1929. TEMPLE.
25 Ibid.
26 PH to Bruce, 24 August 1929.
27 PH to Bruce, 14 June 1929.
28 *TLWO*, 60.
29 *Tragedy II*, 280. In this original version, Bruce mistakenly remembered Hamilton's offer as having come at the same time as his announcement that *Rope* was a success. He recalled it as a decisive influence on his decision to resign his teaching job and return to Britain: 'I have never been quite able to decide whether or not my return was a mistake.' (Ibid.) Thus the moment of Hamilton's first great success was seen by Bruce also as a moment of betrayal.
30 *TLWO*, 59.
31 *20,000*, 66–7.
32 *TLWO*, 59–60. The phrase 'too splendid' is from *Tragedy I*, 134.
33 PH to Ellen Hamilton, 2 November 1929. BH.
34 PH to Bruce, 29 October 1929. 'You Were Meant for Me' featured in *Broadway Melody*, *Hollywood Revue of 1929* and *The Show of Shows*.
35 PH to Ellen Hamilton, 2 November 1929. BH.
36 F. V. Morley to Patience Ross, 21 November 1929. FABER.
37 Arthur Conan Doyle to Bruce, 26 March 1930. BH.
38 Ibid.
39 *Tragedy II*, 227.
40 On Lalla – 'too exigent sexually' were Bruce's actual words (*Tragedy I*, 142); on his mother, 'her respect, before old age, for *tabu*, and perhaps

her history as a wife, is suggestive of sexual frigidity.' (*Tragedy II*, 13.)

41 PH to Bruce, 14 June 1929.
42 *Tragedy I*, 135.
43 *Tragedy I*, 141.
44 *Tragedy II*, 234.
45 Hamilton's own typescript of *John Brown's Body* is possessed by the New York Public Library. I am grateful to Timothy Boulton for letting me see his photocopy of this text.
46 *Radio Times*, 26 September 1930.
47 *The Evening World*, 3 March 1930.
48 Ibid.
49 Ibid.
50 *Boston Evening Transcript*, 21 June 1930.

11 Marriage and *The Siege of Pleasure*

1   PH to Ellen Hamilton, n.d. [early August 1930]. BH
2   *TLWO*, 64.
3   Ibid., 57.
4   PH to Bruce, 10 June 1955.
5   *TLWO*, 64–5. Bruce had some struggle in finding the right words. Originally he wrote: 'For Hamilton discovered that he was quite unable to consummate a sexual arrangement with Loïs.' Also he originally referred to 'one of those *physiological* incompatibilities' (my italics, as against 'psychological', to which he changed it in the published memoir). (*Tragedy I*, 144.)
6   PH to Bruce, 22 August 1930.
7   *Hue and Cry*, 215.
8   Ibid., 23.
9   Ibid., 73.
10 F. V. Morley to Bruce, 15 January 1931. FABER.
11 Bruce to F. V. Morley, (misdated) 15 January 1931. FABER.
12 PH to Bruce, 2 September 1931.
13 *Tragedy I*, 147.
14 PH to Bruce, May 1931.
15 PH to Bruce, n.d. [1931], quoted in *Tragedy I*, 147a.
16 PH to Michael Sadleir, 9 July 1931. TEMPLE.
17 PH to Bruce, n.d. [July? 1931].
18 PH to Bruce, n.d. [July or August, 1931].
19 Ibid.
20 PH to Bruce, September 1931.
21 PH to Martha Smith, October 1931. TEMPLE.
22 PH to Michael Sadleir, 8 November 1932. TEMPLE.

23   PH to Michael Sadleir, 26 December 1931. TEMPLE.
24   PH to Bruce, May 1927.
25   PH to Bruce, December 1928.
26   *20,000*, 226.
27   *Craven House*, 198–9.
28   Ibid., 199.
29   *20,000*, 36.
30   Ibid., 248.
31   Ibid., 287.
32   Ibid., 329.

12 Accident

1   PH to Bruce, January 1932.
2   See Val Gielgud, *Years of the Locust*, Nicholson and Watson (1947), 93, and *Years in a Mirror*, Bodley Head (1965), 59.
3   PH to Martha Smith, n.d. [January 1932]. TEMPLE.
4   *TLWO*, 71–2.
5   A couple of weeks after Hamilton's accident, Bruce also had an accident, if accident it was. He described it in his memoirs:

For many years I have been subject to severe nightmares, probably springing from some forgotten childhood trauma, but the immediate occasion was nearly always eating too much too late. So it was this night. It must have been about three o'clock in the morning when, impelled by the terrors of heaven knows what dream, I jumped out of bed, smashed the lower window-pane, and returned to bewildered half-consciousness finding myself on a narrow fragile kind of pergola. (I learned afterwards that it was the roof of a tiny veranda to the room below and about forty feet from the ground, the distance I would have fallen if the flimsy structure had broken under my weight.)

I had no idea where I was. I called out loudly, 'Help!' three or four times; and at last I heard a man's voice calling, 'Where are you?' I answered, and this I remember distinctly, 'I don't know, but I think I'm on the roof of the hospital.' Within a few seconds the man was in the room, and he pulled me through the broken window. His name was Mr Olive, the landlord of the house, and almost certainly he saved my life. But Loïs, who visited the scene a day or two after the mishap, told me that he remained unshakeable in the conviction that I had meant to commit suicide, but funked it before the job was finished. (*TLWO*, 75.)

Compare this with an incident reported by Lalla during a summer holiday when she was about ten, Bruce eight and Patrick four: 'Patrick has been stung on his hand, but not badly. In the middle of tea one day Bruce cried out he was stung on his ear, but when the nurse looked he wasn't stung at all.' LALLA to Ellen Hamilton, undated. SF.

6   *Tragedy I*, 210.
7   PH to Bruce, 30 January 1957.
8   Kenneth Robinson to the author, 15 August 1992.
9   *TLWO*, 78; author's conversation with Ara Calder-Marshall.
10 Introduction to *Twenty Thousand Streets Under the Sky*, CONSTABLE (1935), x.
11 BBC Radio talk by Arthur Calder-Marshall, 5 September 1951. BBC.
12 Ibid.
13 PH to Bruce, 11 March 1932.
14 PH to Bruce, May 1933.
15 PH to Bruce, 3 June 1933.
16 *TLWO*, 19.
17 'Hegel remarks somewhere that all facts and personages of great importance in world history occur, as it were, twice. He forgot to add: the first time as tragedy, the second as farce.' This is the first sentence of Karl Marx's political pamphlet, *The Eighteenth Brumaire of Louis Bonaparte*, David McLennan (ed.), *Karl Marx: Selected Writings*, Oxford University Press (1977), 300.
18 PH to Bruce, 25 September 1933.
19 PH to Bruce, 26 October 1932.
20 PH to Bruce, n.d. [May 1934].
21 PH to Bruce, 10 October 1933.
22 Ibid.
23 *The Spring Term*, 6.
24 *TLWO* 5–6.
25 PH to Bruce, 26 October 1933.
26 Ibid.
27 PH to Bruce, 16 November 1933.
28 *TLWO*, 82 and PH to Bruce, 29 November 1933.
29 *TLWO*, 1.

13   *The Plains of Cement*

1   PH to Bruce, n.d. [early 1934].
2   PH to Michael Sadleir, October 1933. TEMPLE.
3   PH to Bruce, n.d. [early 1934].
4   PH to Michael Sadleir, 26 February 1934. TEMPLE.
5   PH to Martha Smith and Michael Sadleir, 18 March 1934. TEMPLE.

6   *20,000*, 509–10.
7   Ibid., 338.
8   Ibid., 341.
9   Ibid., 343.
10 Ibid., 480.
11 See for example, Sonia Orwell and Ian Angus (eds.), *The Collected Essays, Journalism and Letters of George Orwell*, Secker and Warburg (1968), Volume IV, 130–1, 135.
12 *20,000*, 335.
13 Ibid., 504.
14 Michael Sadleir to PH, 4 January 1935. TEMPLE.
15 PH to Michael Sadleir, 5 January 1935. TEMPLE.
16 Michael Sadleir to PH, 11 January 1935. TEMPLE.
17 *20,000*, 436.
18 Ibid., 355.
19 *Gorse*, 561.
20 *TLWO*, 84.
21 Charles Mackehenie to Bruce, 2 March 1963. SF.
22 PH to Bruce, n.d. [early 1934].
23 Ibid.
24 PH to Bruce, 22 June 1934.
25 *Tragedy I*, 163. It must be added that Ellen and Lalla did not like her much either, nor, for that matter, did Kenneth Robinson, who after the Second World War was to become one of Bruce's closest friends. (Author's interview with Kenneth Robinson, 11 February 1992).
26 Ibid.
27 More precisely, Aileen took pills designed to bring on a miscarriage. Bruce adds later in the paragraph: 'Aileen was [at a later date] found to be incapable of conception. There remains a possibility that she had never been otherwise.' Ibid.
28 *Tragedy I*, 164.

14 *Money with Menaces* and *Gaslight*

1   PH to Bruce, 19 December 1935.
2   Val Gielgud to PH, 11 February 1936. BBC.
3   *Money with Menaces*, vi.
4   Ibid., 42.
5   PH to Val Gielgud, 16 November 1936. BBC.
6   PH to Bruce, 25 January 1937.
7   *Middle Class Murder*, 77.
8   PH to Bruce, 11 December 1958.

9   *Middle Class Murder*, 12.
10 Ibid., 56. After his return from the Soviet Union, Bruce had contributed two propagandist articles to the magazine *Russia To-day* – a celebration of the Moscow underground railway and an attack on those who claimed that freedom of expression was restricted in the Soviet Union. *Russia To-day*, April and May 1934.
11 *The Brighton Murder Trial*, 9.
12 Ibid., 10.
13 See Robert Conquest, *The Great Terror: A Reassessment*, Pimlico (1992), 167.
14 Quoted in David Caute, *The Fellow Travellers*, Weidenfeld and Nicolson (1973), 119–20.
15 *The Brighton Murder Trial*, 158.
16 Ibid., 159
17 Ibid., 376.
18 Ibid., 386.
19 *Tragedy I*, 159.
20 *New Statesman*, 19 June 1937; Henry T. F. Rhodes, *New English Weekly*, 14 June 1934.
21 PH to Bruce, n.d. [early 1937].
22 *Tragedy I*, 167.
23 PH to Lalla, October 1937. BH.
24 Ibid.
25 PH to Bruce, 24 October 1937.
26 PH to Val Gielgud, 22 January 1938. BBC.
27 *TLWO*, 85.
28 PH to Bruce, 12 February 1938.
29 *Money with Menaces*, 90.
30 *To Be Hanged*, 128.
31 *Gaslight*, 13–14.
32 PH to Bruce, 23–7 April 1939.
33 PH to Bruce, 23 March 1948.

15 *Impromptu in Moribundia*

1   Lionel Trilling, *The Last Decade*, Harcourt Brace Jovanovich: New York (1979), 140–1.
2   See Igor Golomstock, *Totalitarian Art*, Collins Harvill (1990), 85–9.
3   Ibid., 85–6. The phrase 'engineers of human souls' had been coined by Sergei Tretiakov, himself to die in a labour camp in 1923. Ibid., 26.
4   Anthony Blunt in 'Art Under Capitalism and Socialism' in C. Day Lewis

(ed.), *The Mind in Chains: Socialism and the Cultural Revolution*, Frederick Muller (1937), 120.

5   Philip Henderson, *The Novel Today*, John Lane The Bodley Head (1936), 7.

6   Ralph Fox, *The Novel and the People*, Lawrence and Wishart (1936), 101.

7   Robert Conquest, *The Great Terror*, 297.

8   See Robert Conquest, ibid. The most revered was the first to die. Maxim Gorky died on 18 June 1936, reportedly of natural causes, though there are serious grounds for believing Stalin ordered his poisoning. In exchange for a promise of immunity, Karl Radek agreed to give fabricated evidence against Bukharin in December 1936 that the two of them had plotted to kill Stalin. Bukharin was arrested in February 1937. After torture and trial, he was sentenced to death on 13 March 1938 and executed soon afterwards. Radek was murdered by May 1939 by cell mates reportedly acting on official instructions. In July 1938 Stetsky was one of 138 of the Soviet Union's political élite whose execution was ordered by Stalin and who were summarily shot in the days afterwards. Zhdanov survived the longest, because, as First Secretary of the Leningrad Communist Party, he willingly enacted a purge of the local party that was drastic even by prevailing standards, wiping out virtually the entire organization. He became a Soviet hero when presiding over Leningrad during the wartime siege. This very success roused Stalin's suspicions that the city would be a centre of discontent. His star began to fall, and though he attempted to redeem himself with a public denunciation of certain writers, among them Anna Akhmatova, he died in July 1948, a victim of the alleged Doctors' plot which was used as a pretext for Stalin's final purge; in fact he was almost certainly killed on the instructions of Stalin.

9   PH to Bruce, 23–7 April 1939.

10   E. R. Dodds (ed.), *Collected Poems of Louis MacNeice*, Faber (1966), 22.

11   Edward Mendelson (ed.), *W. H. Auden Selected Poems*, Faber (1979), 53–4. But these lines were the first to be cut. See the version printed in Edward Mendelson (ed.), *The English Auden: Poems, Essays, and Dramatic Writings*, Faber (1977), 210–12.

12   PH to Bruce, 12 February 1938.

13   PH to Bruce, n.d. [early 1938].

14   *Impromptu in Moribundia*, 42.

15   Sonia Orwell and Ian Angus, op. cit., I, 258.

16   *Impromptu in Moribundia*, 39.

17   Ibid., 136.

18   Ibid., 143–4.

19   Ibid., 246.

20   Ibid., 248.

21   Ibid., 250–1.

22   Ibid., 252.

23   Ibid., 284.

24   Claud Cockburn, introduction to Patrick Hamilton, *The Slaves of Solitude*, Oxford University Press (1982), xii.

25   *Lay Sermons Addresses and Reviews*, Macmillan (1870), 36, quoted in PH to Bruce, 16 December 1959.

26   *Time and Tide*, 18 February 1939.

27   PH to Bruce, 23 April 1939; *New Statesman*, 11 February 1939.

28   PH to Bruce, ibid.

29   Ibid.

30   *Traitor's Way*, 198–9.

31   Ibid., 252.

32   *TLWO*, 86.

33   Bruce reveals this secret motive in his autobiographical novel, *A Cause for Cain*, 372. SF.

16 The War and *Hangover Square*

1   PH to Bruce, 23 April 1939.

2   Ibid.

3   *TLWO*, 93.

4   *Time and Tide*, 20 May 1939.

5   *Time and Tide*, 3 June 1939.

6   Ibid.

7   'He did not like the work, and one of the editors at the paper remembered him complaining once that he could not bear to go to another "bloody play".' Michael Shelden, *Orwell: The Authorised Biography*, Minerva (1992), 353. The editor was Lettice Cooper, who had favourably reviewed *Impromptu in Moribundia* for *Time and Tide*.

8   PH to Bruce, 8 September 1939.

9   PH to Bruce, 30 November 1939.

10   Ibid.

11   PH to Bruce, 31 December 1939.

12   Letter to Bruce, 28 April 1940; *TLWO*, 95.

13   PH to Bruce, 3 June 1940.

14   PH to Bruce, 3 July 1940.

15   PH to Bruce, 28 April 1940.

16   PH to Bruce, 2 October 1940.

17   PH to Bruce, 3 July 1940.

18   PH to Bruce, 28 April and 2 October 1940.

19   Ibid.

20   PH to Bruce, 3 June 1940.

21 PH to Martha Smith, July 1940. TEMPLE.
22 *Tragedy I*, 197–8.
23 PH to Bruce, 15 January 1941.
24 PH to Martha Smith and Michael Sadleir, 18 September 1950. TEMPLE.
25 PH to Bruce, 22 March 1941.
26 *Hangover Square*, 44.
27 Ibid., 233.
28 Ibid., 124–5.
29 Ibid., 130.
30 Ibid., 29.
31 Ibid., 35.
32 Ibid., 178.
33 This aspect of the novel may well have been suggested by G. S. Marlowe's initially successful, but now forgotten, novel, *I Am Your Brother* (Collins, 1935). Julian Maclaren-Ross cogently sums it up as the portrayal of 'the repulsive mother of the schizophrenic young composer, shuffling and snuffling about the Soho markets in search of offal on which to nourish her other, perhaps imaginary son', Julain Maclaren-Ross, *Memoirs of the Forties*, Penguin: Harmondsworth (1984), 39. When Julian (the composer) is arrested for the Soho murder of a prostitute, he speaks to the officer in words that could have come from *Rope*:

'I'm sure you must think me an awful fellow, but you know, officer, sometimes it gets one. One laughs, and sneers, feels very superior to this bunch of useless people. It's only at times I feel like this. It's only envy. It is a curse to be a little different from them all. Talent, great talent, genius – what is it? Words. It's only bloody sweat and agony – yes – how much I envy them their lives – their little passions – their little foods and drinks – their little lives and deaths. Why does God always choose the weak ones – men with some ailment, poor and humble, just worry-loaded creatures – to stand up for him?' (*I Am Your Brother*, 279–80.)

Julian ends, looking out of the window of an asylum at ordinary life outside:

'How gay life can be! Strange that I once was one of them. The little house in Greek Street, Brighton. The concert. Dreams and hopes. And Viva. Yet, it's all so far from me.' And to the nurse who has just put the tray with his dinner on the table: 'You know, sometimes I wonder why it had to come like this. Life is a grand show if one is not miscast — hideous make-up, hideous part I had.' (Ibid., 285).

Curiously, in the 1944 film version of *Hangover Square* that travesties Hamilton's novel, George Harvey Bone becomes a composer.

34 PH to Bruce, 15 August 1941.
35 PH to Bruce, 26 November 1941.
36 PH to Bruce, 6 June 1942.
37 PH to Bruce, 22 March 1941.
38 PH to Bruce, 15 August 1941.
39 PH to Bruce, 27 August 1941.
40 PH to Bruce, 19 May 1941.
41 PH to Bruce, 6 June 1942.
42 *Hangover Square*, 73.
43 Ibid., 260.
44 *Tragedy I*, 202.
45 Ibid.
46 Ibid.
47 Ibid.
48 *TLWO*, 103.
49 Claud Cockburn, introduction to *The Slaves of Solitude*, x.
50 PH to Bruce, 19 May 1941.
51 Ibid.
52 PH to Bruce, 26 November 1941.
53 Rudy Behlmer (ed.), *Memo from David O. Selznick*, Macmillan (1973), 340.
54 PH to Bruce, 26 November 1941.

17 *The Duke in Darkness*

1   PH to Bruce, 22 March 1941.
2   PH to Bruce, 19 May 1941.
3   PH to Bruce, 20 November 1928.
4   PH to Bruce, n.d. [November 1928].
5   *The Duke in Darkness*, 7.
6   Milton Rosmer to Bill Linnit, 24 March 1942. BH.
7   PH to Bruce, 5 August 1959.
8   Arnold Rattenbury, 'Total Attainder and the Helots' in *The 1930s: A Challenge to Orthodoxy*, Harvester Press: Hassocks, Sussex (1978), 150–2.
9   *The Duke in Darkness*, 56.
10 Michael Sadleir to PH, 8 January 1940. TEMPLE.
11 Val Gielgud, to PH, 14 February 1940. BBC.
12 Michael Sadleir to PH, 13 May 1942. TEMPLE.
13 *Craven House* (1925), 241.
14 *Craven House* (1943), 190.
15 *Craven House* (1925), 309; *Craven House* (1943), 247.
16 PH to Bruce, 6 June 1941.
17 Ibid.

18 PH to Bruce, 24 December 1942.
19 *Pro*, 236.
20 PH to Bruce, 9 December 1943.
21 PH to Bruce, 18 September 1943.
22 Ibid.
23 PH to Bruce, 13 December 1948.
24 Ibid.
25 *Gaslight*, 35.
26 *Hangover Square*, 76.
27 *The Slaves of Solitude*, 35.
28 PH to Bruce, 18 September 1943.
29 PH to Bruce, 15 April 1944.
30 PH to Bruce, 9 December 1943.
31 James Agate, *The Tatler*, 7 March 1945.
32 *News Chronicle*, 7 March 1945.
33 PH to Bruce, 5 May 1944.
34 Rudy Behlmer, op. cit.
35 PH to Bruce, 22 August 1944.
36 PH to Bruce, n.d. [November 1944].
37 Flora Robson to Bruce Hamilton, 26 October [1968?]. BH.

18 *The Slaves of Solitude* and Peace

1 PH to Bruce, 15 April 1944.
2 *The Slaves of Solitude*, 8.
3 PH to Bruce, 27 May 1927.
4 *Mem I*.
5 *The Slaves of Solitude*, 169.
6 After the doctor has reassured Miss Roach that there is no connection between the fall she caused and Thwaites's death, it occurs to him 'that it was conceivably arguable by medical men that a fall might be put down as some sort of secondary cause.' (*The Slaves of Solitude*, 223.)
7 Hamilton may have been influenced here by Rudyard Kipling's First World War story, 'Mary Postgate'. The similarities are numerous: Mary is a spinster, cruelly called Postie as Miss Roach is called Roachie. Both take a maternal interest in young military men. Both achieve fulfilment through death and the victory over a German which, for them, is a personal version of the war being fought elsewhere. In the earlier story, Mary watches a crashed German pilot die while offering no help. Both celebrate their violent triumph with a luxurious bath. The end of Kipling's story could have ended *The Slaves of Solitude*:

Then the end came very distinctly in a lull between two rain-gusts. Mary Postgate drew her breath short between her teeth and shivered up to the house, where she scandalized the whole routine by taking a luxurious hot bath before tea, and came down looking, as Miss Fowler said when she saw her lying all relaxed on the other sofa, 'quite handsome!' Craig Raine (ed.), *A Choice of Kipling's Prose*, Faber (1987), 313.

8   *The Slaves of Solitude*, 157.
9   PH to Bruce, November 1944.
10 PH to Bruce, 4 September 1945.
11 PH to Bruce, 22 May 1945.
12 Ibid.
13 *Hangover Square*, 144–8; *The Duke in Darkness*, 48–9.
14 Sonia Orwell and Ian Angus (eds), op. cit., IV, 201.
15 Ibid.
16 Author's interview with Kenneth Robinson, 11 February 1992.
17 Ibid.
18 Sonia Orwell and Ian Angus, ibid.
19 *TLWO*, 119.
20 PH to Bruce, 7 November 1945.
21 *TLWO*, 111–12.
22 The story is told in *Tragedy I*, 213. It was on this occasion, 'that I told him (but only after he had, with his extreme sensibility to the moods of others, realized that I was out of humour and almost bullyragged me for the reason) that I thought his behaviour to Claud had been a bit undignified, and though I would probably have said no, I wouldn't have minded being at least asked to go behind myself.' This passage is typical of what was lost when Bruce's memoir was cut and reworked for publication. Gone are the specific incident and the personal resentment that may have influenced Bruce's judgement. All that remains is the general statement that Hamilton abased himself before his friends. This return trip of Bruce's apparently produced a series of what he considered to be humiliations. On one occasion Bruce was with Hamilton when Hamilton was due to meet Eric Ambler to give him some professional advice, 'and I was, after not more than a brief introduction, almost packed off by my brother. Feeling quite capable of leaving of my own accord when they got down to business I rather resented this, as I greatly admired most of Ambler's work and would have been glad of a few minutes' talk with him.' (*Tragedy I*, 214a.)
    While in England, Bruce had considered applying for a job with the British Council. Hamilton suggested Michael Sadleir as a referee but, as Bruce had nervously anticipated, Sadleir refused, saying 'he could hardly say more than that I seemed an amiable fellow, the brother of one of his closest friends, and that I could sing "Love in Bloom" very nicely – which would perhaps

be no very weighty point in my favour. I felt this was an unnecessary humiliation, for which Patrick was entirely responsible.' (Ibid.)

23 *Barbados and the Confederation Question*, ix.
24 *Tragedy II*, 487.
25 Bruce's unpublished 1946 journal. SF.
26 *TLWO*, 112–13.
27 *The Slaves of Solitude*, 230–4.

19 *Rope* on Film

1 'Whenever I collaborate with a writer who, like myself, specializes in mystery, thriller, or suspense, things don't seem to work out too well.' François Truffaut, *Hitchcock*, Simon and Schuster: New York (revised edition, 1984), 193.
2 Donald Spoto, *The Life of Alfred Hitchcock*, Collins (1983), 255–6.
3 Rudy Behlmer (ed.), op. cit., 287.
4 François Truffaut, *Hitchcock*, 142.
5 PH to Bruce, n.d. [early June 1947].
6 Ibid.
7 Ibid.
8 PH to Bruce, 5 August 1947.
9 PH to Bruce, n.d. [early June 1947].
10 PH to Bruce, 23 March 1948.
11 Ibid.
12 PH to Bruce, 5 August 1947.
13 Spoto, *The Life of Alfred Hitchcock*, 303–8.
14 PH to Bruce, 11 December 1947.
15 Ibid.
16 PH to Bruce, 23 March 1948.
17 PH to Michael Sadleir, 22 May 1948. TEMPLE.
18 PH to Bruce, 13 December 1948.
19 Ibid.
20 PH to Bruce, 7 August 1949.
21 Ibid. and 20 September 1949.
22 PH to Bruce, 20 September 1949.
23 Ibid.
24 Ibid.
25 Ibid.
26 Truffaut, *Hitchcock*, 180.
27 Ibid., 346.
28 Ibid., 345.
29 *TLWO*, 122.

20 Ursula and the Death of Lalla

1 PH to Bruce, 20 September 1949.
2 PH to Bruce, 8 January 1950.
3 Ibid.
4 See Polly Devlin, introduction to Laura Talbot's *The Gentlewomen*, v.
5 Ibid., vi.
6 Audrey Morris, quoted in ibid.
7 *Tragedy II*, 509.
8 PH to Bruce, 1 March 1951.
9 Ibid.
10 PH to Bruce, 16 September 1951.
11 PH to Bruce, 31 January 1951.
12 Bruce's account is impossible as it stands. He writes (*TLWO*, 121–2) that they began their affair after meeting to discuss her book 'a year or two' before the première of *Rope*. But La's first novel was not published until 1950, and, at least in its final form, could not, have been the book they discussed at their first meeting, since it contains a partial portrait of Hamilton. (See p. 208). Bruce confuses the issue even more by saying that the novel concerned was '*The Gentlewoman*' [*sic*]. In fact *The Gentlewomen* was not published until 1952. It may have been written first, though in her introduction to the re-issued edition, Polly Devlin considers that it 'echoes themes to be found in [Hamilton's] work' (viii).
13 *Prairial*, 55–6.
14 Ibid., 72.
15 Ibid., 183.
16 Ibid., 118.
17 Ibid., 220.
18 *Gorse*, 80.
19 PH to Bruce, 5 May, 1950.
20 Ibid.
21 Author's conversation with Fiona MacCarthy, whose mother, Yolande MacCarthy, was a close friend of La's for many years. She deplored Hamilton's influence on her friend, and even suspected him of forbidding her to write letters. Hamilton's reluctance to socialize, his awkwardness in female society, may well have led him to be unmannerly, even cruel, over La's friendships. Against this, and with a lack of direct evidence either way, it should be said that La was forty-three years old and if she was assertive enough to break up a marriage, she could also have stayed in touch with her friends had she wished. Her fiction could be seen as expressing a distaste for the world in which she had grown up.
22 PH to Bruce, 1 March 1951.
23 PH to Bruce, 31 January 1951.

24 Ibid.
25 Loïs Hamilton to Bruce, 16 December 1951. BH.
26 Ibid.
27 PH to Bruce, 30 June 1951.
28 Ibid.
29 PH to Bruce, 31 January 1951.
30 Frank Bridger to Bruce, 14 March 1951. BH.
31 PH to Michael Sadleir, 28 May 1951. TEMPLE.
32 PH to Bruce, 30 June 1951.
33 Ibid.
34 PH to Bruce, n.d. [September 1951].
35 PH to Bruce, 16 September 1951.
36 PH to Bruce, 7 October 1951.

21 *The West Pier*

1 Michael Sadleir to PH, 27 July 1950. TEMPLE.
2 PH to Michael Sadleir, 18 September 1950. TEMPLE.
3 Ibid.
4 For example: 'There is a sociological gloss to Mr. Hamilton's investigations of the Brighton scene.' John Russell, *The Listener*, 30 August 1951. 'For sheer sociological observation this book could hardly be bettered. . . .' Marghanita Laski, *The Spectator*, 31 August 1951. The anonymous *TLS* reviewer struck a variation, calling Hamilton an 'anthropologist, not an advocate for the prosecution', 7 September, 1951.
5 *Gorse*, 14.
6 Ibid., 285.
7 Ibid., 333.
8 Ibid., 565
9 Sonia Orwell and Ian Angus (eds), op. cit., IV, 101. And see also 'The Spivs' by David Hughes in Michael Sissons and Philip French (eds), *The Age of Austerity 1945–51*, Oxford (1986), 75.
10 Arthur Calder-Marshall, BBC broadcast, 4 November 1955. BBC.
11 *20,000*, 282
12 *Gorse*, 301.
13 Ibid., 316.
14 Ibid., 418, 437
15 Ibid., 237
16 Ibid., 133
17 Ibid., 561
18 John Russell, *The Listener*, 30 August 1951.
19 Michael Sadleir to PH, 3 November 1950. TEMPLE.

20 PH to Michael Sadleir, 20 April 1951. TEMPLE.

21 Ibid.

22 J. B. Priestley to Michael Sadleir, 16 April 1951. TEMPLE.

23 Michael Sadleir to J. B. Priestley, 18 April 1951. TEMPLE.

24 Ibid.

25 By Arthur Calder-Marshall, for example. Information supplied by his widow, Ara, in conversation with the author.

26 *Middle Class Murder*, 10.

27 PH to Bruce, 16 September 1951.

28 PH to Bruce, 31 January 1951.

29 PH to Bruce, 31 January 1951.

30 *The Man Upstairs*, 79.

31 Orson Welles to PH, 1 August 1956. BH. Welles wondered optimistically whether Hamilton would 'be willing to enter into some profit-sharing arrangement for the rights'. Hamilton was severely ill at this time and it seems unlikely that he ever replied to Welles's letter.

32 PH to Bruce, 10 November 1951.

33 PH to Bruce, n.d. [early December 1951].

34 PH to Bruce, 28 February 1952.

35 Ibid.

36 *Tragedy II*, 502 [*TLWO*, 125].

37 This episode is an example of one of the more obviously puzzling differences between the typescript and the final published version of Bruce's memoir. According to *Tragedy II* (504), the argument came after a drunken Hamilton invited a casual acquaintance along to Bruce's room and then insisted that each should relate the most embarrassing experience of his life: 'I don't remember what story he told, but his friend, who was quite sober, passed if off with some light-hearted yarn. I myself, though fairly sober – I think the fact that I had not kept up with him drink for drink was one of the reasons building up in Patrick a hostile feeling towards me – was beginning to feel distress and could not readily respond. He asked angrily what was the matter with me, why couldn't I let my hair down. I did at last come out with the story of a genuinely humiliating experience, which I had never thought to tell anybody, least of all a stranger. Presently the friend went away, and I was left to face a rage which Patrick had to some extent controlled so long as a third person was present.' This must have been a bizarre scene, in which Bruce attempted to out-embarrass Hamilton by humiliating himself. In *TLWO* (125–6) the story is misleadingly defused to the point of virtual meaninglessness: 'I got across him by being unable to "let my hair down" when he suggested that each of us should relate the most embarrassing experience of his life; but he managed to control himself until the friend went away.'

38 Until read by the author in July 1992, many of the pages in the British Library copy of the book were uncut.

39 *Let Him Have Judgement*, 176–7.

40 PH to Bruce, 16 September 1951.

41 *TLWO*, 132.

42 Michael Powell, *Million Dollar Movie*, Heinemann (1992), 208. But not one of his most reliable memories, of Bruce's book at any rate, for Powell's account of the plot is largely inaccurate.

43 Ibid., 211.

44 *TLWO*, 58.

45 Michael Powell, *Million Dollar Movie*, 210.

46 *TLWO*, 132.

47 PH to Bruce, n.d. [April or May 1954].

48 *The Gentlewomen*, 116.

49 *TLWO*, 122.

22 *Mr Stimpson and Mr Gorse*

1 PH to Bruce,23 April and 28 April 1952.

2 PH to Michael Sadleir and Martha Smith, 25 May 1952. TEMPLE.

3 PH to Bruce, 27 May 1952.

4 PH to Michael Sadleir and Martha Smith, 27 May 1952. TEMPLE.

5 PH to Michael Sadleir and Beryl, 29 June 1952. TEMPLE.

6 PH to Michael Sadleir and Martha Smith, 18 August 1952. TEMPLE.

7 Michael Sadleir to PH, 7 September 1952. TEMPLE.

8 Edmund Wilson to Vladimir Nabokov, 30 November 1954. Simon Karlinsky (ed.), *The Nabokov-Wilson Letters: Correspondence between Vladimir Nabokov and Edmund Wilson 1940–71*, Weidenfeld and Nicolson (1970), 288.

9 Vladimir Nabokov to Edmund Wilson, 19 February 1955. Ibid., 290.

10 George Plimpton (ed.), *Writers at Work: The Paris Review Interviews, Second Series*, Penguin: Harmondsworth (1977), 107.

11 *Gorse*, 318–23.

12 *20,000*, 67.

13 *Gorse*, 558.

14 Antony Rhodes in *The Listener*, 16 July 1953: 'He has picked on a set of people to loathe, and with pitiless satire he exposes their particular vice, snobbism.' L. A. G. Strong in *The Spectator*, 17 July 1953: 'Mr. Hamilton has a fiendishly accurate ear for the horrors of shoddy provincial dialogue, and he dissects brilliantly, but his book seems to me to suffer from two weaknesses. He loathes his characters, often to the point of anger; and one needs to be a genius in order to create rounded characters from dislike

alone. Futher, Gorse, the predestined villain, is not as interesting as his role demands.'

15   *New Statesman*, 27 June 1953.
16   PH to Michael Sadleir, 18 September 1950. TEMPLE.
17   PH to Bruce, 1 December 1954.

23 Divorce and *Unknown Assailant*

1   PH to Bruce, 28 June 1954.
2   PH to Bruce, 16 November 1953.
3   *Barcelona Road*, 40.
4   Ibid.,185.
5   Ibid., 213–14.
6   PH to Bruce, n.d. [15 June 1953].
7   Ibid.
8   Ibid.
9   PH to Bruce, 29 January 1954.
10   Ibid.
11   Ibid.
12   PH to Michael Sadleir, 15 March 1954. TEMPLE.
13   PH to Michael Sadleir, 6 April, 1954. TEMPLE.
14   Letter from Michael Sadleir to PH, 9 April 1954. TEMPLE.
15   PH to Bruce, 30 October 1954.
16   PH to Bruce, 28 June 1954.
17   PH to Bruce, 30 October 1954.
18   PH to Bruce, 28 June 1954.
19   PH to Bruce, 29 September 1954.
20   PH to Bruce, 30 October 1954.
21   Ibid.
22   Wyn Craig Wade, *The Fiery Cross: The Ku Klux Klan in America*, Simon and Schuster (1987), 289.
23   PH to Bruce, 1 December 1954.
24   Ibid.
25   Ibid.
26   Ibid.
27   PH to Bruce, 6 May 1955.
28   Ibid.
29   *Gorse*, 569.
30   Ibid., 605.
31   Ibid., 605–6.
32   Ibid., 649.
33   Ibid., 643.

34 Ibid.

35 Ibid., 656.

36 Ibid., 669–70.

37 PH to Bruce, 6 May 1955.

38 Michael Sadleir to PH, 6 May 1955. TEMPLE.

39 *New Statesman*, 1 September 1951.

40 *New Statesman*, 29 October 1955.

41 *Spectator*, 18 November 1955.

42 PH to Martha Smith, 3 March 1956. TEMPLE.

24 Breakdown

1 PH to Bruce, 10 June 1955.

2 Ibid.

3 Ibid.

4 He is mentioned twice, for example, in Hugh David, *The Fitzrovians: A Portrait of Bohemian Society 1900–55*, each time only as a recipient of a letter from Dylan Thomas.

5 PH to Bruce, 10 June 1955.

6 Ibid.

7 *TLWO*, 149.

8 Ibid., 151.

9 PH to Bruce, 6 May 1955.

10 PH to Martha Smith, 27 November 1955. TEMPLE.

11 Ibid.

12 PH to Val Gielgud, 22 March 1956. BBC.

13 PH to Val Gielgud, 16 June 1956. BBC.

14 PH to Martha Smith, 5 July 1956. TEMPLE.

15 Ibid.

16 PH to Bruce, 10 June 1955.

17 Stanley Gillam, Secretary and Librarian of the London Library, to Michael Sadleir, 14 September 1956. TEMPLE.

18 Loïs Hamilton to Martha Smith, 20 September 1956. TEMPLE.

19 PH to Bruce, 30 January 1957.

20 Ibid.

21 See Ludovic Kennedy, *Ten Rillington Place*, Gollancz (1961), 232.

22 PH to Bruce, 30 January 1957.

23 Ibid.

24 Michael Gelder et al (eds), *Oxford Textbook of Psychiatry*, Oxford University Press (1989), 679.

25 Ibid., 680.

26 PH to Martha Smith and Michael Sadleir, 4 December 1956. TEMPLE.

27 Ibid.
28 PH to Bruce, 30 January 1957.
29 Ibid.
30 See Colin Wilson and Pat Pitman, *Encyclopaedia of Murder*, Arthur Barker (1961). They were found guilty, sentenced to death but then reprieved because of the difficulty in establishing exactly how the wife and child died.
31 PH to Bruce, 30 January 1957.
32 Ibid.
33 PH to Michael Sadleir and Martha Smith, 4 December 1956. TEMPLE.
34 Ibid.
35 Ibid.
36 Ibid.
37 *The Spectator*, 28 December 1956.

25 Recovery

1   PH to Bruce, 25 February 1957.
2   *Monday Morning*, 16.
3   J. B. Priestley, introduction to *Hangover Square*, 8.
4   PH to Bruce, 30 January 1957.
5   Ibid.
6   Ibid.
7   Ibid.
8   PH to Bruce, 25 February 1957.
9   *TLWO*, 166.
10 Ibid., 168-9.
11 Ibid., 173–4.
12 PH to Bruce, 7 November 1957.

26 Sedate Decay

1   PH to Bruce, 8 February 1958.
2   Ibid. Hamilton had lent Sylvane £25 when he had fallen on hard times. The IOU is dated 7 October 1944.
3   Ibid.
4   PH to Bruce, 11 July 1958.
5   PH to Bruce, 8 February 1958.
6   PH to Bruce, 3 June 1958.
7   George Gissing, *The Private Papers of Henry Ryecroft*, Oxford University Press (1987), 132–3.

8   *Mem II.*
9   *Mem I.*
10 Ibid. A slightly revised version of this passage appears in *Mem II*. See page 22.
11 These memories form the basis of my account of Hamilton's childhood experiences in Chapter Two.
12 The Rector's name is Walter Somerville. Walter was of course Hamilton's first name, and Somerville sounds like a reference to his spiritual home of Brighton.
13 See page 239.
14 *The Elopement*, 152–3.
15 Ibid., 154.
16 *Too Much of Water*, 272.
17 PH to Bruce, 10 June 1958.
18 PH to Bruce, 11 April 1959.
19 PH to Bruce, 10 June 1958.
20 Ibid.
21 PH to Bruce, 11 November 1958.
22 PH to Bruce, 20 January 1959.
23 *Mem II.*
24 PH had used this expression before. See *The Slaves of Solitude*, 214.
25 *Mem II.*
26 PH to Bruce, 14 September 1959.
27 Ibid.
28 Ibid.
29 Ibid.
30 PH to Bruce, 3 February 1960.
31 Martha Smith to PH, 3 April 1959. BH.
32 Martha Smith to PH, 15 March 1960. BH.
33 Ibid.
34 Ibid.
35 PH to Bruce, March 1960.
36 *TLWO* 178.
37 PH to Bruce, n.d. [March 1960].
38 PH to Bruce, 22 March 1960.
39 *TLWO*, 179–80. Hamilton mentioned his affection for Wodehouse to Angus Hall, *Books and Bookmen*, July 1968.
40 Author's interview with Timothy Boulton, 4 February 1992.
41 PH to Bruce, 3 July 1961.
42 PH to Bruce, 20 August 1961.
43 *The Last of the Tenants*, 12.

27 The End

1 PH to Bruce, 28 July 1961. Patrick had seen a good deal of Robinson in the late thirties. Robinson then became closer to Bruce, who dedicated his novel *So Sad, So Fresh*, to him. Three years later, Labour won the general election and Robinson was appointed Minister of Health.
2 PH to Bruce, 20 August 1961.
3 The Earl of Shrewsbury and Talbot to the author, 19 February 1992.
4 PH to Bruce, 20 August 1961.
5 Angus Hall to PH, 1 October 1958. BH.
6 Angus Hall, *Books and Bookmen*, July 1968.
7 Ibid.
8 Ibid. Hamilton had already used the phrase 'happy hunting ground' in *Mr Stimpson and Mr Gorse,* but not of London: 'Then Gorse had a feeling that Reading might be a happy hunting-ground for a car-speculator – new and interesting territory.' (*Gorse*, 316.)
9 PH to Bruce, 17 April 1961.
10 *TLWO*, 188.
11 PH to Bruce, 14 July 1962.
12 John Davenport to PH, 21 July 1962. BH.
13 The Earl of Shrewsbury and Talbot to the author, 19 February 1992.
14 Ursula Hamilton to Bruce, quoted in *Tragedy II*, 664. Bruce was furious: 'That Hamilton should have formed an affection for him was perfectly natural. But what La wrote to me seems almost intended to suggest that Hamilton had a "thing" about her nephew.' Bruce suspected that La had manufactured the incident to justify what Bruce considered to be her illegitimate influence on Hamilton's will.
15 PH to Bruce, n.d. [July or August 1962].
16 *TLWO*, 188.
17 Loïs Hamilton to Bruce, 14 July 1962. SF.
18 Ursula Hamilton to Bruce Hamilton, [27 September 1962], quoted in *Tragedy II*, 666.
19 Ibid.
20 *TLWO* 152.
21 Ursula Hamilton to Bruce, [27 September 1962], quoted in *Tragedy II*, 667.
22 See PH observing Lalla's funeral, p. 212 above.

28 Aftermath

1 *Tragedy II*, 667–8.
2 PH to Shelley, *Poetical Works*, Oxford University Press (1971), 561–2.

3 PH to Bruce, 3 June 1933.
4 PH to Bruce, 27 August 1961, quoted in an Appendix that Bruce wrote for
   TLWO, though it was not ultimately published. The letter was stolen from
   the car of his Barbadian lawyer.
5 Ibid.
6 Ursula Hamilton to Bruce, 2 November 1962. SF.
7 *Tragedy II*, 655–6.
8 Ibid., 651.

Index